the

APPRECIATION
and
AUTHENTICATION
of
CIVIL WAR
TIMEPIECES

Clint B. Geller

National Association of
WATCH&CLOCK
Collectors, Inc.

Library of Congress Cataloging-in-Publication Data

Names: Geller, Clint B., 1954- author. | National Association of Watch and Clock Collectors, issuing body.
Title: The appreciation and authentication of Civil War timepieces / by Clint B. Geller, PhD, FNAWCC.
Description: Columbia, PA : National Association of Watch & Clock Collectors, Inc., 2019.
Identifiers:
  LCCN 2018042500 (print)
  LCCN 2018042952 (ebook)
  ISBN 978-1-944018-06-1 (alk. paper)
  ISBN 978-1-944018-07-8 (ebook)
  ISBN 978-1-944018-08-5 (hardcover)
Subjects: LCSH: Pocket watches—Collectors and collecting—United States. | Antiques—Expertising. | United States—History—Civil War, 1861-1865—Equipment and supplies. | United States—History—Civil War, 1861-1865—Antiquities.
Classification: LCC NK7492 (ebook) | LCC NK7492 .G45 2019 (print) | DDC 739.3—dc23
LC record available at https://lccn.loc.gov/2018042500

Published by
The National Association of Watch & Clock Collectors, Inc.
514 Poplar Street, Columbia, PA 17512

Editorial Director: Christiane Odyniec
Designer: Saul Bottcher
Copy Editor: Freda Conner
Proofreader: Gillian Radel

This book is dedicated to my father-in-law, the late Captain Albert Frank Magone, US Army re-tired (1921–2016). Shortly after our country entered into World War II, Albert enlisted and was selected for officer training. Though a native Pennsylvanian, he served with the "51ˢᵗ Dixie" Infantry Division in the Pacific Theatre. He commanded first a platoon and later a company in combat op-erations for eighteen months on Morotai, Papua New Guinea, Borneo, the Solomon Islands, and especially on Mindanao in the Philippines. He led his men through an especially brutal encounter battle along the Pulangi River on Mindanao. Albert had already seen his fill of the horrors of war when he received an opportunity to return stateside to assume a training position, but he turned it down to remain with his men. In his time in service he received promotions to first lieutenant and to captain, and earned a bronze star for distinguished service in a combat zone. Captain Magone personified all the traits, behaviors, and dedication to our nation that are celebrated in this book.

CONTENTS

Timeless Testaments

This book is a companion to the exhibit, *Timeless Testaments: Civil War Watches and the Men Who Carried Them*, at the National Association of Watch & Clock Collectors Museum, Columbia, PA. The exhibit will run for six months beginning July 6, 2019, the Saturday after the anniversary of the Battle of Gettysburg that took place a mere forty miles away. The exhibit will showcase many of the watches illustrated in this book, as well as numerous other watches of Civil War interest. Horologists and history enthusiasts interested in Civil War timekeeping and related artifacts are encouraged to enhance their reading experience with a visit to the Museum during this special exhibit.

Please visit *www.nawcc.org* for more information on the exhibit.

"'Watch in hand, they await[ed] the approach of the half hour, and as the last second of the last minute [was] marked on the dial plate,' Captain George S. James 'pull[ed] the lanyard; there [was] a flash of light and a ten inch shell traced its pathway towards Fort Sumter.' It was 4:30 AM on April 12, 1861 . . . "

—from *Army Letters*, by De Fontaine,
as quoted in *Civil War Time*, by Cheryl A. Wells[1]

"Woe to those who began this war, if they were not in bitter earnest."

—Diary of Mary Chesnut, April 12, 1861

1

INTRODUCTION

THE AMERICAN Civil War hastened an ongoing transformation in watchmaking from a craft primarily serving privileged elites to a mass-manufacturing industry providing reliable timekeepers to the multitude of ordinary citizens. In the mid-nineteenth century, personal timepieces were not only useful but they could mark an owner's status and confer prestige. Many hundreds of thousands of Civil War soldiers, who had new, often compelling reasons to know the time, came to think of watches as essential war-fighting equipment.

Watches also served personal needs. They occasionally became the objects on which owners recorded their own deeds, and even more often became the medium through which soldiers expressed their respect and admiration for comrades in arms. Surviving soldiers' letters also indicate that having what they considered a reliable watch held psychological importance for many soldiers, perhaps by making them feel that they had some small amount of control over at least one aspect of their often perilous and unpredictable circumstances.

Useful in both war and peace, often cased in precious metal, and combining state-of-the-art manufacturing technology with elegant craftsmanship, better watches were popular for presentation purposes, especially at the end of the Civil War, when many officers were transitioning back to civilian life. Thus, surviv-

1. President Abraham Lincoln (February 12, 1829–April 15, 1865) and his son Tad (1853–71), both wearing watch chains. The photo was taken in the White House on February 5, 1865, by Alexander Gardner. *Image from the Library of Congress (140) Digital ID No. CPH-3A05994.*

ing presentation watches are precious pieces of history as testaments to the relationships that existed between specific soldiers and their peers, their subordinates and their superiors, and as evidence of the rapidly evolving state of watch manufacturing technology in the mid-nineteenth century.

In seeking to provide an enhanced appreciation and understanding of Civil War timepieces, this book sets out to cover a lot of ground. It seeks to explain not only how to collect pocket watches from the American Civil War period but why. It provides a guide to the characteristics of the watches actually known to have been carried and used by Civil War combatants and a primer for assessing associated issues of authenticity and correctness.

But that is only the "how" of it. To understand why a horologist might wish specifically to collect watches associated with the Civil War, the book endeavors to impart a sense both of the importance of that defining struggle in American history, and the role that personal timekeepers played in it. Generally collectors of railroad watches and collectors of military watches already understand that placing horological artifacts in a larger historical or technological context is a rewarding exercise that enhances the appreciation of the artifacts themselves and lends additional fascinating dimensions to the watch collecting pastime.

Civil War-related watches in particular represent the intersection of horology with the single most important and formative event in American history other than the American Revolution itself. Apart from the watch collecting community per se, Civil War watches also are of interest to the community of Civil War reenactors. These motivations for collecting Civil War timepieces suffice for many, but a deeper appreciation of these artifacts may be possible by examining the mutual impacts that American watch-making and the Civil War had on each other, and the significance that watches often carried for Civil War combatants.

The impact of the Civil War on American watch-making has been dealt with before, to a degree, in various sources. [2,3] In this book, I attempt to add some depth to those narratives by bringing additional information sources into

2. One of two watches known to have been owned by President Lincoln. *Image from the Smithsonian website (June 10, 2018).*

the discussion. It then blazes a fresh—if still narrow—trail through mostly uncharted territory by beginning to explore the degree to which the revolution in American watch-making in the decade preceding the Civil War may have influenced the conduct of the war itself.

In the final sections some examples are presented of identified, inscribed Civil War timepieces, along with discussions of the men who carried them, the units in which these men served, and some of the battles in which they fought. It is my hope that some readers, who may be afforded opportunities in the future to own or examine similar timepieces firsthand, may feel the same shiver up their spines as does the author when they contemplate the connection of these artifacts to momentous events in American history.

What Is a "Civil War Watch?"

The phrase *Civil War watch* can be remarkably elastic, so the term needs to be defined if it is to be discussed. The most restrictive definition of a Civil War watch, and the one that horologists, historians, and serious artifact collectors

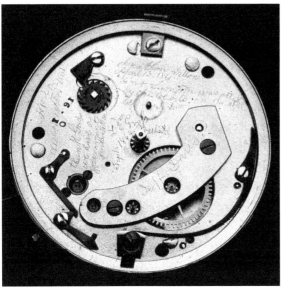

3. This gold cased, reportedly Liverpudlian, "lever" watch had a "secret message" inscribed on the pillar plate underneath the dial by a watch maker, Jonathan Dillon: "April 13, 1861 Fort Sumpter [misspelling in original] was attacked by the rebels on the above date, J Dillon April 13, 1861 Washington. [T]hank God we have a government Jonth Dillon." In 1864 a second watch maker, L. E. Gross, signed his name. Some third person, a joker or a rebel sympathizer, inscribed the name of "Jeff Davis" inside the watch as well. Lincoln very probably was unaware of these inscriptions, which remained hidden behind the dial for over a century. The elegant "bluing" on the steelwork and the superior English mercury vapor gilding are evident in the picture. Bluing is a process of imparting an optical interference color on steel by heating, which creates a hard, scratch-resistant oxidized surface that is durable as well as attractive. *Image from the Smithsonian website (June 10, 2018).*

4. A view of Lincoln's watch showing the front of the engine-turned case with blank shield. Here it is shown attached to a different chain terminating in a "shepherd's hook," a method popular during the Civil War for attaching watch chains, instead of the more formal T-bar and signet fob seen in FIGURE 2. *Image from the Smithsonian website (June 10, 2018).*

should prefer, is a watch, whether American or foreign, for which there is documentary evidence (on the watch itself or elsewhere) that it was owned by a Civil War combatant or other individual of Civil War significance during or immediately at the conclusion of the conflict. An extraordinary example of a Civil War watch satisfying this definition is documented in FIGURES 1–4, which show President Abraham Lincoln wearing a watch chain, and the watch that was likely at the other end of that chain. Direct evidence that a timepiece actually was carried by a Civil War participant makes a watch especially of interest.

A looser and more commonly used definition of a Civil War watch, which contains within it nearly all of the watches in the first category, is a watch made during or shortly before the Civil War whose make and model were known to have been popular among Civil War soldiers. As explained herein, most of the watches carried by American Civil War soldiers were of *foreign* make. [4] Thus, I include in this second category those foreign men's watches, and especially foreign movements in American cases, which give evidence of having been sold in the United States (including within the states then in rebellion) during or shortly before the Civil War.

The term *Civil War watch* is also commonly applied—mostly by sellers and mostly inappropriately—to any watch of indeterminate age whose features are claimed to be compatible with the general characteristics of watches that were known to have been manufactured and sold in the Civil War period.

This last, often purposely nebulous third category of watches may suffice for use in reenactment impressions, especially if a watch is of a generic foreign type. However, the following discussion is restricted to the second definition for American-made Civil War watches and to only the first, most restrictive definition for foreign-made watches. (Note: It was common for foreign-made watch movements sold in the United States during the Civil War to have had cases that were made in the United States.)

Because watches in the third category have no clear connection either to the Civil War or even to the American watch market, the discussions in this book heavily emphasize American-made watches, even though such did not represent the majority of the watches that saw service in the conflict.

Placing the American Civil War in American History: Cause and Consequences

"The first gun that was fired at Fort Sumter sounded the death knell of slavery. They who fired it were the greatest practical abolitionists this nation has produced"

—Brigadier General Daniel Ullmann,
Commander Corps D'Afrique, New Orleans,
June 10, 1863, General Order Number 7

Approximately 750,000 Americans, or nearly one of every fifty Americans who lived in 1861, perished [5] in the struggle that decided whether, in the words of Abraham Lincoln, "…[a] government of the people, by the people, for the people, shall not perish from the earth." [6] The beginning of the Civil War can reasonably be seen as the effective culmination of nearly all prior national history, from the end of the American Revolution in 1783 until the outbreak of full-scale armed internecine conflict in 1861. Similarly, much of subsequent American history can be seen as the unfolding of the profound consequences of the American Civil War. Indeed, the wrenching changes set in motion in the aftermath of the Civil War—Reconstruction, followed by Jim Crow, followed by the Civil Rights Movement and desegregation, followed by many of the struggles of the current period—are still, in some sense, unfolding. As William Faulkner famously observed, "The past is never dead. It's not even past."

Even more than a century and a half after its conclusion, many aspects of the real and alleged causes and the legacy of the Civil War remain hotly debated; however, a few facts are beyond dispute. First, the outcome of the Civil War preserved the Union that was and is the United States. Second, as General Ullman's remarks suggest with near poetic irony, the war led directly to the passage of the Thirteenth Amendment of the U.S. Constitution, ratified on December 6, 1865, abolishing Slavery, thus hastening the very event that secession was intended to prevent. By seceding, eleven Southern states temporarily lost their ability to block the passage of constitutional amendments in Congress and created the circumstances under which Reconstruction legislatures in six Southern states could help to ratify an amendment abolishing Slavery. If not for the secessionists' precipitate act, no such amendment would have been possible in that generation, and very possibly, for several succeeding generations. [7]

Third, emancipation was a far cry from full political equality for the emancipated. The end of hereditary chattel slavery was only one critical step for the emancipated and their descendants on a very long, arduous, and, many (including the author) would say, as yet unfinished journey toward that cherished goal.

Two other Reconstruction-era Constitutional amendments—both radical in their time—followed the Thirteenth. The Fourteenth Amendment, ratified on July 9, 1868, settled the legal status of the millions freed by the Thirteenth Amendment by declaring that all persons born in the United States were U.S. citizens. Furthermore, at least in principle, Section 3 of the Fourteenth Amendment, the Equal Protection Clause, prohibits state and local governments from infringing rights of citizens guaranteed by the Federal Constitution. (However, Section 3 came under almost immediate assault by a reactionary Supreme Court, thus long delaying its practical implementation.) [8]

Then the Fifteenth Amendment, ratified on February 3, 1870, which was perhaps the high-water mark of nineteenth-century American progress toward racial inclusion, declared that the right to vote shall not be denied or abridged on account of race, color, or prior condition of servitude. (But again, the full practical implementation of this amendment required the passage in 1964 of the Twenty-Fourth Amendment outlawing poll taxes and the enactment in 1965—fully one hundred years after the end of the Civil War—of the Voting Rights Act.)

In the 1870s concerns of the Northern political leadership refocused on national reconciliation and on restoring to prewar levels the production of Southern cotton, on which the

economies of both sections had depended before the war. So the political pendulum quickly swung back, and many of the social and political gains won by the former slaves were tragically erased.

Beginning about 1870, nearly forty African Americans gained office in Congress, and many hundreds served in state and local offices. But by 1877, when the last Federal guns left the South and Reconstruction was officially over, the planter class was already in the process of reestablishing its iron grip on the conditions of Southern labor and on local and regional government. [9] Within another decade, broad "vagrancy" laws, selectively enforced against the freedmen, blanketed the South. Thereafter, any rural laborer not under contract to a landowner could be arrested and have his liberty stolen for long periods, while his forced labor was sold to the highest bidder under harsh conditions and to no benefit to himself. Other laws prohibited black workers from leaving a plantation to seek better wages or conditions before their contract was complete—if ever. "Apprenticeship" laws forced women and children into the fields to work with the adults, just as before emancipation, restricting the opportunities to educate children. Laws regulating sharecropping placed the entire crop in the hands of the landowner, to be distributed as only he considered fair, and placed all the financial risks of farming on the tenant. Concurrently, public education for both blacks and whites, but especially for blacks, shriveled and all but died in the South for lack of support.

As for the freedmen's political rights, brutal vigilante violence and police intimidation, which often blurred together, combined with other obstacles to suffrage, effectively negated the voting rights promised to the freedmen by the Fifteenth Amendment in most of the South. In 1901 the last post–Reconstruction era black Congressman, George H. White of North Carolina, left office. It took twenty-eight years before the next African American, Oscar S. De Priest from Chicago, IL, was elected to Congress in 1929.

On the basis of this tragic history, one could conclude that the search for and celebration of Civil War "heroes" is in some sense naive. But it is not. Historian Gary W. Gallagher wrote, "Citizen-soldiers had saved a democratic republic invaluable not only to its own citizens but also as an example of popular self-rule for the rest of the world."[10] The Civil War revealed many individual American men's and women's characters, and through them, the national character, in a manner that almost no other conceivable trial could have done. It put a soldier's principles to the ultimate test, and many responded with dauntless, often reckless bravery and self-sacrifice in the service of causes they perceived to be greater than themselves. The subordination of one's own clear and vital self-interest in the service of one's fellows, one's family, one's country, or even abstract concepts such as liberty and democracy, and then persevering in one's convictions amidst inhumanity and danger inundating one from all sides, approaches the highest ideals of what it means to be human.

In his memoir, *The Passing of the Armies* (Putnam and Sons, 1915), retired Union Major General Joshua Lawrence Chamberlain, who had commanded the 20th Maine Infantry on Little Round Top at Gettysburg, wrote, "War is for participants a test of character; it makes bad men worse and good men better."

Whatever the motivations, racial prejudices, or other moral shortcomings of Federal soldiers or the Union cause, the Union Army's deeds bequeathed a geographically intact and better nation to future generations of Americans. This better nation, for all its continuing imperfections, was and is one in which slave parents were not routinely sold away from spouses and young children. It was and is one in which enslaved farm laborers were not subject to systematic and measured physical torture to extract the greatest possible, health-destroying work output. And it was and is one in which enslaved women were not commonly raped and forced to bear and raise their rapists' children under their rapists' roofs.

Moreover, it was a better nation in which the black community, despite daunting postwar oppression, managed to begin to build autonomous institutions such as schools and vibrant churches, which helped sustain them through the long night of Jim Crow, and from which the Civil Rights Movement would spring nearly a century later. A more detailed discussion of the historical background to the Civil War is provided in the Appendix.

Why the South Seceded

The short answer is that the South seceded to preserve the institution of Slavery, which was the basis of the region's wealth, economy, and society. For a more detailed answer, please see the Appendix and the bibliography.

Why the North Resisted Southern Secession

Historian Chandra Manning insightfully observes that both Northern and Southern soldiers looked to the American Revolution for justification and inspiration.[11] Numerous personal letters and camp newsletters of Union soldiers and combat units described the American experiment in democracy as something precious to all of mankind. They identified the U.S. system of government as "our political temple of liberty." This same sentiment was echoed by Abraham Lincoln in his second annual message to Congress in December 1862, when he called the Union and its system of government "the last best hope of earth." But Manning points out that although Northerners saw the revolution's most important legacy as the democratic government and the U.S. Constitution it bequeathed to future generations, Southerners primarily found in the American Revolution justification of their absolute right to rebel when a government ceased to serve their individual interests.

Northerners could be excused for regarding the idea of unilateral Southern secession as tantamount to theft, since all or most the land on which seven of the eleven seceding states resided either entered the Union or was opened for white settlement through expenditures of the entire nation's blood and treasure. (The financial expenditures of the Federal Treasury were paid for by tariffs, with the support of the South. [12]) For the South's Northern creditors and investors, Southern secession also raised a prospect of staggering financial losses,[13] although the war that ensued to prevent it may have been just as costly. The inevitable wars that would have resulted as two competing nations expanded westward were also easily foreseeable, and the threatened loss of river access to the Gulf of Mexico was a major issue for the Upper Midwest. To be sure, other powerful economic considerations also played into the equation. An editorial in the *Chicago Daily Times* of December 20, 1860, observed:

> In one single blow our foreign commerce must be reduced to less than one-half what it now is. Our coastwise trade would pass into other hands. One-half of our shipping would be idle … We should lose our trade with the South, with all its immense profits. Our manufactories would be in utter ruins … If [our tariff] be wholly withdrawn from our labor … it could not compete with the labor of Europe. We should be driven from the market and millions of our people would be compelled to go out of employment.

But the fear of financial losses would not have convinced many men to risk life and limb. More fundamentally, the North went to war because it was unwilling to validate the principle of unilateral secession, which would foreseeably have spelled doom for what remained of the unique American experiment in democracy once the principle was legitimated that any part of it could withdraw at any time for any reason. The concept of a free and fair election arguably no longer meant anything if its result could simply be negated by the loser through an act of unilateral secession. Southern secession would have been especially deadly for North America's wounded, diminished post-secession democracy, because a feeding frenzy predictably would have ensued among European powers to pick off individual remaining states and draw them into opposing foreign orbits. As Abraham Lincoln so famously said in Gettysburg on November 19, 1863, the "great civil war" in which the nation was then engaged would decide whether a nation "conceived in Liberty, and dedicated to the proposition that all men are created equal, ... or any nation so conceived and so dedicated, can long endure." [6]

The Coming of the War Changes the Calculus

Once the fighting began, the war itself generated its own reasons to keep fighting and to win it. As the cost of the war in blood and treasure mounted beyond all expectation, increasing numbers of Northerners sought a higher purpose more worthy of the horrific price than merely recreating a deeply problematic *status quo ante*. While the North did not initially go to war to free the slaves, the war itself convinced most Northerners that it was imperative to abolish Slavery. Lincoln also appears to have come to understand that the Union would never be safe, and all of the terrible sacrifices so far incurred could be in vain, unless the institution of Slavery were definitively rooted out and destroyed.

Confronted with invading armies, many Southerners were motivated by the desire to protect their families, their property (whether human or other), and their livelihoods; 44.4% of the soldiers in Robert E. Lee's Army of Northern Virginia came from families who held slaves, compared with less than 24% of all Southern households. [14] But even most Southern soldiers who did not own slaves did not relish the thought of large Northern armies marauding in their countryside. In his book *Reluctant Rebels* historian Kenneth W. Noe studied the letters of Southern "later enlisters," Southern men who came to the stars and bars after 1861. Noe concluded that "kinship and neighborhood, not conscription, compelled

these men to fight: they were determined to protect their families and property and were fueled by resentment over emancipation and pillaging and destruction by Union forces." [15] Similarly, on April 8, 1864, Private Harvey C. Medford of the First Texas Partisan Rangers opined in his diary that "we are fighting for property [a generic phrase that when undifferentiated, prominently included slaves] and homes; they for the flimsy and abstract idea that a negro is equal to an Anglo American." [16] (Medford was wrong, sadly. Few white Northern soldiers, even among the many who despised Slavery, fought for racial equality.)

Thus, the outbreak of armed hostilities added powerful new incentives for many Southerners to support secession and to fight for the Confederate cause. Nevertheless, these new motivations never displaced the original ones behind the war. In *For Causes and Comrades: Why Men Fought in the Civil War*, Pulitzer Prize-winning historian James M. McPherson wrote that in 15th Arkansas Infantry Captain Thomas Key's diary entry of April 10, 1864, he was incensed by the idea that if the Yankees won, his "sister, wife, and mother are to be given up to the embraces of their present dusky male servitors." [17] McPherson continued that "Another Arkansas soldier [William Wakefield Garner], a planter, wrote his wife that Lincoln not only wanted to free the slaves but also 'declares them entitled to all the rights and privileges as American citizens. So imagine your sweet little girls in the school room with a black wooly headed negro and have to treat them as their equal.'" Historian Chandra Manning [11] wrote that in a letter to his mother dated March 6, 1864, "Alabamian [Private] Joseph Stapp [41st AL Infantry] worried about the high prices, food shortages, social unrest, and 'desolation and ruin' that plagued the Confederacy, but told his mother that white Southerners would have to 'bear any hardships' in order to 'live independent of old Abe and his negro sympathizers.' " She added that "War-weary as men might be, much of the Confederate rank and file concurred with [9th LA Infantry Captain Reuben Allen] Al Pierson's desire for 'everlasting war in preference to a union with a people who condescend to equalize themselves with the poor, ignorant and only half civilized negro.' " This thought Pierson expressed in a letter to his father, dated March 22, 1864. Thus, preserving white supremacy remained a critical motivating and unifying issue for Southern fighting men to the bitter end.

While these sentiments remained prevalent among Southern soldiers, an increasing number of Northern soldiers came to be inspired by the noble idea that they were setting other men free. For nothing often bred disgust and revulsion with Southern Slavery more than confronting its reality close up. James M. McPherson wrote:

> While restoration of the Union was the main goal for which they [the Union soldiers] fought, they became convinced that this goal was unattainable without striking at Slavery. 'I believe that slavery (the worst of all curses) was the sole cause of this Rebellion,' wrote a private in the 5th Iowa in January, 1862, 'and until this cause is removed and slavery is abolished, the rebellion will continue to exist.' A corporal in the 64th Ohio likened slavery to a cancer. 'We are now fighting to destroy the cause of these dangerous diseases, which is slavery and the Slave Power.' A private in the First Minnesota Infantry [a unit whose heroic, nearly suicidal charge on the second

day of the Battle of Gettysburg continues to inspire awe even 155 years later] put the point succinctly: 'The war will never end until we end slavery.' [17]

Thus, on July 17, 1862, Congress passed the Second Confiscation Act, freeing slaves who had masters in the Confederate Army. Two days later Congress abolished Slavery in the Federal territories. Then on September 22, 1862, seizing on the ambiguous Union victory at Antietam five days earlier as his opportunity, President Lincoln used his Constitutional war powers to issue the Emancipation Proclamation declaring that beginning January 1, 1863, all slaves in rebel-held territory were to be then and forever free. This proclamation, a dramatic expansion of the previous Confiscation Acts, resulted in the immediate liberation, on the day it went into effect, of 20,000 slaves under Federal control in contested areas. Far more momentous was that it created new, effectively irreversible facts on the ground with every new square mile the Union regained from the rebellion, preparing the way for the subsequent passage of the Thirteenth Amendment that comprehensively abolished slavery throughout the nation. Elsewhere in slaveholding territory, the prior leak of escaping slaves swelled to a flood, especially since the Union Army had begun enlisting freedmen, and self-emancipated slaves were not returned to their former masters. Thus, the Emancipation Proclamation struck a heavy blow at the institution of Slavery all over the South even before the Federal armies had arrived. Furthermore, the proclamation paved the way for the entry of nearly 200,000 badly needed freedmen into Northern ranks, including 179,000 soldiers and 19,000 sailors, 40,000 of whom died of enemy action or disease. Last, but of crucial importance, Lincoln's proclamation eliminated with one deft stroke any immediate possibility that European powers would intervene on the side of the Confederacy. From that point on the war became, to the relief and satisfaction of many Northerners and to the disgust of some other Northerners, about not just restoring the Union as it had been, but about forging in the crucible of war a more perfect Union free of the national disgrace of Slavery.

Southern Soldiers and the Issue of Slavery

The same Southern sentiments regarding the centrality of slavery to secession and the war often rose up from the ranks of fighting men, as those which descended from the Confederate leadership. McPherson (REF. 16, page 20) writes of the correspondence among three brothers, all of whom enlisted to fight for the Confederate cause early in the war:

> One of three brothers who enlisted in a South Carolina artillery battery believed that 'a stand must be made for African slavery or it is forever lost'. The Confederate states were united by the institution of 'slavery, a bond of union stronger than any which holds the north together,' wrote the second brother. Therefore, added the third, the South's 'glorious cause of Liberty' was sure to triumph.

As McPherson's passage suggests, it was commonplace for white Southerners to conflate the preservation of African Slavery with the preservation of white liberty. Indeed the notion was actively promoted by Southern leaders that African Slavery made all Southern whites members of a privileged "aristocracy," regardless of their particular economic circumstances.

Chandra Manning provides a brilliant perspective on the centrality of the question of Slavery in the minds of the Civil War enlisted men of both the North and the South. In their own personal letters, diaries, and camp newspapers, the enlisted men of both sides overwhelmingly affirmed that they well understood that the war in which they were fighting was caused by, and was being fought, above all else, to determine the future of Slavery. She wrote:

> … to many of its participants, the Civil War was nothing less than a clash between competing ideas about how Americans should interpret and enact their founding ideals. The problem, as soldiers on both sides saw it, was that the opposing section posed a direct threat to everything that mattered. The opposing side threatened self-government. It threatened liberty and equality. It threatened the virtue necessary to sustain a republic. It threatened the proper balance between God, government, society, the family and the individual. And no matter which side of the divide a Civil War soldier stood on, he knew that the heart of the threat, and the reason that the Civil War came, was the other side's stance on slavery. … In the early months of the conflict, little budged in Confederates' initial understanding of the war as necessary resistance to the destruction of slavery. In contrast, Union soldiers' newfound acquaintance with the South, firsthand observations of slavery, and first taste of combat quickly led them to take a much firmer stand on slavery than many could have imagined before the war. [18]

Northern Soldiers and the Issue of Slavery

Among the Union combatants, ending Slavery was not, at least initially, a popular motivation for enlistment. Many Northern whites had never even seen a black person, and most shared a belief in white racial superiority with their Southern white countrymen. However, once large armies of Northern citizen-soldiers reached the South and began to witness, first-hand, some of the dismal realities of Southern Slavery, many became ardent abolitionists. Thus, in October of 1861, a soldier in the 3rd Wisconsin Infantry told the *Wisconsin State Journal*, "The rebellion is abolitionizing the whole army." [19] Time in the South forced the troops "to face the sum of all evils, and cause of the war [Slavery]." "You have no idea of the changes [concerning Slavery] that have taken place in the minds of the soldiers in the last two months." Now that they saw Slavery with their own eyes, "men of all parties seem unanimous in the belief that to permanently establish the Union, it is to first wipe [out] the institution" of Slavery. Lieutenant Charles H. Brewster of the 10th Massachusetts Infantry, stationed in Maryland, vowed in March 1862 that "I never will be instrumental in returning a slave to his master in any way, shape, or manner. I'll die first." [20] And when Sergeant Cyrus Boyd of the 5th Iowa Infantry encountered a young child about to be sold by her own father, who was also her master, he vowed, "By God I'll fight till Hell freezes over and then I'll cut the ice and fight on." [21]

Soldiers' attitudes also were reflected in the popular songs they sang around campfires, in bivouacs, and on the march. Perhaps most popular of all songs in Union camps was "John Brown's Body," based on an older song, "Say Brothers, Will You Meet Us." The song acquired new lyrics in 1861–62, linking it forever after with the radical abolitionist John Brown. Thus, the image of an erstwhile extreme fringe abolitionist widely regarded as a lunatic fanatic before the war had quickly evolved during the war into a heroic, popular figure. In the same period Julia Ward Howe wrote other words to the same tune, and the deeply religious "Battle Hymn of the Republic" was born, exhorting believers to be willing to "die to make men free." [22] In "Rally Round the Flag" soldiers were reminded that they were fighting for a country in which though a man might be poor, he would not be a slave. (By contrast, the chorus of a popular Confederate camp song, "Run, Yank, or Die," sung to the tune of the traditional "Root, Hog, or Die," began, "Hurrah for Slavery, for Southerners are the boys.")

Notwithstanding this evidence, support for abolition among Northern soldiers was not universal. McPherson writes:

> Of the Union soldiers in the sample [i.e., his sample] who expressed a clear opinion about emancipation as a war aim at any time through the Spring of 1863, more than twice as many favored it than opposed it: 36% to 16%. If we apportion those who did not comment on the subject evenly between the two sides, the picture would conform with the results of a poll in March 1863 in the 15th Iowa, a fairly typical regiment. Half of the men endorsed the Emancipation Proclamation, a quarter opposed it, and the other quarter did not register an opinion. [23]

But as the war progressed, Northern soldiers'

hatred of Slavery increasingly predominated. Thus, in 1864 a more definitive and official national poll was taken when roughly 80% of Union soldiers voted to reelect their "Father Abraham" as president, even though he had run against a popular Union General, George B. McClellan. McClellan would have reversed Lincoln's Emancipation Proclamation and re-admitted the seceded states to the Union under conditions preserving Slavery, in order to end the war immediately while preserving the Union. Much to the contrary, the man for whom the troops voted by a nearly four-to-one margin [24] promised in his second inaugural speech that if necessary to preserve the Union *and end Slavery*, the war would "continue until all the wealth piled by the bondsman's two hundred and fifty years of unrequited toil shall be sunk, and until every drop of blood drawn with the lash shall be paid by another drawn with the sword."

The Devotion of Civil War Soldiers

Whatever the diverse motivations of Civil War soldiers, behaviors provide a revealing window on their levels of commitment. Soldiers of both sides displayed the full gamut of behaviors from craven cowardice and self-promotion to fearless, even reckless devotion and selfless sacrifice. Writer and historian Richard Slotkin wrote:

> The morale of Civil War regiments has been a wonder to historians and a challenge to the military for a hundred and fifty years. What was it that kept men with the colors when desertion and evasion were so easy? What enabled men to march, shoulder-to-shoulder with loud cheers, into blasts of musketry and canister that they knew would destroy one man in three—understanding that to be wounded was often tantamount to a sentence of death, screaming through amputations without anesthetic or suffering the slow torture of gangrene? … wartime service was seen as more than a civic obligation. It was a test of one's personal character and social identity—a demonstration to yourself and your community that you were willing to live up to the expectations embodied in the concepts of 'manhood' and 'honor.' … Young men enlisted to affirm their identity, and they stayed with the colors to maintain their character. [25]

With now some background on the motivations and the commitment of the men who carried some of the watches shown in this book, one can perhaps gain a fuller appreciation of these historical artifacts and the importance of the events in which they participated.

2

IMPACT OF THE CIVIL WAR ON AMERICAN PERCEPTIONS OF TIME

IN THE year 1860, 53% of all Americans, and about 44.5% of all *free* Americans, were engaged in agriculture: 40% and 39%, total and free, in the North, and 84% and 66%, total and free, in the South. [26] Thus, counting small entrepreneurs and the like, possibly fewer than half of free Americans who worked likely received regular cash wages, while the rest operated primarily or partly within a barter system. In the antebellum North, farms tended to be small, and the task of coordinating efforts among individuals tended to be fairly simple. In the antebellum South, the rural economy in many areas was dominated by large plantations, sometimes involving the labor of hundreds of individuals, most of whom were slaves. Not unlike large industrial enterprises, large agricultural enterprises required higher degrees of coordination among workers. A mid-nineteenth-century small farmer's life was regulated by natural cycles of sunup and sundown, and it often mattered little to such a farmer what the hands on a clock or a watch may have said when these natural events occurred. Yet even here, time consciousness and the beginnings of time discipline were hitching a ride on the burgeoning railroad network from the population centers out to the countryside.

Thus, perhaps counterintuitively, by the time of the Civil War, clock time had gotten a purchase on rural culture in the even more agrarian South, on account of the larger scale of Southern agricultural enterprises. When traveling through the rice-producing region of South Carolina in 1853, the distinguished American landscape architect, Frederick Law Olmsted, observed that a "ploughing gang was superintended by a driver, who was provided with a watch; and while we were looking at them, he called out that it was twelve o'clock. The mules were immediately taken from the ploughs, and the plough boys mounting them leapt the ditches and cantered off to the stables to feed them." [27]

Olmstead's account was not an isolated example of the penetration of clock time into labor organization in slave plantation agriculture. In *Mastered by the Clock: Time, Slavery and Freedom in the American South*, historian Mark Smith observes:

> Conversations about time, similar in both substance and meaning to the one recounted by Olmsted, were carried out throughout the nineteenth-century world. ... Of all nineteenth-century societies, the literature suggests, only the American free wage labor North managed to inspire country dwellers to adopt, and in turn promote, clock consciousness. But Southern slaves and their masters were in advance of most of these societies

because, along with their bucolic Northern brethren, they were one of the few agricultural peoples in the nineteenth century world to embrace clock time. [28]

Military organizations carried the need for synchrony of action a big step further than even large capitalist organizations, whether they were Northern mills and factories or Southern plantations. In military matters, not only profitability depended on synchrony of action but sometimes life-and-death survival. In military camps or on campaign, the activities and movements of large numbers of soldiers had to be rigorously coordinated lest chaos or even disaster ensue. Even the most mundane aspects of camp life were regulated by watches. Watches told a soldier when his guard watch began and ended and his relief was due, or when reveille, roll call, and meals were to be expected. In a letter dated August 28, 1862, Sergeant George Oscar French, 11th VT Infantry, Company C, wrote, "I shall send some of my Bounty money home I guess, though I must have a watch for my duty as Sergt requires it for I must know when to post guard." [29] Watches could tell an officer how much time had elapsed since a message was sent or received. Last and most importantly, operational orders not infrequently specified the time of day at which they were to be executed. [30]

Thus, hundreds of thousands of newly enlisted soldiers, who never before thought they needed or even could afford a watch, very quickly came to decide that they could not afford to be without one. Fortuitously, the new compelling motivation to own a watch often was enabled by new means to pay for one, because enlistment was often the first time

in many soldiers' lives when they received a regular cash wage. For all officers, including the most junior, the need for a watch was even more inescapable, because it fell to the officers to carry out and coordinate orders from superiors. Confederate soldier Douglas John Cater of Greer's 3rd TX Infantry and later Co. I, 19th LA Infantry, likened the Confederate army itself to a watch mechanism. He wrote, "A soldier in the army is like a wheel in a watch, a part only of its mechanism." [31]

In her book *Civil War Time: Temporality and Identity in America, 1861–1865,* author Cheryl Wells observes:

> The Union and Confederate military complexes were aware that '[t]ime pervade[d] all decision making in war' and 'dictate[d] the design of weapons, the course of strategy, the organization of armed forces, … and the training of military leaders.' Presidents Lincoln and Davis knew that '[t]emporal considerations dictate[d] military doctrines, and ultimately destroy[ed] them as well. Time [came] before, follow[ed] after, and order[ed] the sequence and tempo of military operations.' … the Union and the Confederacy tried to organize their war efforts and instill order among green troops by basing tasks on the clock … . [32]

Synchrony of action on a battlefield was a far more complicated and challenging problem than merely having accurate timekeepers available, especially in the mid-nineteenth century, before the advent of standard time conventions. Nevertheless, watches were at least essential enablers, even if not sufficient guarantors, of synchrony, and the officer corps of both armies were keenly aware of this fact. [33]

The cheapest, most inferior imports aside, one can dispense with the spurious argument that watches being turned out in large numbers during the Civil War, especially by the U.S. watch industry, were not sufficiently accurate to be genuinely useful to Civil War soldiers. Keeping time even to within several minutes a day was an accuracy standard that was demonstrably well within the capabilities of very ordinary watches of the period, because many of the same exact ordinary watches can considerably exceed that standard today! Coordinating unit movements, even to within a few minutes, could greatly enhance a battle plan's chances of success. And even a few minutes a day was still plenty accurate enough to provide useful estimates of how many hours remained before sundown or until sunrise. This was priceless information, because night engagements in the Civil War were rare. In a passage underscoring the importance of the coming of dawn, historian Noah Trudeau described the beginning of Day Two of the Battle of Gettysburg as remembered by Union soldiers atop Cemetery Hill:

> Dawn ended the spirit of live-and-let-live that had been nurtured by the darkness. Trouble brewed almost immediately, … "As soon it was light on the 2nd of July, we could see the Johnnies moving along the fences in our front …" remembered an Eleventh Corps officer. "It was not long before 'zip' came the bullets from them, and our boys promptly returned their fire, although it was difficult to see them." [34]

On Civil War battlefields, fighting generally ended at or before sundown and did not resume until some light had returned, as in the example just cited. Civil War soldiers often thought in terms of three distinct "sunrises": when it was light enough to march; when it was light enough to shoot; and the actual rising of the sun.

3

IMPACT OF THE CIVIL WAR ON AMERICAN WATCH-MAKING

WHEN THRUST into harm's way, mortals tend to seek every marginal advantage available, and pocket watches clearly came to be seen in that manner during the Civil War. On June 21, 1863, Union Sergeant Isaac Newton Parker wrote home to his wife. [35] According to author Cheryl Wells, his letter:

> … resonated with anxiety, tension, and terrible concern [for his watch]. Although not broken, Parker's watch had not been serviced in seven years. Rather than trust the task to unreliable North Carolina watch repairers, Parker implored his wife to take his watch to O. E. Silbey's in Buffalo, New York. She was to have the watch cleaned and repaired regardless of the cost. She was to test the repaired watch for accuracy by measuring it against a clock in Silbey's shop and was also to wind the watch and let it run down the 'full 48 hours' it was supposed to run without stopping. The fact that Parker mailed his watch more than seven hundred miles attests to the importance of having an accurate timepiece. A functioning watch was not a luxury. Like canteens, shoes, rifles, and water, it was essential for Parker's work as a Union sergeant in the 132nd New York Infantry Regiment as well as for the war effort generally.

Thus, many thousands of men found themselves in a situation in which knowing the correct time could conceivably become vitally important to them. The American watch industry, which primarily meant the American Watch Co. of Waltham (sometimes subsequently abbreviated herein as "AWCo"), responded with increased output, a less expensive line of watches, and an intensive advertising campaign directed at soldiers that emphasized superior quality and American pride. Just how effective these measures may have been in stimulating demand for their products is revealed by some of the information following. In short, by 1863 the AWCo Treasurer could report that the company was selling nearly every watch they could make, even at increased prices, and in 1864, five new American watch companies were capitalized.

Evidence of Widespread Use of Watches among Civil War Soldiers

In assessing the impact of the Civil War on American watch-making, it is important to have a sense of how many American and foreign watches likely saw service in Civil War field camps and battlefields. Watches were the personal property of Civil War soldiers; therefore, few government records, other than occasional probate records or inventories of effects, exist to inform current research concerning the number of watches in use in Civil War armies. But definitive proof that Civil War soldiers

5. The 3ʳᵈ New Hampshire Infantry band, photographed by Henry P. Moore at Port Royal, SC, on February 28, 1862. The city had been retaken by Union forces on November 7, 1861. *Image from ourwarmikepride.blogspot.com/2015/07/a-musician-takes-his-sons-to-war.html (June 10, 2018).*

found watches useful—if not even indispensable—is available in other kinds of abundant and multifarious evidence that soldiers purchased and carried them in great numbers throughout the war. This evidence, direct and indirect, is reviewed here.

Written Personal Accounts of the Use of Watches by Civil War Enlisted Men and Officers

Civil War soldiers' letters home and diary entries mentioning, or at least implying the presence of watches, are not too difficult to find. For instance, officers' official reports and personal memoirs are replete with relatively precise citations of specific times of day, or of precise time intervals, which in many cases, could only have been informed by a watch. The previously quoted passage describing South Carolina Captain George James consulting his watch before firing the first shell at Fort Sumter on April 12, 1861, is a particularly consequential example that imparts shivers even a century and a half later. The excerpt from Sergeant Parker's quoted letter home likewise testifies to the im-

6. Union Major General August Valentine Kautz (1828–1895). Born in Ispringen, Baden, Germany, Kautz immigrated to the United States with his parents in 1832. He was a Union cavalry commander who served with distinction throughout the Civil War and who wrote several manuals that were eventually adopted by the U.S. Army. In 1866 Brigadier General Kautz was breveted to Major General by President Andrew Johnson. *Image from the Library of Congress.*

portance of a watch to many men in uniform. But the following, much more prosaic and even amusing example, which appeared on page 103 of an 1893 book, *The Third New Hampshire and All About It,* by Captain D. Eldredge of the 3ʳᵈ New Hampshire Volunteer Infantry, provides clear evidence of the omnipresence of watches in at least some Civil War army camps:

> During the winter of 1861–62 our camp was visited with the 'watch fever,' so called; and it raged with such fury at one time that nearly every man was affected with it, and had a watch in each pocket. Many got nipped so badly by their first trade, that it also became

their last one. The desire for watch trading ran so high that small knots of men could be seen hovering over a few embers, almost into the small hours of the night (morning), trading watches. The guards were finally instructed to arrest anyone who appeared like a watch fiend, after taps.

The 3rd New Hampshire Infantry band, one of many regimental bands in both armies, is shown in **FIGURE 5**.

That the 3rd NH Infantry was not some unique horophilic anomaly may be concluded from an account given by Union Major General August V. Kautz (**FIGURE 6**) of a typical "Inventory of Effects" of a Union enlisted man as "A pair of trousers worth $2, and a watch worth $25." [36]

Kautz's remark is quite consistent with that of correspondent and journalist (and occasional libertine novelist), G. A. Sala (**FIGURE 7**). In *My Diary in America in the Midst of War*, Sala described a Union sentry in early 1864 in the following terms:

> The sentinel was a common soldier, very slovenly, and not at all clean in his person and attire; but he wore a handsome watch and chain, and a carbuncle ring on his finger. There are numbers of young men of education and of wealth serving as private soldiers in the American army—serving from pure patriotism and devotion to that which they deem a righteous cause … . [37]

Typical of references to watches in surviving personal letters of Civil War combatants is the example of Union Colonel (and postwar, Brigadier General) George W. Gallup, whose watch and career are described in Chapter 9 (p. 135). A

7. British writer George Augustus Sala (1828–95), one of the most popular and prolific journalists of his time, wearing a watch chain and fob on his vest. The photo was taken in 1860 by the famous American portrait photographer, Mathew Brady. *Image from the Library of Congress.*

collection of Gallup's letters and a terse war diary are preserved in the Filson Historical Library in Louisville, KY. In one surviving letter to his wife, dated May 18, 1864, Colonel Gallup confides to her, "We go to the front tomorrow. I report direct to General [John M.] Schofield, Cmmndg, the 23rd Army Corps. … Will [Gallup's servant] took my watch in the trunk back with him." This letter, one of two that mention his watch, implies that he had carried the watch with him through several battles in Kentucky since receiving it from his men the previous year. However, Colonel Gallup greatly feared it would be stolen if he were killed or captured during the upcoming campaign, so he decided to send it home for safekeeping. Indeed, evidence cited later in this book indicates that his fear was well founded.

In his personal memoirs Confederate Colonel John S. Mosby (**FIGURE 8**), an elusive irregular cavalry commander dubbed the "Gray Ghost," described the events of October 14, 1864, known as "The Great Greenback Raid." In the telling he observed that "… I believe I was the only member of my command who went through the war without a watch, but all of my men had watches …" [38]

The letters of Sergeant James Beitel, 153rd PA Infantry, describe his brisk business selling and repairing watches in camp. He documents the strong demand for watches and watch repair within the Army of the Potomac, including some typical prices for reworked watches: $4 for French watches, which were not considered desirable, and up to $15 for somewhat better watches, probably Swiss or English, which were "strong runners." [39] Similarly, historian Alexis McCrossen wrote, "over the course of two months, the soldier [Luman A. Ballou, Co.

8. John Singleton Mosby (December 6, 1833–May 30, 1916), a.k.a. the "Gray Ghost," was a Confederate Army cavalry battalion commander who eventually rose to the rank of colonel. His command, the 43rd Battalion, Virginia Cavalry, more popularly known as Mosby's Rangers or Mosby's Raiders, was a partisan ranger unit that was alternately renowned or reviled for its stunning raids and its ability to elude pursuit and vanish into the local populace of farmers and townspeople.

Union officers at times viewed and treated the men of Mosby's controversial command as spies in that they wore no uniforms—the better to infiltrate Federal lines and the quicker to blend back in with the civilian population. The three stars on Mosby's collar, after the Austrian system of rank insignia, indicate that he was a full colonel when this image was taken. (Many have been confused by the fact that General Robert E. Lee also often wore a colonel's rank insignia and that Confederate general officer's rank insignia also included stars, albeit partly enclosed by gold wreaths.)

Mosby had opposed secession before the war. After the war Mosby became a Republican and worked as an attorney. He supported his former adversary, U.S. President Ulysses S. Grant, and not unlike former Confederate General James Longstreet, who served in Grant's cabinet, Mosby served as the American consul to Hong Kong and in the U.S. Department of Justice.

Given their postwar allegiances, it is not surprising that despite their military accomplishments, neither John Mosby, who possessed all the essential ingredients of a folk hero, nor James Longstreet, who was one of the Confederacy's few most important generals, were much celebrated by the "Lost Cause" secession apologists who erected Confederate monuments all over the South. *Image from the Library of Congress.*

G, 7th VT Infantry] 'bought a watch,' went 'up to the new regiments to trade watches,' 'sold a watch chain,' 'traded watches,' traded his watch for a fiddle, and bought a watch for five dollars (which he sold a few days later for twelve dollars). ... Another officer [Sergeant William H. Johnson, Co. E, 7th CT Infantry] also earned extra money by speculating in watches. He wrote to his family, 'I am glad the watches are acoming, as I think I can dispose of them to good advantage.'" [40]

A famous reference to the presence of a watch on a Civil War battlefield is attributed to Confederate Captain Richard Beard, who recorded in his diary the death of Union Major General James B. McPherson during the Battle of Atlanta on August 22, 1864. (General McPherson is not to be confused with the previously cited historian, James M. McPherson.) The general was in transit between two parts of the Federal line when he stumbled into the vanguard of a surprise Confederate attack. Author Stephen Davis relates:

> McPherson and his staff were riding down a wagon road when they unexpectedly ran into part of [Confederate Major General Patrick] Cleburne's line. 'He came upon us suddenly,' remembered Capt. Richard Beard of the 5th Confederate [Infantry Regiment, a unit composed primarily of Irish immigrants]:
>
> 'I threw up my sword as a signal for him to surrender. He checked his horse, raised his hat in salute, wheeled to the right and dashed off to the rear in a gallop. Corporal Coleman, standing near me, was ordered to fire, and it was his shot that brought General McPherson down.'
>
> McPherson's subordinates dashed off. One Union officer struck a tree in his flight; the

blow smashed his pocket watch and froze the time of the general's death—2:02 p.m. Confederate Captain Beard came up to the body and saw a bullet hole in the back, near the heart. [41]

A watch also was recovered on the battlefield from the body of Confederate Brigadier General Richard B. Garnett. [42] Garnett met his end during the storied assault known as Pickett's Charge on the third and final day of the Battle of Gettysburg, July 3, 1863. One of Garnett's aides, a Private Irvine, reportedly saw the general shot off his horse about twenty yards from the stone wall that the Federal troops were defending. Irvine freed the general's dead body from beneath his horse, which had fallen on top of the general, and the aide then recovered Garnett's watch and returned it to the proper authorities. The horse eventually made it back to the rebel lines with a large quantity of blood on it, but Garnett's body was never recovered.

A Union officer, Lieutenant Frank Haskell, an assistant to General John Gibbon, recalled the Confederate artillery barrage that preceded the same fateful charge in which General Garnett perished:

> We dozed in the heat, and lolled upon the ground, with half open eyes . . . A great lull rests upon the field. Time was heavy; - and for want of something to do, I yawned and looked at my watch; - It was five minutes before one o'clock. I returned my watch to its pocket, and thought possibly that I might go to sleep, and stretched myself out accordingly.

But Lt. Haskell's nap was rudely interrupted:

> What sound was that? - There was no mistaking it! - The distinct sharp sound of one of the

9. The Friend to Friend Masonic Memorial, sculpted by Ron Tunison and dedicated in 1993, and located in the Gettysburg National Cemetery Annex off Taneytown Road near Steinwehr Avenue. The Union officer shown receiving Armistead's watch, Captain Henry Harrison Bingham, would subsequently win a Medal of Honor at the Battle of the Wilderness in May 1864, where he "rallied and led into action a portion of the troops who had given way under fierce assaults of the enemy." After the war ended, Bingham was breveted to the rank of brigadier general by President Andrew Johnson, and he would go on to serve a long and very distinguished career in the House of Representatives. The fact of Armistead's Masonic distress signal has been disputed, but that he gave his watch to Bingham in safekeeping for General Hancock was confirmed by Bingham himself. This famous battlefield incident was earlier memorialized as a detail in the foreground of a panoramic 1876 painting in the Library of Congress Collection, by artist James E. Walker, titled, "Gettysburg, Repulse of Longstreet's assault." *Image by Laura Magone & William Fuller.*

enemy's guns, square over to the front, caused us to open our eyes and turn them in that direction, when we saw directly above the crest the smoke of the bursting shell, and heard its noise. In an instant, before a word was spoken, as if that were the signal gun for general work, loud, startling, booming, the report of gun after gun, in rapid succession, smote our ears, and their shells plunged down and exploded all around us.

Perhaps the most poignant story involving a watch on a Civil War battlefield is immortalized in polychrome bronze (**FIGURE 9**). Also during Pickett's ill-fated charge, Major General Winfield Scott Hancock, commanding the Union center, had already been wounded when the Confederate brigade of Brigadier General Lewis Addison Armistead, a close friend and former comrade in arms, penetrated the Union line and was struggling to take control of Federal batteries there. It was then that Armistead suffered the wound that would end his life two

10. The gold pocket watch, engraved "S. I. Tobias & Co., Liverpool," found with the remains of Lt. George E. Dixon in the Confederate submarine, CSS *Hunley* in 2004, shown after extensive cleaning.

The possibly fifteen-jewel watch with uncompensated balance and simple regulator was found in a partially-wound state, indicating that it had stopped suddenly, quite possibly when saltwater had inundated the movement on the night of February 17, 1864. If so, the time showing on the dial, around 8:23, was probably close to Dixon's time of death.

Also found with Dixon's remains was a $20 double eagle gold piece whose reverse is inscribed, "Shiloh, April 6, 1862, My life Preserver, G. E. D." The legend survives that the coin, which according to the story, had been given to Dixon by his sweetheart, Queenie Bennett, had absorbed most of the impact of a minie ball when he was shot in the thigh during the Battle of Shiloh. Upon chemical examination, both the coin and Dixon's femur showed traces of lead. *Image from www.nbcnews.com/id/22266374/ns/technology_and_science-science/t/watch-civil-war-sub-raises-new-puzzle/#.wybim0gvwdu (June 10, 2018).*

days later. When he was wounded, it has been reported that he gave a distress signal recognizable to fellow freemasons and that officers in both gray and blue responded. The *Friend to Friend* Masonic Memorial in the Gettysburg National Cemetery Annex portrays Union Captain Henry Harrison Bingham, a staff assistant to General Hancock, rendering aid to Armistead. Armistead, already seeming to know his fate, is shown handing his watch and chain, with a square-and-compass Masonic watch fob, to Captain Bingham to be taken to

his friend, General Hancock. Armistead, Bingham and Hancock were all freemasons.

The efforts of General Garnett's aides to retrieve his dead commander's watch despite his personal peril and the touching concern of a mortally wounded General Armistead to see that his friend received his watch attest to the importance that many men placed on their watches, and suggests how much other men often identified watches with their owners.

Another outstanding story of a watch actually bearing witness to its owner's demise attaches to the remnants of the watch belonging to a former steamboat engineer, Lieutenant George E. Dixon, skipper of the CSS *H. L. Hunley* (**FIGURE 10**). After a century and a half of immersion in the saltwater of Charleston Harbor, little is left of the inner workings of the watch that belonged to Lt. Dixon, the skipper of the first submarine to sink an enemy vessel. [43] Yet even in death, the watch may continue to record the time of its owner's end on February 17, 1864, at about 8:23 PM.

Finally, a most extraordinary instance of a recorded death of a Union combat officer exists in which not only is there documentary evidence that the officer carried the watch at the time of his death but the actual, remarkably intact watch is available for examination. This watch and its owner's story are presented in Chapter 9 (p. 135).

Apart from direct references to watches in diaries and public memoirs, such as those just mentioned, abundant references exist in these kinds of documents to events occurring at relatively precise times. Some of these times might have been supplied by a public clock, but in most cases they could only have been determined by consulting a watch—whether the correspondent's or that of someone else nearby. A sampling of such indirect references to watches follows.

Accounts of the Battle of Bull Run/First Manassas

This battle, the first major clash of arms of the war, was a confused and disorganized melee in which both sides were still learning to fight. No consistency yet existed in either uniforms or equipment, with some Union units in gray and several Confederate units in shades of blue. The consequences were predictable. Friendly fire was frequent, often deadly and sometimes disastrous. Military training or discipline on either side was mostly conspicuous by its absence, with troops falling out of line without orders to drink at every stream or even to pick berries. Coordination, much less anything resembling synchrony of action, was virtually impossible under the circumstances. Rather than being instruments of order, the many watches on the field mostly bore witness to the chaos enveloping them. At Bull Run and for a long period afterward many recruits of both armies had to assimilate whole new conceptions of time and relearn their own relationships to time. Cheryl Wells [29] relates several examples of events or plans referring to or depending on precise times supplied by watches:

> July 18, 1861: " … at 8:15 AM, he [General Irvin McDowell, commanding the Union Army of Northeastern Virginia, later renamed the Army of the Potomac] looked at his watch and instructed Brigadier General Daniel Tyler's brigade to advance on Blackburn's Ford …"

> Then later that day, "According to Tyler, 'from 3:15 until 4 o'clock,' Federal cannons fired 415 shots, which were 'answered by the enemy's batteries shot for shot.'"

> On Saturday, July 20: "McDowell issued General Order 22. It called for a three-pronged attack coordinated by the clock [i.e., by the timekeepers then to hand, namely, watches], with success hinging on regiments functioning within a monolithic time. Tyler's first division, excluding Richardson's brigade, was to 'move at 2:30 AM precisely on the Warrenton Pike to threaten the passage of the bridge, but [not to] open fire until full daybreak [a mixture of clock and natural time appearing in the order].' … Colonel David Hunter's Second Division was to start at 2:00 AM, and Colonel Samuel P. Heintzelman's division was 'to march at 2:30 AM.'"

> And later that same day: " … By J. G. Barnard's watch, Tyler's division finally cleared Cub Run at 5:30 AM, two and a half hours after their departure."

> On July 21: "The Confederates also created a clock-regulated offensive battle plan. [The commanding Confederate General, P. G. T.] Beauregard issued orders at 4:30 AM on July 21 by [General Albert Sidney] Johnston's account, but at 5:00 AM by [General James] Longstreet's account."

Gettysburg

In his book *Gettysburg*, historian Stephen Sears describes the gallant stand of Federal Brigadier General John Buford's cavalry against the advance of Confederate Major General Henry (nicknamed Harry) Heth's infantry division on the first day of the battle, July 1, 1863. Buford stood fast against an enemy force that greatly outnumbered his two dismounted brigades, hoping to hold the high ground long enough for Major General John Reynolds to arrive with the Federal First Corps. Sears relates:

During these early morning hours of July 1, from the cupola of the Lutheran Theological Seminary [which had no public clock] on Seminary Ridge, Federal signalman Aaron Jerome tracked the expanding fight in front of him, and in turn with his strong glass anxiously scanned to the southeast for Reynolds's corps. At last, on the distant Emmitsburg Road, he sighted a column of troops. Jerome promptly reported his sighting to General Buford … **With that, at a few minutes after ten o'clock**, Buford wrote out a dispatch for General Meade [commanding general of the Federal Army of the Potomac (AoP)]. [44]

Later that day, Major General Oliver Otis Howard and his Federal 11th Corps reached the field. Only the second to arrive of the AoP's seven corps, the Union troops were still heavily outnumbered in the developing battle. Sears describes (p. 182) the circumstances when Howard learns that General Reynolds has been killed and that he, Howard, was then in command of all Federal forces on the field:

Howard noted the time as 11:30 AM—when one of General Reynolds staff called up to him [on the observation deck of the three-story Fahnestock Building in Gettysburg] that the general had been killed and that he [i.e., Howard] was [then] the ranking officer on the field.

But General Howard's watch was not the only timepiece on the field to record Reynolds's demise. Wells reports (p. 37):

Shortly after arriving with his men, Reynolds fell victim to a Confederate bullet and died at either 10:15 AM (by the watches of Major General Abner Doubleday and Brigadier General James Wadsworth), or 10:30 AM (by Colonel Charles S. Wainwright's recollection). According to Jesse Bowman Young of the Eighty Fourth Pennsylvania Infantry, 'At a little before 11 o'clock, … Major General Oliver O. Howard … arrived at Gettysburg to find himself … by the death of Reynolds in command of the whole field.' Howard claimed that he learned 'the sad tidings of' Reynolds death 'about 11:30 AM,' at which time he assumed command of the left wing of Reynolds's forces.

And on the third day of the battle, Stephen Sears describes the tense lead-up to Pickett's Charge, Lee's last effort to break the Federal lines and salvage a victory from imminent defeat. On page 415, Sears relates:

Exactly what time Pickett stepped off would become a matter of some debate. By taking Pennsylvania College's Professor Jacobs [who likely had access to a clock] as the benchmark—Jacobs carefully noted the Confederate bombardment [preceding the assault] as starting at 1:07 PM, a fairly close confirmation of the 1 o'clock starting time [Confederate artillery commander, Colonel] Porter Alexander recorded for it—and then considering the times marked on Alexander's notes to Pickett, it appears that Pickett's Charge commenced about 2:30.

Evidence That Watches Were Sometimes Given to Enlisted Men by Their Units

The watch pictured in **FIGURES 11–14** bears a most interesting presentation on its inner rear lid (a.k.a. the dust cover or cuvette): "25th Michigan Infantry, Co. B, to [Sergeant] James

11. Cuvette of the four-ounce silver Waltham watch presented to Sergeant James A. Sage by his unit. The presentation reads, "Company B 25ᵗʰ Mich. [Infantry] to J. A. Sage, 1862."

A. Sage, 1862." Sergeant Sage was on the roster of the 25ᵗʰ Michigan Infantry when it was first mustered into service on September 22, 1862. Inside this four-ounce coin silver case is a seven-jewel Waltham P. S. Bartlett grade Model 1857 movement with a solid steel balance and SN 42,888, which indicates it was finished between June 1 and July 31, 1862. Comparison of the year, 1862, on the case presentation with the known data for the 25ᵗʰ Michigan Infantry and the movement's factory production date makes it clear that the watch was presented to Sergeant Sage either when or shortly after Sergeant Sage was recruited. The fact that James Sage was enlisted as a sergeant also indicates that he was considered an especially desirable recruit. Indeed, Sage was promoted to second lieutenant soon after he received the watch and later to first lieutenant of his company. The diary of Sergeant William H. Shaw of the 37ᵗʰ

12. Dial of the James A. Sage watch, signed "American Watch Co."

MA Infantry documents a second example of a watch presented to a noncommissioned officer by his company, this one just before the Battle of Fredericksburg. His diary entries for May 2nd and 3rd, 1863 state, "In the evening, received a nice watch from my company just before we crossed the river. 3rd, at daylight we marched into Fredericksburg, had been there for a short time when the rebel batteries opened their batteries on us …" The cuvette of the silver hunting case of Shaw's seven-jewel William Ellery grade Model 1857 Waltham watch is engraved, "Wm. H. Shaw, Presented by Co. D, 37th Mass Vols." [45]

13. P. S. Bartlett grade, seven-jewel Waltham Model 1857 full-plate movement of the James Sage watch, with steel balance. Movement SN 42,888 was finished between June 1 and July 31, 1862.

An example of a watch gifted to a Union line officer by his company is shown in **FIGURES 15–17**. The presentation reads, "Presented by CO H, 52 Reg. P.V. [Company H, 52nd Regiment, Pennsylvania Volunteer Infantry] to Capt. E. R. [Edwin Ruthven] Peckens at Beaufort, SC, April 30, 1863." The movement of the watch is a basic, no-frills English

half plate, right angle lever with seven jewels, a monometallic brass balance, and a device called a *fusee*. (A fusee is a conical pulley with a chain wrapped around it that is used to equalize mainspring torque over the running period; see Chapter 5 starting on p. 75.) The movement is signed "Adams & Co., Liverpool, 99006." The five-digit movement serial number matches

14. Engine-turned interior of the front lid of the James A. Sage hunting-case watch, marked "Warranted, Coin Silver."

that on all three lids of the gold case, marked "R. & W., 99006." Loomes [46] lists a Nathaniel Adams making watches in Liverpool in 1851. Ten or eleven years later, when the current watch in question was made, Adams seems to have been signing his movements "Adams & Co." The mark "R. & W." could be either a retailer's mark or a case maker's mark, almost certainly American. The movement appears to have been made with some of the provisions for it to be hinged into a swing-out case, which would have been standard if the movement

15. The movement of the Peckens watch. The quintessentially English-style ratchet tooth escape wheel is visible beneath the top plate at the upper right of the image.

had been cased in England. However, this gold case is not of the swing-out style, it lacks English hallmarks, it has a hinged cuvette with a lift tab, and it features a prominent eagle with spread wings and an American flag shield on its breast on the front lid. Thus, it is exceedingly likely that this case was made in the United States specifically for the English movement of the same serial number. The single-sunk Roman numeral dial is unsigned and the hands are slender spades.

Edwin R. Peckens was born in Plymouth, PA, and graduated from the University of Lewisburg (later renamed Bucknell University) in

16. The cuvette of the watch presented on April 30, 1863, to Captain Edwin Ruthven Peckens of the 52nd Pennsylvania Volunteer Infantry by his Company H.

1854. After the war he came to manage several collieries for various coal companies in Pennsylvania. Captain Peckens (**FIGURE 18**) was commissioned on August 22, 1861, and fought at the battles of Lee's Mills, Williamsburg, Seven Pines (a.k.a. Fair Oaks), and White Oak Swamp during the AoP's Peninsula Campaign of March–July, 1862. Fellow Pennsylvanians often called the 52nd Pennsylvania the "Luzerne Regiment," referring to the county from which most of its men were recruited. At Seven Pines

they lost 129 men killed or wounded out of a total of 259 men engaged. Captain Peckens received his watch from his comrades in arms as a parting token of their esteem at the time he resigned his commission on account of ill health on April 28, 1863. [47] (Some sources give his resignation date incorrectly as September 4, 1863.)

About six months after Captain Peckens withdrew, the men of the 52nd Pennsylvania were situated on Folly Island off the coast of South Carolina, in position to witness the cou-

17. The engine-turned front lid of the Peckens watch, which is marked "R. & W., 99006" on its interior. The eagle with spread wings, especially with the shield motif on its breast, adapted from a detail of the Great Seal of the United States, was a popular patriotic Civil War decorative motif.

18. Captain Edwin Ruthven Peckens (1831–1903) looking quite elegant in a dress uniform. *Image from suvcw.org/past/edwinruthvenpeckens.htm*

rageous charge of the 54th Massachusetts Infantry at Fort Wagner that was immortalized in the Hollywood film *Glory*. On February 18, 1865, the men of the 52nd PA were those who hoisted the stars and stripes above Fort Sumter, which had been abandoned earlier by the Confederates, for the first time since the fort's surrender in 1861. (Robert Anderson, by then a major general, would not return to his old post to hoist his original banner until the following April.) The dedicated 52nd PA regiment served throughout the entire war, despite losses not only from enemy action but from typhoid and smallpox. Despite these hardships, many among them reenlisted in November of 1863 when their original obligations were completed. A portion of the regiment was also taken prisoner on July 3, 1864, after an unsuccessful assault on Fort Johnson, and about fifty of these men perished in the notorious Confederate POW camps of Columbia and Andersonville before they could be freed. It was a noteworthy accomplishment for Captain Peckens to have earned the respect of such men. [48,49,50]

19. Cuvette of the 18-kt. gold Waltham watch presented to Major Josiah B. [Botsford?] Cobb of the 12th Indiana Cavalry. The presentation reads, "Presented by Col. Edward Anderson, 12th Ind. Cav., to Maj. J. B. Cobb, of ours."

Evidence of Watches Gifted to Officers by Their Superiors

An Appleton, Tracy & Co. (AT&Co) grade Waltham Model 1857 watch in an 18-kt. gold hunting case, shown in **FIGURES 19–24**, was presented to Major Josiah B. (possibly Botsford) Cobb (**FIGURE 21**) of the 12th IN Cavalry by his commanding officer, Colonel Edward Anderson. The serial number of the watch, 85,082, fixes the movement's date of completion in October 1863, suggesting that it was probably presented to Major Cobb on the occasion of his promotion from the rank of captain early

20. Dial of the J. B. Cobb Waltham watch, ca. 1863. The hands are slender blued spades with polished tips.

22. Front of the 18-kt. gold hunting case of Major J. B. Cobb's Waltham watch.

21. Major Josiah B. Cobb (January 1834–April 13, 1919), 12ᵗʰ Indiana Cavalry. The 12ᵗʰ IN Cavalry took the field in March 1864, at which time Cobb, a veteran of the 2ⁿᵈ IN Cavalry (the first Indiana cavalry unit to serve in the Civil War) was "elected" captain of Company D. He was promoted to major later that year.

According to his obituary in the Indianapolis Times, Cobb had helped to organize the 12ᵗʰ IN Cavalry in the winter of 1863. The 12ᵗʰ IN Cavalry saw action in Mississippi, Alabama, and Tennessee against Nathan Bedford Forrest's irregular cavalry and the forces of John Bell Hood. They were involved in the battles of Wilkinson's Pike (a.k.a. Third Murfreesboro), Overalls Creek, Spanish Fort, and Fort Blakely, among others.

Of the 1,357 men who served in the 12ᵗʰ IN Cavalry throughout the war, 168 were either killed in action or died of wounds or disease. Seven other men of the unit were unaccounted for. *Image from U.S. Army War College Archive, June 10, 2018.*

23. The elegantly engine-turned interior of the front lid of the J. B. Cobb watch, showing the "G. W. & Co." mark, standing for the horologically well-known firm of Giles, Wales & Co., founders of the United States Watch Co. of Marion, NJ, in 1864. (Also see REF. 2.)

24. Waltham Model 1857, Appleton, Tracy & Co. grade full-plate movement, SN 85,082, finished between October 1 and October 31, 1863, with gold alloy balance wheel, stopworks, and fifteen jewels in screwed-down top plate settings.

in 1864. The photogenic Major Cobb had previously served as a sergeant in the 2nd IN Cavalry, which participated in several momentous engagements, such as Shiloh (April 6–7, 1862), the Siege of Corinth (April 29–May 30, 1862), Perryville (October 8, 1862), Chickamauga (September 18–20, 1863), and possibly Stones River (December 31, 1862–January 2, 1863), during his service with the unit. Cobb returned to his hometown of Goshen in 1863, where he raised a company of the 12th IN Cavalry. The company elected him Captain. [51] After the war Cobb raised horses, a fitting occupation for a former cavalryman, and operated a racetrack on his property outside of town. He served terms as the Mayor of Goshen (1884) and as an Elkhart County Commissioner (1901).

Evidence of Watches Gifted to Officers by Their Subordinates and Peers

A sufficient number of examples of watches gifted to respected commanding officers and military colleagues survive to conclude that such gifts were fairly frequent occurrences. This practice made perfect sense, because gold pocket watches combined elements of luxury, prestige, and desirability with practical military utility, making them ideal for presentation purposes. Moreover, unlike swords or some other known kinds of presentation objects, watches would remain useful to the recipient when he returned to civilian life, making timepieces especially favored for end-of-service presentations. Quartermaster officers seem to have been frequent recipients of such largesse. A similar case is that of the 18-kt. gold, 20-size watch, whose dust cover is pictured in **FIGURE 25**, which was presented *during* the war to Major Jonathan Ladd, a man known to have engaged in some extralegal commercial activity for which he was court martialed, but later pardoned. [38]

The presentation reads, "Presented to Paymaster Major Ladd, by the Officers of 2nd C.V.A. [Connecticut Volunteer Artillery], March, 1864." The watch is reported to have been a gift arranged by Colonel Elisha Kellogg of the 2nd C.V.A, who fell at Cold Harbor barely three months later.

A second, equally impressive 20-size gold watch (**FIGURES 26–30**) was presented to Captain John Eddy "by his friends in the Q.M. Department" of Camp Butler, a recruit collection and training camp near Springfield, IL. Captain Eddy (**FIGURE 31**) had previously served in the 95th IL Infantry and had fought at

25. Cuvette of the 20-size 18-kt. gold Waltham watch presented to Union Major Jonathan Ladd, previously shown in the NAWCC Bulletin (see **REF.** 38). The presentation reads, "Presented to Paymaster Major Ladd, by the Officers of 2nd C.V.A. [Connecticut Volunteer Artillery], March, 1864." The watch is reported to have been a gift arranged by Colonel Elisha Kellogg of the 2nd C.V.A, who fell at Cold Harbor barely three months later. *Image courtesy of Paul Mellen.*

Island Number 10 and in several battles of the Vicksburg Campaign (December 1862–July 1863) as the Federal army battled its way down the Mississippi River.

An 18-size gold watch, the movement and dial of which are shown in **FIGURE 32** and **FIGURE 33**, is even more impressive than the preceding two. The 18-kt. gold hunting case is marked "R. & A.," for the firm of Robbins & Appleton, the AWCo's principal sales agency of the period. It houses an American Watch Co. grade Model 1859 movement likely costing

26. Cuvette of the 20-size 18-kt. gold watch "Presented to Captain John Eddy by his Friends of the Q. M. [Quartermaster] Dept. Camp Butler, near Springfield, Ill., Apr. 1865."

more than its substantial gold case. Although there is no evidence that this watch was a gift, one may wonder, because the watch likely cost four to five months of a captain's pay. Captain Fuller's name appears on the personalized double-sunk dial shown in **FIGURE 33**, in place of the usual American Watch Co. signature.

Several additional outstanding examples of watches presented to Civil War officers by appreciative subordinates and comrades in arms are shown and discussed in Chapter 9 (p. 135).

Photographic Evidence of Civil War Soldiers Wearing Watches

Not all Civil War soldiers who carried watches wore them in a conspicuous manner, especially

27. Single-sunk enamel Roman numeral dial of Captain John Eddy's Waltham watch, signed "American Watch Company."

because, as documented here, watches were such desirable objects of plunder on the battlefield. Fortunately, watches were easy to conceal underneath officers' frock coats and enlisted men's sack coats, or in packs. Hence, most of the pictures we have of Civil War soldiers wearing visible watch chains are posed pictures taken in

secure locations removed from harm's way. Indeed, wearing a watch prominently into battle might even have made one a more appealing target for enemy fire. Nevertheless, most soldiers, who were typically far from home, had no access to bank vaults or other secure repositories for their valuables. Thus, if they used a

28. The 20-size Appleton, Tracy & Co. grade three-quarter-plate movement of John Eddy's watch, SN 100,822, finished May 1864, with fifteen jewels in screwed-down top plate settings, stopwork (not visible), and temperature-compensated bimetallic balance.

watch during their service at all, they probably carried it with them on campaign, although usually not ostentatiously. McCrossen (REF. 4, page 68) writes, "The very design of the Union's uniforms suggests that officers and enlisted men were expected to carry a watch. ... Pocket watches were typically carried in vests, but since not all soldiers wore vests, a watch pocket lined with white cotton might have been sewn to the right of the fly of soldiers' trousers, as is the case with three pairs held by the New York Historical Society." Soldiers' shirts also had pockets suitable for watches. The Revised U.S. Army Regulations of 1861, Section 1485,

29. Split pusher, or push piece, in the pendant of the Waltham watch presented to Captain John Eddy, indicating the presence of lift springs actuating both lids of the hunting style case. The attractive milling on the edge of this case is a dot pattern. A second form of decoration, "reeding," also widely used on coinage of the period, is visible along the edges of the case lids above and below the case edge in this image. As on coins, reeding was used even more widely on case edges than milling.

specified the standard Federal fatigue blouse, or "four button sack coat," as follows: "For Fatigue Purposes - a sack coat of dark blue flannel extending half-way down the thigh, and made loose, without sleeve or body lining, falling collar, **inside pocket on the left side**, four coat buttons down the front." [emphasis added] A coat pocket right in front of one's heart might also have seemed like an especially appealing place to keep a substantial piece of metal. (The Civil War Museum of Philadelphia has in its collection a bullet-struck watch that belonged to Sgt. John O. Foering of the 28th Pennsylvania Infantry, and that example is not unique.)

With the preceding considerations in mind, some mostly posed pictures of Civil War soldiers wearing watches, in most instances as evidenced by their exposed watch chains, are shown in **FIGURES 34–42**. As can be seen, watches were by no means a luxury restricted to officers. In one or two of these instances, the watches at the other ends of these chains are known.

In **FIGURE 40**, not only the chain but the watch itself is seen in the soldier's hand. This circa 1861 image from the Library of Congress Collection likely shows a twenty-year-old Private Florentine Ariosto Jones of the 13th Massachusetts Infantry, who listed his pre-enlistment occupation as "watchmaker." [52] F. A. Jones worked at E. Howard & Co. of Boston (often subsequently abbreviated herein as "EH&Co") before the war. After the war, he then famously went on to become the Factory Superintendent at EH&Co around 1865, succeeding George P. Reed in that position, before relocating to Switzerland to found the International Watch Co. of Schaffhausen in 1868. The details in the image are too hazy to know for certain, but the watch seems to be about the right size and to have the right kind of flat profile to be an N-size Howard product, and the center post and the boss of the minute hand seem sufficiently narrow for the watch in Jones's hand to be a rear-setting Howard.

Last but not least, the Union's leading general, Ulysses S. Grant, is shown in **FIGURE 41** as a major general, and in **FIGURE 42** after his promotion to lieutenant general (the Union's only active lieutenant general at that time).

30. Front of the 18-kt. gold hunting case of the John Eddy Waltham watch. The case shows considerable careful use, which is perhaps ideal for a provenance watch like this one.

Commercial Pocket Watch Advertising Targeting Civil War Soldiers

FIGURE 43 (p. 49) is a copy of an advertisement widely disseminated from late 1861 throughout the Civil War by Robbins & Appleton (R&A). Through R&A, the AWCo touted their William Ellery grade watches in "Sterling silver" hunting cases as being "expressly designed for Soldiers." There are some clear misstatements of fact in this ad, as nearly all American-made silver cases are coin silver (90% pure), not Sterling silver (92.5% pure), and the Model 1859

31. Captain John Eddy (1821–86), born in Devonshire, England, immigrated to the United States in 1837. Captain Eddy served with the 95th Illinois Infantry, where in addition to Island Number 10, he fought at the Battles of Raymond, Jackson, Champion's Hill (the pivotal battle of the Vicksburg Campaign), and Big Black River.

In 1864 the 43-year-old farmer was sent back home to Coral, IL, McHenry County, to recruit more troops for the cause. According to the Daily Illinois State Journal of January 6, 1865 (page 3), he was appointed Acting Assistant Quartermaster for Camp Butler at the beginning of that year, remaining throughout April. In May 1865 Captain Eddy marched with the First Division at the head of the Lincoln funeral procession. He was active in the Grand Army of the Republic (GAR) after the war and actually "fell dead," probably of a heart attack, while addressing a GAR gathering in Marengo, IL, where he is buried.

The "History of McHenry County," Illinois, (Chicago: Inter-State Publishing Co., 1885) relates that John Eddy "served in many local offices of trust, such as Sheriff, Supervisor, Justice of the Peace, School Trustee and Director." *Image from civilwardata.com (June 10, 2018).*

32. Waltham watch movement SN 40,134, finished in November 1860, of Captain Charles Fuller's watch: American Watch Co. grade, nineteen-jewel three-quarter-plate Model 1859 movement. This flagship product features a temperature-compensated bimetallic balance and D. B. Fitts's patented reversing center pinion, marked on the top plate in an arc around the winding arbor washer. The Fitts's pinion unscrews harmlessly in the event of a mainspring breakage, dissipating the violent reverse impulse associated with it and protecting the fragile escapement down train. Part of the novel mechanism is visible in the picture as a steel disk concentric with the center wheel. American Watch Company grade movements like this one were the AWCo's highest-grade products and were made in very limited numbers. Like the example shown, these watches were more often than not cased in gold. Captain Fuller's watch likely commanded a price of $200 or more. Many American wage laborers, not to mention Union privates, earned less than $200 in a year. *Image courtesy of Craig Risch.*

design, presumably their "new style," predated the Civil War, thus documenting that inaccuracy and hyperbole are hardly new phenomena in commercial advertising. The ad also claims that Waltham watches are sturdier and more dependable than the "worthless, cheap watches of British and Swiss manufacture with which

the country is flooded," which they may have been. These allegedly superior American alternatives are "of a moderate price," which is presumably higher than the "cheap, worthless" foreign watches that the ad disparaged, but is nevertheless, "nearly as low … as the fancy-named Ancres [lever escapement watches] and

33. Personalized dial of Captain Charles Fuller's watch. Double-sunk dials like this one were very scarce in the Civil War period. The Fuller watch dial is the only example known to the author of a personalized dial, whether double-sunk or otherwise, on a Civil War provenance watch. (The dial is said to be "double-sunk," because the seconds bit carrying the seconds indications is set below the central disk, two levels below the chapter ring.) In this period, double-sunk dials only appeared on some very limited runs of the AWCo's highest-grade Model 1859 watches. The "teardrop"-style hands, with polished bosses and slender spade tips, are more common on E. Howard & Co. watches than Waltham watches. *Image courtesy of Craig Risch.*

Lepines of foreign make …" Lepine calibre watch movements [53] were an abundant Civil War-era style (actually several related styles; see Chapter 5 on p. 75).

Several aspects of this ad are noteworthy. First, it targets Union soldiers specifically, claiming that the watch model being offered was designed with soldiers in mind. Second, the AWCo ad states that the American watch market was "flooded" with cheap foreign watches. Such a flood would presumably have occurred in response to exploding demand, which in 1863 could have had only one plausible cause. Thus, the ad provides additional corroboration, if any were necessary, that the entry of more than a million Northern men into uniform—and in many cases, into the Northern wage economy—convinced many who had never felt a need to own a watch that they could no longer do without one. For similar reasons an upsurge in demand for watches could be expected to have occurred in the South as well, although the unavailability of American-made watches due to the absence of watch manufacturers in the South, and the Federal naval blockade restricting imports, might well have

34. An unidentified Union sentry with a prominent watch chain. This man appears to be carrying the watch in a pouch on his belt, where it would have been more conveniently accessible for frequent consultation, rather than in his coat pocket. *Image from the Library of Congress.*

35. Lieutenant Josiah Mahoney, a proud Southern Unionist of the 8th Tennessee Volunteer Cavalry, Company D, sporting a prominent watch chain on his vest. The 8th TN Cavalry participated in the Knoxville Campaign (fall of 1863), the Siege of Knoxville (September–December 1863), and the Second Battle of Saltville (December 20–21, 1864). *Image from fortcampbellcourier.com (June 10, 2018).*

36. Black soldiers also wore watches. Shown here is an image of First Sergeant James H. Harris of the 38th U.S. Colored Troops (USCT), Company B, one of approximately 200,000 freedmen and other African Americans who fought for emancipation and for the Union. Harris was awarded the Medal of Honor for his heroic actions during the Battle of Chaffin's Farm, on September 29, 1864. His regiment, part of a division of black troops, assaulted the center of the Confederate defenses at New Market Heights. Harris and two other men of the 38th USCT, Private William H. Barnes and Sergeant Edward Ratcliff, were in the lead of the assault. The three men were the first to reach the Confederate defenders and engage them in hand-to-hand combat. The rest of their division followed, and the Confederates were routed. In all, over half the men of the black division had been killed, captured, or wounded in the battle. Harris's Medal of Honor citation was awarded for "gallantry in the assault." Private Barnes and Sergeant Ratcliff also were awarded Medals of Honor for their heroism that day. (In REF. 4, McCrossen discusses another image of a black soldier, posing similarly with a revolver and a prominent watch chain. She remarked about that picture, "Watches were signs and symbols of power, equal to pistols and rifles . . .") *Image from the Library of Congress.*

37. A highly produced picture of six proud soldiers of the 63rd New York Infantry, part of Meagher's celebrated Irish Brigade, immortalized in numerous songs. Two of the men in the picture, all of whom are likely line officers (i.e., lieutenants or captains), are wearing visible watch chains. All wear happy smiles in this posed picture, but during the Battle of Fredericksburg (December 11–15, 1862), the Irish Brigade suffered 41.4% casualties in its assault on the stone wall atop Marye's Heights, a charge in which they shouted "Faugh-a-Bellagh," ("Clear the way"), advancing over their own dead and wounded. In that battle, the color sergeant of the 69th NY Infantry, another part of Meagher's brigade, was found dead with his flag concealed and wrapped around his body, a bullet having pierced the flag and his heart. At Antietam on September 17, 1862, eight color bearers of the Irish Brigade were shot down at Bloody Lane, but the brigade carried the position. The men of the Irish Brigade were among the 150,000 Irish Americans, mostly recent immigrants who had fled the Irish Potato Famine (1845–52), who fought for the Union. Irish Americans also served in significant numbers in the Confederate army. The 33rd Virginia Infantry, part of the famed Stonewall Brigade, was composed of Irish immigrant volunteers. During the Battle of First Manassas/First Bull Run this regiment may have been the first unit to utter the "rebel yell," a shrill, piercing battle cry that sent shivers up many a Union spine. *Image from the Library of Congress.*

frustrated much of the demand that was generated. Third, the Waltham watch ad shows that despite the economies of scale and the advantages of automation achieved by the AWCo by 1863, the AWCo was not competing with foreign suppliers purely on price. Rather, American mass-produced watches were neither the cheapest nor the most expensive on the market, but were being marketed as allegedly best-value alternatives based on superior quality for the money. Fourth, Robbins & Appleton was

attempting to exploit the patriotic zeal of the times, touting, "American Watches for Americans" to appeal to proud American consumers, and to soldiers in particular.

Other advertisements from the same source, which ran just as widely more or less concurrently with the first, took the patriotic theme a step further, playing not only to national pride but stirring resentment toward the Confederacy's alleged covert European allies and their allegedly inferior products. For instance, a watch

38. Corporal David Urbansky (also spelled Orbansky) of the 58th Ohio Volunteer Infantry, Company B. Born in 1843 in Lauten-burg, Prussia, he immigrated to the United States in 1857, settling in Columbus, OH, and enlisting in the Union army about six months after the Civil War began. Corporal Urbansky became one of six Jewish soldiers to win the Medal of Honor during the Civil War. His medal was awarded for "gallantry in actions" at both Shiloh (1862) and again at Vicksburg (1863). During the Siege of Vicksburg, the 5'3" tall Urbansky rescued his commanding officer, who was lying wounded in a no-man's land, by carrying him to safety under heavy enemy fire. The officer recovered as a result of the prompt medical attention he was able to receive after his rescue by Urbansky.

    Of the nation's small population of 150,000 Jews, about 6,700 Jewish men, including at least four generals, served in the Union army, and 3,000 served in the Confederate army. About 600 Jewish men died during service. Urbansky also counted as one of over 200,000 native Germans, the largest single immigrant contingent, and one of over half a million immigrants to serve in the Union army. A major reason for the surge in German immigration in the period before the Civil War was the series of failed revolutions that spread across the German states in 1848. These uprisings were unsuccessful bids for greater democracy and representative government. In their aftermath many thousands left to build a new life with greater opportunity in the only democracy available: America. It is no surprise that so many of these same men subsequently chose to fight to preserve that democracy. This writer would dearly love to know where Corporal Urbansky's watch is today. *Image used with permission of the Jacob Rader Marcus Center of the American Jewish Archives, Cincinnati, OH.*

39. A studio picture of three Union soldiers, two wearing visible watch chains. The cocky looking fellow in the middle, with a cigar between his teeth skewed at a jaunty angle and a period, minstrel-style banjo, perhaps made by William E. Boucher, balanced on his shoulder, clearly comes across as the dominant personality of the group. *Image courtesy of James Bollman.*

40. Likely an 1861 image of young Private Florentine Ariosto Jones of the 13th Massachusetts Infantry, "watchmaker," and future Howard Factory Superintendent and IWC founder. Jones appears on the roster of the 13th MA, and the young man in the image bears a strong likeness to the man in a definitively identified photograph of F. A. Jones at a later age. The 13th MA lost four officers and 117 enlisted men killed and mortally wounded and forty enlisted men by disease, a total of 161 casualties, during service. They served at Cedar Mountain, Thoroughfare Gap, 2nd Bull Run, South Mountain, Chantilly, Antietam, Chancellorsville, Fredericksburg, Gettysburg, Wilderness, Spotsylvania, North Anna, Pamunkey River, Totopotomoy Creek, and Cold Harbor, among other battles, mustering out of service in August 1864. *Image from the Library of Congress archives, a sixth plate tintype from the Liljenquist Family Collection.*

advertisement placed by Robbins & Appleton in the *Pittsburgh Daily Post* of March 24, 1862, asked, "Why should an American send gold to England and France, our covert but bitter enemies, when gold is so much needed at home?" Yet another common Waltham watch ad declared "No More English or French Rubbish made to Sell but not to Keep Time."

Three advertisements by two New York watch wholesalers that appeared in *Harper's Weekly* are shown in **FIGURES 44–46**. The first two appeared on June 13, 1863, scarcely two weeks before the Battle of Gettysburg, and the last one, on April 2, 1864, less than a month before the bloody Overland Campaign

commenced in Virginia. All three ads target soldiers. Apparently, even sellers of exceedingly cheap foreign watches in gold-plated (not to be confused with gold-filled) cases were claiming to offer watches "adapted to the Army." One ad offers foreign "calendar watches" and "genuine American lever watches" both for the same price of $22. (A "lever watch" is a watch with a lever escapement, different forms of which are illustrated in Chapter 5, starting on p. 75.)

The reference to "genuine" American watch-

42. Lieutenant General Grant, photographed sometime after March 9, 1864. Notice the three stars on his right epaulette and the four-button groups on his frock coat. *Image from the Library of Congress.*

41. Major General Ulysses S. Grant, photographed sometime between February 1862 and March 9, 1864. Note the two stars on his epaulettes and the three button triplets visible on one side of his double-breasted frock coat. *Image from the Library of Congress.*

es again reflects that Waltham products were already known to be frequent targets of Swiss counterfeiters, an indirect tribute to the AW-Co's recent commercial success and technological accomplishments. Indeed, the title of an advertisement for Waltham watches placed by a retail sales outlet, W. P. Bingman & Co., that appeared in the *Indiana State Sentinel* (Indianapolis, IN) as early as August 4, 1862, was already warning Waltham watch buyers to "Beware of Counterfeits." A more widely disseminated warning, not its first, placed directly by the AWCo shortly after the war ended, appeared on multiple dates in probably dozens of newspapers. It was titled "Caution from

the American Watch Company" and included stern warnings against counterfeit "Walthams" and inferior, imitation "soldier's watches." Yet another ad that ran in the *Detroit Free Press* on November 21, 1862, offers allegedly "American hunting watches sold as low as $20." However, this ad makes no direct reference to the AWCo, which was the only one of the two active American watch manufacturers offering watches anywhere near that price; that omission should raise suspicions high. (Perhaps an Ellery grade Waltham movement in an *albata* [i.e., a nickel alloy] case might have sold that low, but that is questionable. Surviving silver watchcases from the Civil War period greatly outnumber contemporaneous albata cases, despite the frequent remelting of silver cases over

American Watches
For Soldiers
AT REDUCED PRICES.

American Watches for
Americans!

THE AMERICAN WATCH COMPANY give notice that they have lately issued a new style of Watch, expressly designed for Soldiers and others who desire a good watch at a moderate price. These watches are intended to displace the worthless, cheap watches of British and Swiss manufacture with which the country is flooded, and which were never expected to keep time when they were made, being refuse manufactures sent to this country because unsalable at home, and used here only for jockeying and swindling purposes.

We offer to sell our Watch, which is of THE MOST SUBSTANTIAL MANUFACTURE, AN ACCURATE AND DURABLE TIME-KEEPER, and in Sterling Silver Cases, Hunting pattern, at nearly as low a price as is asked for the fancy-named Ancres and Lepines of foreign make, already referred to.

We have named the new series of Watches, WM. ELLERY, Boston, Mass., which name will be found on the plate of every watch of this manufacture, and is one of our trade-marks.

Sold by all respectable watch dealers in the loyal States.

Wholesale orders should be addressed to

ROBBINS & APPLETON,
Agents of the American Watch Company,
182 BROADWAY, N.Y.

43. A reproduction of an advertisement for Waltham watches, placed by Robbins & Appleton. This was one of several Waltham watch ads widely disseminated throughout "the loyal states" (plus other Union territory) in 1861–1865. Papers in which the ad appeared included the *Washington DC Evening Star*, the *Detroit Free Press*, the *Chicago Tribune*, the *Philadelphia Inquirer*, and the *New South*, of Port Royal, SC (which was recaptured by Union forces in November 1861), among others.

$22. WATCHES. $22.

A Splendid Silver Hunting Case Lever, that indicates the day of the month accurately, for $22; usual price $35 to $45.

$22. Genuine. $22.

Genuine American Lever Watches, in Sterling Silver Hunting Case, for $22 ; worth $35 at retail.

Also every variety of good Watches at equally low rates.

All orders from the Army must be pre-paid, as the Express Companies will not take bills for collection on soldiers.

J. L. FERGUSON, IMPORTER OF WATCHES,

208 Broadway, New York.

44. A reproduction of a June 13, 1863, advertisement in *Harper's Weekly*, from an importer, J. L. Ferguson, offering, among other items, "Genuine American Lever Watches," for $22 retail, but again making no mention of the only plausible authentic source. One can almost smell the snake oil.

the years. This fact indicates that albata cases were not very popular.)

American Watch Factory Production Records

The conclusion that AWCo watch advertisements directed at soldiers significantly stimulated public demand for Waltham watches is consistent with AWCo factory production and employment figures for the Civil War years. Southern secession precipitated a broad economic depression that gripped the North beginning in 1861 and extended into 1862, and this event was reflected in the AWCo's immediate fortunes. But as the North reorganized for war and as provisions were made to equip and supply an army of the greater part of a million men, industrial output rebounded and then

$7. WATCHES. $7.

A Beautiful Engraved Gold-Plated Watch, Lever Cap, small size, English Movements, perfect time-keeper. Sent free by mail, in neat case, for only $7. A Solid Silver, same as above, $7. Specially adapted to the ARMY. CHAS. P. NORTON & CO., 38 & 40 Ann Street, N. Y.

45. A reproduction of a second watch ad appearing in the same June 13, 1863, issue of *Harper's Weekly*, this one for "solid silver watches specially adapted to the Army," for $7.

$47. AMERICAN $47. LEVER WATCHES.

Trade Mark, P. S. Bartlett, Waltham, Mass., Full Jeweled, WARRANTED, in 4 oz. coin silver hunting case, gold joints, fancy push pin, for $47.

Also every variety of good Watches at equally low rates. All orders from the Army must be pre-paid, as the Express Companies will not take bills for collection on soldiers.

J. L. Ferguson, Importer of Watches. 208 Broadway New York.

46. A reproduction of a *Harper's Weekly* advertisement of April 2, 1864, also from retailer J. L. Ferguson, offering P. S. Bartlett grade Waltham watches, which would have been 18-size Model 1857 full plates, in four-ounce silver cases for $47. Here at last is an advertisement for American watches specifying the make and grade of the Waltham watches being offered and with a realistic price. Presumably, because the price of $47 was being touted, the seller regarded this price as an especially attractive one. This ad is a powerful confirmation that not even lesser Waltham products were available at that time for a price as low as $13, as is occasionally claimed.

accelerated despite the manpower drain created by enlistment. Concurrently, the demand for watches exploded. Thus, in 1863, Treasurer Royal E. Robbins of the American Watch Co. was able to report,

"I have the pleasure to say the demand for our productions continues not only without abatement but in quantities we find ourselves wholly unable to supply. Indeed the trouble for the last year has been to divide the watches amongst our very numerous customers as to produce the least dissatisfaction. The several advances in price we have been partly compelled and under these circumstances partly invited to make, have been paid with entire readiness, and although these prices have now reached a very high point the demand continues as brisk as ever." [54]

But in 1864, even after having ramped up production to 250 watches per day, Waltham still could not supply the entire demand for domestic timepieces. Other ambitious entrepreneurs and investors took notice. And thus in that year, as mentioned, five new watch companies were capitalized—the National Watch Co. of Elgin IL; the United States Watch Co. of Marion, NJ; the New York Watch Co. of Providence, RI [sic]; the Newark Watch Co. of Newark, NJ; and the Tremont Watch Co. of Boston, the last of which would assemble parts mostly manufactured abroad. It is noted, however, that none of these companies would produce watches before the Civil War ended, perhaps excepting Tremont, whose first watches reached the market in May, 1865, the month in which the fighting ended. (Henceforth, we will take May 13, 1865, the date of the conclusion of the war's last battle, at Palmito Ranch in Texas, as the effective end of the conflict. Other dates may be quoted in other sources, but we are primarily concerned here with whether a watch might have seen action on a Civil War battlefield.)

The AWCo factory production records indicate that in 1860, the last full year of production prior to the start of the Civil War, 12,484 men's watch movements were made, many of which were cased by the AWCo in silver or gold. In 1861, only 2,360 men's watches were made, an 81% drop! The technologically advanced but undercapitalized Nashua Watch Company would have encountered the same hurricane headwinds in 1861-62, a fact which may well have changed watchmaking history. In 1862, annual production of men's watches was 16,620. Production shot up to 34,121 in 1863, then to 45,940 in 1864, and finally to 46,801 movements in the last year of the conflict. Thereafter, Waltham production and sales remained strong and followed a generally increasing trajectory for many years, punctuated only by unrelated fluctuations in the larger economy. This trend is understandable. The Civil War permanently expanded the potential market for watches. A consciousness of clock time, once imbued by life-and-death experiences in war, tends to remain with a person forever after. McCrossen (REF. 4, page 67) observed that, "War accelerated the transformation of Americans, particularly soldiers, into clockwatchers. During the US-Mexican War (1846-48), most officers and some soldiers carried watches, but it was during the US Civil War that watches spread through the ranks."

Furthermore, the popularity of American watches among soldiers, and the technological strides made by American watch manufacturers during the war both elevated the standing of American watch-making with the American public and brought domestic watches within the financial means of a greater fraction of the population. The AWCo's annual production of women's watches never quite reached 3,000 during any year of the Civil War, but it is quite likely that some of these watches were purchased by female nurses in military hospitals. Civil War nurses, both male and female, would have found themselves with more need of a watch than many, as they would have had to take patients' pulses and perform a myriad of other tasks on a schedule, in order to coordinate their own work with that of many other busy staffers and doctors.

In all, about 146,000 men's watches were made by the AWCo and its predecessors, which would have been available for service during all or some part of the Civil War. Swings in employment levels at AWCo during the Civil War roughly tracked the swings in production rates. The company treasurer, Royal E. Robbins, who was also the principal owner, reported 180 full-time hands at work in fiscal year (FY) 1859 (fiscal years beginning on February 1). [3] As the secession crisis loomed in 1860, 160 employees were at work but were reduced to four-fifths time, constituting a full-time equivalent workforce of only 128. During part of FY 1861, as the crisis struck, production actually ceased altogether. During FY 1862, employment levels had barely recovered to eighty full-time equivalents, but by FY 1863 the full-time employment level ballooned to 429 hands—between two and three times the size of the prewar workforce!

The AWCo sold nearly all of its watches domestically and in the North during the Civil War. Thus, because a significant fraction of the able adult male population of the North was in uniform at some point during the war and all of these men earned cash wages, there is every reason to conclude that the dramatic commensurate spike in demand for Waltham watches originated principally with the soldiers specifically targeted by the company's marketing campaigns in that same period. (Indeed, the AWCo introduced the first William Ellery grade Model 1857 movements in May of 1861, [56] scarcely a month after President Lincoln's initial call for 75,000 troops.) Hence, one may conclude that a significant fraction, and perhaps even a majority of the nearly 150,000 men's watches produced by American watch manufacturers prior to the end of the Civil War, most of which were produced *during* the war, might have found their way into soldiers' pockets. To this number must be added an even larger number of foreign watches, which remained the most affordable (if not necessarily always the most reliable) watches available during the entire Civil War period. McCrossen reports that in 1865 alone, the last year of the war, Swiss makers exported 226,000 watches to the United States, more than Waltham's cumulative production. Throughout the war, British makers exported about 30,000 watches to the US annually. [4]

Many of the watch production records of E. Howard & Co. also survive from the Civil War period and are located at the Smithsonian American History Archives Center in Washington, DC. These records indicate that any of about 6,000–7,000 expensive, luxury market Howard watches made before the end of the Civil War might have found their way into the pocket of an officer or a well-heeled enlisted man. Howard movement serial numbers began at 101, but Howard movements were never completed in strict serial order, and some serial numbers never were made at all. Nevertheless, it is a useful reference point that as the last battle of the Civil War was concluding on May 13, 1865, the EH&Co production records indicate that movement SN 7,000 was finished and added to inventory in the Howard factory. (In May 1865, and in fact until 1874, ladies' watch movement production at Howard had been limited to only one hundred movements.)

Court Testimony Referring to the Purchase of Watches by Civil War Soldiers

Paymaster Major Jonathan Ladd received the watch previously shown in **FIGURE 25** (see p. 36) from grateful officers of the 2nd Connecticut Volunteer Artillery. He was an interesting character whose greatest claim to notoriety is that he and his watch may have been present in the boardinghouse across from the Ford Theatre on the evening of April 14, 1865, where President Lincoln lay dying. [38] It may even be that Ladd's watch, doubtless among numerous others, recorded the time of our greatest president's last moments. Shortly after those more impactful moments, Major Ladd was court-martialed on June 10, 1865, for having engaged in the illegal profiteering on sales of—what else?—watches, to fellow servicemen. The following excerpt, from the same source, [44] of the testimony at Ladd's court-martial given, presumably under oath, by a sutler (a civilian provisioner for troops) named Luther Caldwell, shines an unflattering light on the dimensions of part of the trade in watches to Union troops:

> **Caldwell:** "We accordingly made an arrangement by which he [Major Ladd] was to have one quarter of the profits of all the watches we sold at the barracks."
>
> **Lawyer:** "Which was how much on a watch?"
>
> **Caldwell:** "Well the watches cost us $33.50

and we sold them for $60. He [Ladd] had a quarter of that, which was $6.50, or something like that."

Lawyer: "How many watches did you sell under that arrangement?"

Caldwell: "Well I don't know exactly. I should say, something over four hundred."

And this was the magnitude of the watch business conducted, or more precisely, admitted to, by only one sutler, probably over the course of less than a year in Elmira, NY, which was the site of a recruit collection and training base and a collocated prison camp for Confederate POWs. The fact is also quite noteworthy that four hundred soldiers, most of whom likely would have been enlisted men rather than officers, were willing to pay what was about four to five months of a private's pay for what they regarded as a desirable watch. The cheapest foreign imports in gilded brass cases may have been available for as little as $7, and refurbished watches perhaps were available even more cheaply. And yet, Caldwell's testimony tells us that many common soldiers were willing to pay several times more than was probably necessary to have just any watch, to have what they considered a quality, reliable watch to carry into harm's way with them. If Caldwell was selling Waltham watches, which seems very possible, one could infer from this fact that the AWCo's ads clearly had achieved an impact.

Of course, there was also a brisk, completely legal trade in watches by itinerant merchants to Civil War troops. Author Carlene Stephens wrote that, "Roving merchants sold thousands of cheap watches to eager customers in wartime encampments." [55]

Accounts of Watches as Battlefield Plunder

After a battle, pocket watches were one of the first items looked for by looters and scavengers on either side. William Keating Clare of the 9th New York State Militia (83rd NY Infantry) relates part of his experiences while burying Confederate dead after the Battle of Gettysburg, in a letter dated July 5, 1863:

> Then several regiments were detailed to bury the dead, which occupied all day. ... While burying the rebel dead many valuables were found. The idea of searching dead men's pockets may strike you with indignation, - but what's the use of burying gold and silver? **Our men secured thousands of watches,** chains, "greenbacks," and, strange to say, thousand in gold coin with which the Southern Army is well supplied. [58]

Similarly, Lieutenant Colonel John I. Nevin of the 28th Pennsylvania Infantry recorded in his diary on July 3, 1863, that "A man of the 62nd New York came to our camp tonight with eight watches to sell." [59] There should be little doubt how he got them.

Much the same went for the plundering of the possessions of live prisoners. Historian Allen C. Guelzo reports:

> One officer of the famed Louisiana Tiger battalion [it likely was Captain William J. Seymour, who is known to have left a diary] was shocked after [the battle of] First Bull Run [which Confederates called "First Manassas"] to find '30 or 40' of his men 'marching up with new uniforms on, gold rings on their fingers, and their pockets filled with watches and money that they had stolen.' [60]

Similarly, McCrossen (REF. 4, page 70) mentions the memoir of a Union prisoner in the infamous Confederate prison camp at Andersonville, Georgia, who wrote that prisoners were searched "and robbed of everything valuable—watches, money, knives." As the Lieber Code suggests (see "The Lieber Code"), Confederate prisoners likely had similar experiences.

Watches Recorded among the Exhumed Union Dead at Gettysburg

Large numbers of Union and Confederate dead were buried in mass graves immediately after the Battle of Gettysburg. Soon afterward, the process of exhuming and then reinterring many of these bodies in the Gettysburg National Cemetery began. This process was carried out with great care and respect for the dead, especially with Union soldiers. In particular, the possessions found with each soldier were carefully recorded and kept in separate containers for possible retrieval by loved ones. Of course, many, and probably even most of the dead had been relieved of their valuables prior to burial (often, probably in one of the various hospitals before even reaching the cemetery). Nevertheless, the *Revised Report to the Select Committee to the House of Representatives, Soldiers National Cemetery, Gettysburg, with Accompanying Documents*, authored by Samuel Weaver in March of 1864, records approximately thirty Union bodies discovered with valuables still on their persons from among 270 bodies whose personal effects were cataloged in the report. For this purpose I have somewhat arbitrarily defined as a "valuable" either any precious metal object specifically identified as such or cash totaling amounts over 20¢ (smaller amounts might having been missed). Of these thirty individuals, four were found with silver or gold watches, although, oddly enough, no watch keys. Three other deceased soldiers, not among the aforementioned thirty, were found with watch keys or a watch chain, but no watches. One might infer from these data that in 1863 at least four in thirty soldiers in the Army of the Potomac, or about 13%, carried a watch.

However, this 13% watch ownership rate estimate is almost certainly a lower bound, because the four-in-thirty ratio would overlook any person who had only a watch among his valuables and had it taken away prior to burial. Furthermore, several examples are reported here of a dying or a dead man's watch being given to or taken away by respectful comrades in arms for return to the deceased's family. Several other examples are known of men who gave their watches or other valuables to noncombatants (e.g., chaplains, servants, quartermasters, surgeons, or cooks) before a major anticipated action. Typical of these was a note recorded at Gettysburg by Confederate Major G. B. Gerald of the 18th Mississippi Infantry (Barksdale's Brigade):

> Second day's fight … The field officers dismounted from their horses, the reason for this being that an order had been issued sometime before that no officer below the rank of brigadier or acting brigadier general should ride into battle, because of the fact of difficulty in replacing the horses killed. **I gave my horse and watch as well as some other belongings to my servant.** [61]

Nevertheless, we have this 13% lower bound figure to fall back on. Inasmuch as more than three million soldiers served in the Union and Confederate armies, combined, over the course of the war, even this modest lower bound rate would give us a minimum of about 400,000 watches that saw service! The real total was almost certainly considerably higher than that.

The Lieber Code of Military Conduct Reference to Pocket Watches Carried by Prisoners of War

Live Confederates captured by Union troops may have fared no better than Union soldiers captured by the Louisiana Tigers, as far as their valuables were concerned. Indirect evidence of this is the issuance of Article 72 of the Federal Army's "Instructions for the Government of Armies of the United States in the Field," known as the "Lieber Code of Military Conduct," dated April 24, 1863. It stated:

> Money and other valuables on the person of a prisoner, such as watches or jewelry, as well as extra clothing, are regarded by the American Army as the private property of the prisoner, and the appropriation of such valuables or money is considered dishonorable, and is prohibited.

The fact that such a regulation was considered necessary and that it specifically mentioned watches attests to a widespread practice that was being addressed, which could not have been widespread if pocket watches were not frequently found among Confederate prisoners and dead. (Issuance of the regulation likely did little to curtail the prohibited practice.) This piece of evidence is one of a few sources

that speak, at least indirectly in this case, to the prevalence of watches in the Confederate army. And of course, apart from some number of American watches plundered from living or dead Union soldiers, or purchased before the war, watches carried by Confederate soldiers would have been overwhelmingly of foreign make.

Watch Prices versus Soldiers' and Civilians' Pay

The affordability of watches to soldiers was obviously another factor bearing on the number and nature of watches in soldiers' pockets. Most of the information currently available is relevant only to watch prices available to Union soldiers, because new American-made watches were not much available within the Confederacy after 1861, and even foreign watches might have been more expensive in the South than in the North because of the Federal naval blockade of Southern ports. However, in the North the advertisements previously shown provide some landmarks, as does the Robbins & Appleton trade catalog of April 12, 1864. The R&A catalog, information from which is provided in **TABLE 1**, thus establishes nominal wholesale prices for Waltham movements in 1864. It is not known whether discounts may have been applied or how deep they might have been, although the predecessor firm, AT&Co, was offering discounts to retailers of 20% to 30% as late as 1858, when the country was still in the throes of the financial depression of 1857. [62] However, given R. E. Robbins's exuberant sales report of 1863 cited earlier, it is unlikely that the AWCo was discounting their catalog prices in 1863, or for that matter, even in late 1862. It is similarly unlikely that actual retail prices were any lower than nominal wholesale prices.

As observed earlier, the AWCo had positioned its most high-volume products in the market as mid-priced, best-buy options that supposedly were specifically designed for soldiers. This fact may surprise some, because one can find undocumented assertions spread around the literature and the Internet that complete, cased William Ellery grade Waltham watches were available to Union soldiers at a retail price of $13, which would have made them competitive on price with all but the cheapest foreign goods. There is no evidence I have found to support this contention. According to TABLE 1, in 1864 the list wholesale price of a William Ellery grade Model 1857 or Model 1859 watch (the most common models) with a silver hunting case (the most common casing choice) was $26 for a seven-jewel watch or $27.50 for an eleven-jewel watch, and more for heavier cases. (In 1860–61 Waltham did offer some watches at deep discounts to stay afloat, but total Waltham output at the time was small compared with ramped-up production rates later in the war.) The wholesale prices listed in the 1864 R&A trade catalog would be broadly consistent with the sworn military court testimony of sutler Luther Caldwell given in 1865, who averred that he paid $32.50 each for the many watches he sold to the troops in Elmira, NY, if they were Waltham products as seems very possible.

As a prominently American manufacturer, the AWCo doubtless also benefited from the patriotic fervor in the country, as suggested by a line in one of its ads, "American watches made for Americans." The AWCo's best-buy marketing strategy was well suited to a situa-

tion in which many soldiers seem to have been keener on having a reliable timepiece in their pocket than the most affordable one. As mentioned, some kind of small size "English" watch, in a gold-plated brass case apparently was advertised for as little as $7, which was less than a month's pay for even a Union private (see TABLE 3). McCrossen mentions that there was at this time also a lively trade in second-hand watches, which presumably were cheaper than new ones. A wider variety of new watches, perhaps of somewhat better quality, was available for around $22. And according to the testimony of sutler Luther Caldwell previously cited, he allegedly did a brisk, if somewhat illicit, business in watches among Federal troops at $60 apiece. This fact documents the strong demand for quality timepieces among soldiers. Caldwell reported that he had paid $33.50 for these same watches, so his markup was 79%. That kind of margin is not unusual in the modern retail jewelry business, where turnover of inventory is slow, and not infrequently glacial. One can only wonder whether Caldwell's markup was typical or unusual of watch sellers supplying the Civil War Federal troops. However, considering that Caldwell was sharing his commission with Ladd, and Ladd apparently risked court martial for his involvement with the sales, one may surmise that Caldwell's markup may have been significantly higher than was considered "legitimate" to justify that jeopardy.

As indicated in the R&A wholesale ("For the Trade Only") catalog, William Ellery grade movements, presumably of either the three-quarter-plate (Model 1859, famously advertised for soldiers) or full-plate (Model 1857) models ranged in price from $16.50 for seven-jewel movements to $18.00 for eleven-jewel

			Grade		
		Wm. Ellery	PS Bartlett	AT&Co[C]	AWCo[D]
Model 1857 (18-size, full plate)[A]	7 jewels	$16.50	-	-	
	11 jewels	$18.00	$19.00	-	
	15 jewels	-	$20.50	$33.00	(not made)[E]
	w/gold balance	+$0.75	+$0.75	-	
	w/comp. balance	-	+$3.50	+$5.00	
	w/temp. adjust	-	-	+$5.00	
Model 1859 (18-size, ¾ plate)[B]	7 jewels	$16.50	(unknown)[F]	(not made)[G]	(not made)[G]
	11 jewels	$18.00			
Model 16KW/20KW (both ¾ plate)	15 or 19 jewels[C,D]	(not made)	(not made)	$52.50[H]	$120.00
	+Stratton's Barrel[I]			$62.50	$135.00
	+Stratton/Fogg[J]			$75.00	$150.00
Model 1861 (10-size Ladies' ¾ plate)	7 jewels		$23.00	-	
	13 jewels		$27.50	-	
	15 jewels	(not made)	-	$35.00	(not made)
	w/comp. balance		-	+$5.00	
	w/temp. adjust		-	+$7.50	
Open-Face Cases			$7.50–$9.00		
Coin Silver Hunting Case	2 oz.		$9.50		
	2 oz. w/silver cap		$10.50		
	"heavier"[K]		$11.50		
	"even heavier"[K]		$12.50		
	gold case joints		+$1.00		

TABLE I: Wholesale prices for movements and silver watchcases from the April 12, 1864 Robbins & Appleton Trade Catalog. (From Ehrhardt, REF. 63.)

A) In a full-plate movement, the barrel bridge and train plate together completely enclose the entire side of the movement opposite the dial, and the balance wheel pivots above the top plate. For an example, see FIGURE 11. B) In a three-quarter-plate movement, all train wheels are carried in the train plate, like a full-plate movement, but the balance wheel pivots adjacent to, and in or below, the plane of the top plate. For an example, see FIGURE 28. C) With only rare exceptions, all Appleton, Tracy & Co. grade movements had fifteen jewels. D) Except for movements with C. W. Fogg's vibrating stud, nearly all American Watch Co. grade movements had nineteen jewels in this period. E) One AWCo grade Model 1857 movement is known. F) No price information available. G) No longer made in this grade by 1864. H) This price includes $5.00 for a compensated balance and $7.50 for adjustment to temperature. I) N. P. Stratton's patented mainspring barrel protected the escapement from damage from the violent reverse impulses often accompanying mainspring failures. J) C. W. Fogg's patented vibrating hairspring stud was a form of regulator that was believed to perturb isochronism less than regulators with fixed curb pins. AWCo grade movements with Fogg's stud had twenty jewels, rather than nineteen. K) The "heavier" case possibly weighed three ounces and the "even heavier" possibly four ounces.

movements. Silver cases made in the AWCo's own case department cost from $7.50 to $9.00 for open-face cases, depending on weight, or from $9.50 to $12.50 for hunting-style cases (the most popular Civil War choice), with a $1 extra charge for gold joints. Thus, complete Ellery grade AWCo silver watches wholesaled for from $24 to $31.50, depending on particulars—at least, without undisclosed discounts. (The close coincidence of this price with those paid by Luther Caldwell for his inventory is highly suggestive.) The next grade up, the P. S. Bartlett (PSB), was also popular among enlisted men. Uncased movements sold for as little as $19.00 (with steel balance wheel and seven jewels) up to as much as $27.50 (with gold balance wheel and fifteen jewels), so complete silver PSB grade watches wholesaled for prices from $26.50 to $41.00, depending on particulars. The upper grades, "Appleton, Tracy & Co." and "American Watch Co.," were often carried by officers and were often in gold cases. All the Waltham watches this author has seen with inscribed presentations to Civil War commissioned officers were of one of these two grades.

Complete watches of the top two Waltham grades nominally wholesaled for as little as $40.50 for an AT&Co grade Model 1857 movement with gold balance and fifteen jewels in a silver open-face case, to up to $163.50 for a twenty-jewel AWCo grade 20-size key wind ("Model 1862") watch in a heavy silver hunting case with gold joints (more than a year's pay for a private!). Significant additional price increments would have applied due to a gold case and retail markups. The top-of-the-line AWCo grade silver 20-size watch costing $163.50 wholesale was adjusted to temperature, isochronism, and five positions. It featured twenty

ruby and diamond jewels, a bimetallic expansion balance and Breguet overcoil hairspring, which was considered more isochronous than a flat spiral hairspring. These movements had Stratton's patent mainspring barrel, which, like the previously mentioned Fitts's patented center pinion, protected the escapement against damage due to the reverse shocks associated with mainspring breakages. The twenty-jewel movements also featured Fogg's patent vibrating hairspring stud (a form of regulator), in which the hairspring stud turned in a jeweled pivot hole.

The other American watch manufacturer active during the Civil War, E. Howard & Co., was selling watch movements of their own unique "N" size, which was slightly greater in diameter than a standard Lancashire Gauge 19-size. The Howard company sold these movements to its direct factory customers for prices probably ranging from about $58 to $116, based on the available post-war pricing information. The $58 dollar movements had conventional gold gilding, simple regulators, and were adjusted only to isochronism. Their most expensive $116 movements featured gold-flashed ray damaskeening, R. S. Mershon's patent compound rack and pin regulator, all top plate train jewels in settings (either spun into the plate or screwed down), and adjustments to isochronism, temperature, and six positions. Nearly all Howard movements of the period had fifteen jewels; seventeen-jewel examples are rare. They were *quick train* (i.e., they beat 18,000 times per hour); they had Reed's patented (Nov. 24, 1857) protective barrel with integral maintaining power, which both protected the wheel train and escapement from damage during mainspring breakages and kept the watch running during winding; they had Geneva-style stop-works (see: Escapement Features); and they were adjusted at least for isochronism (i.e., uniformity of timekeeping accuracy over the running period). Many EH&Co movement examples with compensated balances were adjusted to temperature (i.e., "Heat & Cold"), and some were adjusted to six physical positions as well (dial up, dial down, pendant up, pendant right, pendant left, and pendant down).

The earliest Howard watch movement serial number for which factory wholesale pricing information is available is SN 17,601, a $106 movement finished in January 1869. **TABLE 2** gives the wholesale price structure for late (i.e., post-Civil War) Model 1862 ("Series III") movements of the kind most similar to those sold during the Civil War.

Howard retail watch price information from the Civil War period is tough to find. Five years after the Civil War, the Howard factory watch production records indicate that movement SN 23,984, with Reed's patent regulator, screwed-down jewel settings and adjusted to temperature and six positions, was sold to the Howard Co.'s Boston sales office on June 2, 1870, for $101. [57] An actual retail sales receipt (**FIGURE 47**) from the Howard company sales office at 114 Tremont St., in Boston, dated September 12, 1870, indicates that this movement was sold in a 61¾ pennyweight (total weight) 18-kt. case for an undiscounted retail price of $232.00, less a 15% discount (including on the case), bringing the final price to $197.20. During the Civil War the Federal government sold most of its $250,000,000 gold reserve to Britain at $16/ounce. As Federal gold reserves dwindled, the price of gold rose from $21/ounce in 1860 up to $30/ounce by 1865,

Feature	Factory inventory value
Base movement price (*adjusted only to isochronism-"U"*)	$58
Patent Regulator (*Mershon's during the Civil War, Reed's post-war*)	+$6
Jewel Settings in Train Plate (*set or screwed down*)	+$5
Adjusted to Temperature (*i.e., Heat and Cold or "HC"*)	+$12
Adjusted to Isochronism, Temperature, and Positions (all 6)—"HCI6P"	+$37
Ray Damaskeening (*with gold flashing*)	+$9
Ray Damaskeening and Nickel Plating (*post-war only*)	+$19

TABLE 2: Factory inventory prices for late 1860s N-size E. Howard & Co. watch movements. (From Table II-12 of **REF. 57**.)

a 43% rise. But by 1870 it was back down to $23/ounce, so the three-ounce 18-kt. watchcase sold in 1870 would likely have contained about $50 worth of gold. Adding a few dollars for the work of alloying the gold and forming it into a case with springs (which would have subtracted from the net weight of gold) and a crystal, and adding that figure to the wholesale movement price (which presumably would have had an undisclosed retail markup added upon sale), gives us about $151. Thus, on the basis of this one example, relative to factory movement inventory values, the retail markup on complete cased watches in the Howard factory sales office seems to have been about 30% in 1870.

A perspective on the preceding Waltham

| Rank | Monthly Pay[C] | |
	Base	Average
Private[B]	$13	
Corporal	$14	
Sergeant	$17	
Sergeant Major	$21	
2nd Lieutenant	$45	$105
1st Lieutenant	$50	$105
Captain	$60	$115
Major	$70	$169
Lieutenant Colonel	$80	$180
Colonel	$95	$212
Brigadier General	$114	$315

TABLE 3: Union Army soldiers' pay,[A] by rank, pre-April 1864 (From REF. 64.)

A) Does not include enlistment bounties. Confederate pay was slightly lower and typically six months in arrears. Pay in both armies increased in April 1864. B) Negro privates earned $10/month. C) Ranks of 2nd Lieutenant and above had a minimum base pay (left column), and received expense allowances.

and Howard watch prices is provided by **TABLE 3**, which lists Civil War Federal soldiers' pay by rank. Average pay for officers by rank is given without and with expense allowances. A private's pay increased by $1 per month in 1864, with proportional increases up the chain of command. But especially late in the war, a Union enlisted man's total compensation often was significantly increased by enlistment bounties, which often raised his effective pay to something like that of an officer. (For instance, when many men in the 52nd Pennsylvania Infantry satisfied their original service obligations in November 1863, they were offered reenlistment bounties of $400 along with one-month furloughs to visit home. [42]) Black soldiers

earned less than white soldiers, reflecting the predominant racism of the time, with a black private earning $10 per month. Black noncoms earned more, and black commissioned officers, who appeared late in the war, were few, but did exist. Confederate soldiers' pay was somewhat lower than Federal soldiers' pay, and typically six months in arrears. As mentioned, in the contemporary civilian sector, much of the labor force did not work for regular wages at all. The monetary economy coexisted in this period with an extensive barter economy that was not conducive to widespread consumption of expensive manufactured goods like watches. Thus soldiers likely made the market for watches in the North.

For those American civilians who did work for wages during the Civil War period, the Federal Census of 1860 provides average pay scales in seventeen different industries in that year, per **TABLE 4**. (Lower-skilled laborers like hod carriers, ditch diggers and railroad navvies would have mostly earned less than the numbers in the table.) The highest paid workers were in the "Foundry and Machine Shop" trade, who earned $392/year ($32.67/month). These jobs existed primarily in the North, because the only significant iron works south of the Mason–Dixon Line was the Tredegar Iron Works in Richmond, VA. The lowest paying trade listed in the 1860 census was the chewing tobacco industry, which was located primarily near tobacco-producing regions in the Middle and Border South. Free workers in this industry earned about $189/year ($15.75/month). Thus, considering that soldiers received food and clothing in addition to pay and had no lodging expenses, an enlisted man's discretionary income appears to have been at least com-

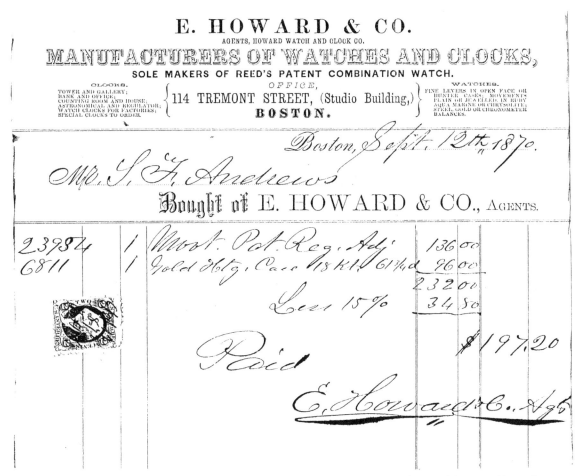

47. A surviving E. Howard & Co. sales office receipt showing that N-size three-quarter-plate Model 1862-N Howard movement SN 23,984 was sold to a retail customer, S. F. Andrews, along with a 61¾ pennyweight ("dwt") 18–kt. gold case on September 12, 1870. (Image from Figure 65, Page 71, of REF. 57.) *Image courtesy of Paul Hartquist.*

parable to, if not perhaps even slightly greater, than that of most civilian wage earners, especially considering enlistment and reenlistment bounties. This fact again points to the likely critical role of soldiers in the watch market.

One may then conclude that the cheapest and least reliable watches available to Northern soldiers during the Civil War—typically bottom-end Swiss watches in brass cases—might have cost a Union private less than a month's pay, whereas an Ellery grade Waltham product in a silver case would have cost him from three to six months' pay. An AWCo grade 20-size watch in a gold case would have cost a Union colonel something like a month's total compensation, or about a year's salary for a typical tradesman, or perhaps more! Top-of-the-line Howard watches of the period were also exorbitant luxuries made for men of means. It is not surprising that not that many of these luxury watches were produced.

The totality of evidence of watch ownership in Civil War armies reviewed herein makes it clear that many Civil War enlisted men were willing to make the investment of several months' pay to purchase an Ellery grade or a PSB grade Waltham watch, and many officers carried an AT&Co grade Waltham watch, often in a gold case. Recognized as valued and useful items, quite a few watches, usually cased in gold, also appear to have been presented to commanding, subordinate, or fellow officers by comrades in arms. Several examples of presentation watches are shown later in this book.

Estimates of Civilian Rates of Watch Ownership before and during the Civil War

Many watches that went to war with their owners certainly were purchased before the war began, or at least before the specific warrior in question became a part of it. Hence, in assessing how common watches were likely to have been in Civil War armies, it is relevant to ask what fraction of the adult male civilian population of either section owned watches immediately before the war. Historian Mark Smith analyzed 2,000 probate records listing inventories of effects from the District of Charleston, SC, and from Laurens County, SC, to assess the percentages of watch and clock ownership in those districts over time. The Charleston District was primarily urban, with a large seaport, whereas Laurens County was primarily rural. On the basis of the numbers Smith reports, **TABLE 5** can be composed for the period 1863–65.

More than half of white households in South Carolina owned slaves, a significant wealth indicator, in 1861, and **TABLE 5** indicates that roughly around 15% of all white SC households may have possessed watches as well. It is

Occupation	Annual Wages
Foundry and Machine Shop Products	$392
Carriages and Wagons	$362
Liquors, Malt	$358
Agricultural Implements	$342
Iron and Steel Rolling Mills	$341
Liquors, Distilled	$324
Glass	$322
Cigars and Cigarettes	$317
Flour and Grist Mills	$315
Leather	$312
Lumber, Sawed	$298
Iron & Steel	$285
Paper	$254
Woolen Goods	$232
Cotton Goods	$196
Brick and Tile	$195
Chewing Tobacco	$189

TABLE 4: Average American laborers' annual wages by occupation. (From 1860 U.S. Census data.)

surprising that the apparent rate of watch ownership among slaveholding (and presumably, therefore, wealthier) residents in those areas of South Carolina was no higher and may even have been slightly lower than among non-slaveholders. (Note that in this case, "non-slaveholders" may not primarily have been small farmers; this group included small merchants, clerks, railroad men, dock workers, merchant ship officers, and so forth, especially because the very poor might have been less likely to have left probate records.) The Charleston District and Laurens County were more prosperous, on average, than most of the rural South, so they perhaps may represent an upper bound to the average watch ownership rate within the South as a whole. At the same time, a Confederate soldier, faced with the same motivations and some of the same opportunities as his Northern adversaries, may have been somewhat more likely to own a watch than the typical Southern civilian. Elsewhere, Smith compares the percentage of probate inventories containing one or more "timepieces" (which could be watches, clocks, or both) from rural Greene County, NY, for the period 1841–50 (the latest period for which he reported data there), with the data for urban Charleston and rural Laurens County in South Carolina for the overlapping, but not identical period, 1839–44. He finds that 73% of the forty-one probate inventories from New York included timepieces of some kind, whereas 51% of the 107 inventories from urban Charleston and 67% of the 127 inventories from rural Laurens County contain one or more clocks or watches. Thus, the average rates of timepiece ownership in rural Greene County, NY, and in rural Laurens County, SC, and therefore, presumably watch ownership in particular, in those areas appear to have been very comparable. The timepiece ownership rate in urban Charleston was actually somewhat lower than those in either Northern or Southern rural areas! However, given the figures in **TABLE 5**, most of these timepieces were probably clocks. Nevertheless, Smith's data, if broadly extrapolated, could be taken to indicate that antebellum rates of both watch and clock ownership were surprisingly uniform throughout most of the United States.

	Slaveholders	F.N.S.
Charleston District	12%	18%
Laurens County	17%	19%

TABLE 5: Percent of slaveholders and free non-slaveholders (F.N.S.) owning watches in the Charleston, SC, District, and in Laurens County, SC, in 1863–1865. (Data from **REF. 28**, Table 1, p.34.)

Estimates of the Frequency of Watches in Civil War Armies

The preceding discussion may inform some crude estimates of the frequency of pocket watches among Civil War armies. It seems reasonable to estimate that approximately 75,000 watches, or about half the men's watches produced by the American watch industry prior to May 1865, may have found their way into one or more Union soldiers' pockets. The rationality of this estimate rests on the facts that (1) most American watches to that point in time were produced during the war; (2) current or discharged soldiers comprised a large fraction of the active Northern adult male population at that time; (3) all soldiers earned cash wages, whereas many other Northern men did not; (4) soldiers had more reason than most to aspire to own a watch; and (5) retail advertising for watches during the Civil War heavily targeted soldiers. More than a few watches probably saw service in more than one soldier's pocket over the course of the war, as soldiers of both sides often bought, sold, traded, gambled, salvaged, looted, and frequently bequeathed possessions among themselves. In view of the Lieber Code, the memoirs of Captain Wm. Seymour of the Louisiana Tigers, and the letters of W. K. Clare and Lt. Colonel Nevin previously cited, it is clear that some watches changed sides during the conflict, perhaps even more than once. Smith's data on watch ownership in Charleston and Laurens County, SC, excerpted in **TABLE 5**, appears broadly compatible with his reported rates of total timepiece ownership in South Carolina and rural New York. From these, one may extrapolate a guesstimate that perhaps one in five men who entered the Union army had a watch in the family, either his own or his father's, prior to the beginning of the war. This watch was overwhelmingly likely of foreign make, and it was probably as likely as not to have accompanied the soldier to war. Furthermore, an even greater number of foreign watches had "flooded" into the North and many ended up in soldiers' hands during the war, as AWCo watch advertisements lamented, and as McCrossen's report of Swiss and British wartime imports confirms. This would have made for a grand total of at least 500,000 watches in Union soldiers' hands, distributed among 2,757,000 men who had served in the Union army or navy at some point during the conflict. [65] This average of about one man in five with a pocket watch is nearly double the lower bound of 13% established by the rate of watches found among exhumed Union dead at Gettysburg, but for the reasons given, it too may yet be a lower bound. The half-million number is about as accurate a lower bound as deserves to be quoted, using this crude estimating basis.

Total Confederate enlistment figures are less precisely known. According to one respected source, between 750,000 and 1,228,000 men served in the Confederate armies over the course of the Civil War. [65] The watches carried by Confederate soldiers were of foreign make, except for a few American watches purchased mostly before the war, subsequently smuggled through Federal lines, plundered from enemy dead or prisoners, or perhaps even traded for between the lines with Yankees. As in the Northern armies, most Southern officers likely would have had some kind of a watch, especially because the Southern army was even more class stratified than the Northern army. Most Southern officers would have owned watches even before the war began, or before they had become officers, as a gentleman's watch was very much a status symbol as well as a utilitarian object. Again extrapolating from Smith's South Carolina data, perhaps between 15% and 20% of Southern recruits may have had a watch in their families before they entered into military service. Because about 75% of able-bodied Southern men between the ages of eighteen and forty-five served in the Confederate army at one point or another in the war, it is likely that more than half of these watches may have gone to war. Conversely, there is scant evidence that many new foreign watches made it into the South through the admittedly porous Federal naval blockade after sometime in 1862. Advertisements for new watches are very hard to find in Southern newspapers for the years of the war, although such ads were not hard to find shortly afterward. Similarly, a list of confiscated cargo from a captured blockade runner reviewed by the author contains only one reference to watch parts. (This fact may be surprising, given that the high value-to-weight ratio of pocket watches, especially in gold cases, should have made them attractive to smugglers. This one cargo could be an anomaly, or it could reflect the shortage of foreign exchange within the Confederacy with which to indulge the purchase of watches.) In addition, there seem to be far fewer surviving Confederate presentation watches than Union provenance presentation watches. This author has seen precisely zero Confederate presentation watch examples, although other kinds of Confederate presentation items, such as swords, are widely known. Likewise, this observation suggests that new watches were extremely scarce within the changing borders of the Confederacy after about 1861.

Consequently, after sometime in 1862, it can be inferred that the population of watches available to CSA soldiers was principally that which already existed in the South prior to the outbreak of war, and which was only modestly augmented by blockade running, battlefield plundering, and etcetera. If Mark Smith's South Carolina data can be taken as roughly representative of the rates of watch ownership throughout the South, then this reasoning would have put a watch in the pocket of about one in six to seven Confederate soldiers, surprisingly close to the estimated Union watch ownership rate.

On the basis of the preceding analysis, somewhere between half a million to one million watches likely saw service in the American Civil War. That reasoning notwithstanding, certain anecdotal information previously cited (e.g., the "watch fever" story, the sutler's court-martial testimony, the recollections of officers such as Kautz and Mosby, the LA Tigers anecdote recounted by Guelzo, and W. K. Clare's letter from Gettysburg, etc.), if extrapolated, could indicate that the true rates of watch ownership among Civil War soldiers could have been considerably higher than the crude estimates just offered.

4

IMPACT OF AMERICAN WATCH-MAKING ON THE CIVIL WAR

Having discussed the impact of the Civil War on the American watch-making industry, we now consider the ways in which that burgeoning industry may have affected the conduct of the war that stimulated it. While the majority of watches carried by Civil War soldiers were of foreign make, the population of surviving presentation watches, which are overwhelmingly American, informs us that American watches held special significance for many combatants. To understand that special significance, it is useful to examine the importance of watches in general to Civil War soldiers. And to that end, we begin by looking at the ways that watches were used in the field.

How Watches Were Used in the Field

As is already clear, the list of ways in which personal timepieces were used on Civil War battlefields runs from the mundane to the momentous. Watches regulated camp life; they informed soldiers of the passage of time and of the imminence of sunrises and sunsets; and they enabled some kind of rough coordination of operational orders among units in the field.

But perhaps the biggest change relative to the use of watches that occurred during the Civil War compared with previous conflicts was likely in the sheer number of watches in military use. The cumulative effect of the presence of all these watches was apt to have changed the course of events in numerous inconspicuous but nevertheless potentially important ways. The outcomes of major battles are sometimes decided by the timing of decisions of any number of subordinate commanders. Some of their decisions would certainly have been affected by the presence of timepieces, but which of those decisions that were affected were truly critical to the outcomes of battles is usually difficult or impossible to determine. A gap in an assault line might not have appeared. Some rendezvous might not have been missed, or some lethal delay might have been avoided. Hence, the overall impact of the presence of timepieces on Civil War battlefields may be mostly concealed within the subtle, cumulative effects of their increased numbers. As author Cheryl Wells observed, a functioning watch was not a luxury.

Watches were used during the American Civil War in many of the same ways as watches had been used in previous conflicts (e.g., the Napoleonic wars in Europe). But in the Civil War, not just affluent generals, who could afford exquisite timepieces like those made by A. L. Breguet, the most influential watchmaker of Napoleonic times, carried watches. If "to carry a fine Breguet watch is to feel like you have the brains of a genius in your pocket," as Sir David Salomons famously put it, [66] then to have carried a Waltham watch in 1863 was in a sense like having had the brains of Charles Vander Woerd, Charles Mosely, Nelson P. Stratton, and other brilliant Waltham mass-manufacturing machine tool inventors in one's pocket. While Breguet's genius was in watch design, the real genius of Waltham's tool designers was in the development of precision machinery and methods that automated and standardized watch-making. They did this not only by automating watch part manufacture but by streamlining the assembly and finishing processes using some fully interchangeable and other batch-matched parts. [2,67] At no time was this achievement more consequential than during the greatest conflict in American history, when the genius of Waltham's machine tool designers placed reliable timepieces in the hands of many tens of thousands of Union Army soldiers. Waltham's accomplishment effectively crystallized a critical cultural difference between the social and industrial organization of the North and the South at that time, a difference mirroring the cause of the war itself and foreshadowing its outcome. [68]

Noteworthy Examples of Watches Affecting Civil War Operations

Several examples already have been cited of orders specifying exact times of day. In most instances, such orders could only have been satisfactorily carried out if the officers charged with the orders had access to watches. Three more especially noteworthy examples of the use of watches in Civil War operations follow:

Siege of Vicksburg (May–July 1863)

Historian Shelby Foote wrote of the efforts to coordinate the actions of Federal land and naval forces during the Siege of Vicksburg:

> For the first time in history, a major assault was launched by commanders whose eyes were fixed on the hands of watches synchronized the night before. This was necessary in the present case because the usual signal guns would hot have been heard above the din of the preliminary bombardment, which included the naval weapons on both flanks. [69]

Battle of Cedar Creek (October 19, 1864)

Control of Virginia's Shenandoah Valley was strategically essential for the Confederacy, both because the valley represented the principal breadbasket for Lee's Army of Northern Virginia (AoNV), and because the valley was a potential attack route for Southern forces toward Washington, which Northern commanders always had to consider in their plans. The Battle of Cedar Creek was the last major battle of the war to take place in the Shenandoah Valley. It began with a surprise Confederate assault on the forces of Union Major General Philip Sheridan, who ultimately won the day. This battle is the one known example in which Confederate commanders synchronized their watches to coordinate their assaults. Author Joseph Whitehorne writes:

> [Confederate Lieutenant General Jubal] Early gave his orders at a commander's conference

48. A spring detent pocket chronometer movement by Thomas Rushton, with helical hairspring and compensated balance with trapezoidal weights. The sterling silver open-face swing-out case carries a Chester date mark for 1839.

at 1400 on the 18th. The officers synchronized their watches in order to meet the attack hour of 0500, 19 October 1864, as closely as possible. Although risky, the scheme of maneuver was a good one. It gave Early's outnumbered attackers the opportunity to achieve local su-periority of mass, allowing them [a chance, which was not realized] to defeat their en-emy in detail in conjunction with the surprise intrinsic to their approach. Early succinctly explained the need for such a gamble: 'I can only say we had been fighting large odds during the whole war, and I knew there was no chance of lessening them … . General Lee … expressed an earnest desire that a victory should be gained in the Valley if possible and it could not be gained without fighting for it. [70]

Siege of Petersburg (June 18, 1864)

Apart from inaccuracies in watches of the period, a more global problem existed in that there was no universally accepted reference time in any particular locale. Instead, local time in each city or town typically was at least slightly different, and it was up to individual watch or clock owners to decide for themselves what the "proper time" was. Railroad lines generally based their schedules on the time determined from a clock in either the headquarters, or the maintenance yard of the lines. The system of standard time zones familiar today would not come into being until after 1883. Thus, different railroad companies whose lines met at the same station often would offer schedules based on different local time references. The lack of standard reference times also further complicated the problem of synchronization for Civil War military planners, especially because these plans sometimes depended on railroads. In effect, the only way to guarantee synchrony between two timekeepers was either to get them both in the same place and there to set them to the same time, or to synchronize them by means of a very high speed communication link. During the Civil War, only one adequate long distance communication technology existed for the purpose: the telegraph.

Writing about Federal Major General George Meade's assault on Petersburg on June 18, 1864, renowned Civil War historian, Edwin

49. Cuvette of a second English pocket chronometer, this one with a Civil War connection. The presentation reads, "Presented by the British Government to Captn Sherman Lewis of the U.S. Barque 'Stampede' of New York for his humanity to the Crew of the Ship 'Perthshire' of Hartlepool in Feby 1864." The British government presented this outstanding watch to Captain Lewis of the Stampede for his humanitarian actions in saving the lives of the crew of the British ship when it foundered in a storm. The Perthshire was reputedly "a notorious blockade runner." *Image courtesy of Heritage Galleries.*

C. Bearss, relates, [71] "The generals involved were to telegraph army headquarters for a time-check to insure that their attack would be launched simultaneously." It was clear that the purpose of the "time check" was to synchronize their watches. (Meade was the commanding officer of the Army of the Potomac during the period in question, although Ulysses S. Grant,

50. The Earnshaw-style spring detent chronometer movement of the English presentation watch, SN 1,604, ca. 1864, freesprung with helical hairspring and chronometer balance made by the British firm of Brockbank and Atkins. *Image courtesy of Heritage Galleries.*

his superior officer, was traveling with him at that time.)

Indeed, Wells [1] and other authors make reference to the telegraph for providing a local time reference with which to synchronize watches. A more novel use of a personal Civil War timepiece is described by Federal Major General John McAllister Schofield. In his memoirs Schofield relates that he measured the intervals between the flash and sound of explosions occurring during the Battle of Atlanta in July and August of 1864, presumably to determine the range of enemy guns. [72] Similarly, Confederate Colonel (and Georgia Militia Brigadier General), George Washington Rains, the "Chemist of the Confederacy," reportedly used his high grade Swiss chronograph "to time guns" in 1861. [73] (A chronograph is a watch with an extra hand, usually a long "sweep hand" running off the center post, for timing intervals. This hand can be started, stopped, and set back to zero independently of the main time train. Most chronographs, like the one used by Colonel Rains, also include small subsidiary dials with additional hands for recording longer intervals of several minutes, or even hours.)

At sea there was an added need to know the time of day accurately when out of sight of land: determining longitude. In the nineteenth century the only really practical way of determining longitude at sea involved knowing the accurate time at a fixed reference location. That information, in conjunction with a local celestial observation using a sextant, could be used to fix longitude. An error in determining longitude could cause a ship to miss a destination island, a ship channel, or a rendezvous, or to fail to avoid an obstacle. Larger ships, or flagships of groups of military ships, usually had one or more marine navigational chronometers on board. So called "pocket chronometers" were smaller versions of these spring-driven clocks. Ships' chronometer clocks were set in shock-absorbing triple-gimballed mounts to cushion them and keep them upright on pitching and rolling ships. The main ship of a squadron would often signal the time read on its chronometer to the other ships by means of a signal cannon or flare at a prearranged time. Smaller

51. Dial of the Brockbank and Atkins pocket chronometer. *Image courtesy of Heritage Galleries.*

ships might only have a pocket chronometer or some other reasonably accurate watch in the captain's pocket to determine the time.

In subsequent years the term pocket chronometer evolved to mean any highly accurate watch, especially so after watches with observatory ratings became more common in the market. However, during the Civil War, the term usually referred very specifically to watches with several of the same particular technical features as full-sized marine navigational chronometers, features that were considered crucial for highly accurate timekeeping: a freesprung (i.e., no regulator) detent escapement (either the predominantly English spring detent style or the predominantly Swiss pivoted detent style); usually, a helical (as opposed to a spiral) hairspring; a fusee (see following chapter); and a temperature-compensated balance (bimetallic, sometimes with moveable trapezoidal weights instead of timing screws). A typical pre-Civil War English pocket chronometer, a spring detent movement in a classic English open-face silver swing-out case carrying a Chester date mark for the year 1839, is shown in **FIGURE 48**. By the 1850s some pocket chronometers incorporated winding reserve indicators (an extra hand on the dial tracking the state of winding), also called "up and down" indicators, and some had combination spiral and helical, called "duo-in-uno," hairsprings. With only very rare exceptions, all pocket chronometers were of European make during the Civil War. Shown in **FIGURES 49–51** is another English pocket chronometer by the prestigious watch-making firm of Brockbanks and Atkins. This watch was presented by the British government in 1864 to an American merchant ship captain for his rescue of the crew of a British ship in distress. (The ship in question was allegedly a "notorious blockade runner." Thus, the American skipper's actions were indeed humanitarian.)

5

GENERAL CHARACTERISTICS
OF CIVIL WAR WATCHES

Thε GENERAL characteristics of watches used during the American Civil War are described here. An understanding of these characteristics will take any collector a long way towards narrowing their search for potentially authentic "Civil War" timepieces and winnowing the chaff of eBay and other market venues.

Domestic versus Foreign Timepieces

Civil War timepieces were largely of American, English, or Swiss make (all others, e.g., German, French, or Danish watches, being scarce or rare). As previously discussed, foreign-made Civil War watches outnumbered domestic ones, but watches carried by Confederate soldiers are especially likely to have been made abroad. That said, watches with identified Union Civil War provenances tend mostly to be American, because so many of these watches are presentation pieces, and domestic watches were highly favored for presentation purposes. Persons interested in acquiring authentic Civil War timepieces, whether "named" or otherwise, should be aware that the authenticity issues are each a bit different with American, than with English, than with other European-made watches. So it is appropriate to begin this

section with a few remarks that apply to both domestic and foreign made Civil War watches. Then some unique aspects of American watches bearing on authenticity will be dealt with. And finally, some issues unique to English, and to Swiss and other foreign watches will be addressed in turn.

Winding and Setting

With only rare exceptions, Civil War period watches, including all American-made watches, were wound and set with a key. All American watches were wound from the rear. The most common American watch model, the AWCo's Model 1857, had its hands set from the front, using a winding square on the "center post," in the center of the watch dial. All other American watches of the Civil War period, whether made by Waltham or E. Howard & Co., were both set and wound from the rear on separate arbors. The manner of setting the time affects the replacement of watch hands, because movements that are set from the rear have hands with narrower post holes in their bosses than hands for watches with a winding square on the dial side. Replacement hands for rear-setting American watches are few and far between, and original 20-size (i.e., AWCo Model 1862) hands, as well as N-size EH&Co watch hands are especially scarce. English watches of the period were predominantly wound from the rear and set from the front (i.e., from the dial side), similar to Waltham Model 1857 watches.

While the first stem-winding watch patent (an English one) dates to about 1820, the first American stem-winding watches reached the market in 1867–68. The first American stem-setting (a.k.a. "pendant setting") watches appeared about the same time. European stem-winding watches were extremely rare in the U.S. market up to the time of the Civil War. One such great rarity, a Danish watch exhibiting several other extremely rare features, such as a spring detent chronometer escapement mounted on a tourbillon (a rarely seen mechanism for reducing positional errors), is shown in **FIGURES 52–56**. This watch by a prestigious maker, Jules Jurgensen of Copenhagen, one of two noteworthy Danish watch makers of the period, somewhat predates the Civil War. The watch was presented in 1854 to G. B. (Gustavus Bartlett) Simonds, Esquire, who served as "Superintendent of Motive Power" for the New York and New Haven Railroad. Simonds held several patents for practical inventions, including U.S. Patent Number 11,094, issued on June 13, 1854. It was this invention, for a spark arrestor for use on locomotive engines, for which Simonds probably received the watch.

Beginning in early 1862 Simonds commanded a squadron of Union mortar boats on the Mississippi River, under Commodore Andrew Hull Foote, until sometime after the Confederate surrender of Vicksburg on July 4, 1863. Simonds was involved in the Siege of Island Number 10 and the capture of Fort Pillow, and he was involved in the capture of the armory in Memphis. Thereafter he commanded the mortar boats in the Union Navy Yard in that

52. The cuvette of the watch by prestigious maker Jules Jurgensen of Copenhagen, a stem-wound and lever-set tourbillon spring detent pocket chronometer presented in 1854 to Gustavus Bartlett Simonds, Esquire. It is engraved, "G. B. Simonds, Supt. [Superintendant of] Motive Power, N.Y. and N.H. RR. [New York and New Haven Railroad]," as well as "Jules Jurgensen, Copenhagen, SN 6557." *Image courtesy of John Cote.*

53. Interior of the front lid of the G. B. Simonds watch. The inscription reads, "Presented to G. B. Simonds Esq.ʳ [Esquire] by the Employees of the N.Y. and N.H. RR as a token of their esteem, May, 1854." One of the "Jurgensen lips" on the case lids, where they envelop the base of the pendant, is evident. *Image courtesy of John Cote.*

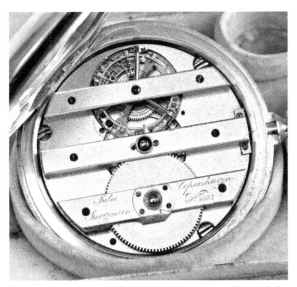

54. The movement of the extraordinary Simonds watch by Jules Jurgensen, showing the tourbillon spring detent chronometer escapement with Breguet (spiral with overcoil) hairspring. Breguet hairsprings require less depth than a helical spring, so perhaps a Breguet hairspring was chosen as a compromise to better accommodate the space constraints of the tourbillon mechanism. *Image courtesy of John Cote.*

55. The exquisite dial of the Simonds watch with elegant calligraphy and Breguet-style hands. *Image courtesy of John Cote.*

city, signing his official correspondence, "First master, commanding mortars of Memphis." There are no known surviving pictures of Simonds, but an 1862 illustration of a Mississippi mortar boat from Harper's Weekly is shown in **FIGURE 57**.

Watch Movement Finishing and Details

Escapement Features

The escapement of a mechanical watch or clock is the oscillator that draws impulse from the power source and determines the timekeeping qualities of the timepiece. The power source would be a spring in the case of watches, or often, a falling weight, in the case of clocks. The escapement contains another spring, the hairspring, which stores and releases energy during the escapement's cycle. Owing to the linear nature of Hooke's Law of spring forces, the period of a spring oscillator is roughly independent of the amplitude of its vibration. That is, it is naturally "isochronous," ignoring second-order effects, such as friction, and very small deviations from Hooke's Law at finite displacements. Thus, a major advantage of the detached lever escapement is that the balance and hairspring assembly (i.e., the oscillator) is in contact with the wheel train, through the lever, for only the small fraction of its period necessary to receive impulse each cycle. The "detached" nature of this escapement helps to maintain constant timekeeping accuracy throughout the running period of the watch, even as the motive impulse supplied to the escapement by the mainspring decreases. Two different varieties of "detached" lever escapements similar to those used in

56. Close-up of the tourbillon and escapement assembly of the Simonds watch. *Image courtesy of John Cote.*

watches in the Civil War period are shown in **FIGURE 58** and **FIGURE 59**. The first detached lever escapement was invented by Thomas Mudge in 1750, but it was not used much until the 1800s. But by 1861 detached lever escapements predominated even on most cheap imported watches. However, many verge watches (which typically had fusees), as in **FIGURE 60**, and watches with cylinder escapements were still in service at that time. Duplex escapement watches, which were common around 1800, also enjoyed a brief resurgence in popularity in the mid-nineteenth century, especially

those by British maker T. F. Cooper. English lever escapement movements and some very early American watch movements (all of which were levers) had ratchet tooth escape wheels, as in **FIGURE 59**. Swiss lever watches, as well as nearly all American lever watches, had escapements with club-tooth escape wheels.

Better American and Swiss watches, which lacked fusees, had stopworks to limit the range of torque exerted by the mainspring on the wheel train over the running period. Stopworks reduced isochronal errors, prevented overwinding, and possibly reduced the frequency

57. An 1862 illustration from Harper's Weekly of a mortar boat of the kind in G. B. Simonds's Mississippi squadron. Designed exclusively for bombardment of land targets, these novel inventions each had one single thirteen-inch mortar mounted in the middle of an open-topped enclosure. The weapon weighed 17,250 pounds and rested on a 4,500-pound carriage. With a twenty-pound charge of powder and the mortar at a forty-one-degree elevation, it could hurl a 204-pound shell loaded with seven pounds of powder more than two and a quarter miles. Crewmen often sheltered behind the wall of the vessel on the edge of the aft deck when the huge mortar was fired, to partly shield themselves from the sonic blast. After the Union gained control of the entire length of the Mississippi River in July of 1863, the role of these mortar boats was over.

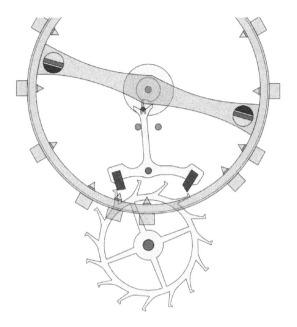

58. A diagram portraying the "in-line" (a.k.a. "straight line") style of lever escapement with a club tooth escape wheel (at bottom in the diagram). This escapement style was used in American three-quarter-plate watches during the Civil War, such as the Waltham Models 1859, 20-size key wind and 16-size key wind, as well as in all E. Howard & Co. watches of the period. Some contemporaneous Swiss and English watches also used in-line escapements.

Like other lever escapement styles, the in-line style consists of an escape wheel (bottom); the lever and its pallet stones (center) that act upon the escape wheel; the roller table(s) and its/their roller jewel (top) that engage with the fork of the lever; the hairspring (concentric with the balance wheel, not shown) and the balance staff and balance wheel, which together determine the timekeeping qualities of the escapement.

(The example shown is of the "double roller" variety, which was used on some, but not all Swiss watches of the Civil War period. Waltham three-quarter-plate watches made during the Civil War had somewhat simpler in-line escapements, in which the groove of the fork, at bottom in the figure, engaged with a jewel extending up from a single roller.) *Image copyright David Penney.*

of mainspring failures. The more common Geneva style of stopwork consists of a star wheel that meshes with a stop finger. The stop finger arrests the rotation of the star wheel when it encounters the one convex arm, limiting the use of the mainspring to its more central coils, where the torque it applies to the wheel train varies least.

In the lever escapement configuration of **FIGURE 59**, the relative positions of the balance staff, the lever arbor, and the escape wheel pinion define a right angle, rather than a straight line. An additional attribute that makes this an "English style" escapement is the ratchet tooth escape wheel. Preferred by most mid-nineteenth-century British watchmakers for the theoretical advantage that they minimized frictional losses, escape wheels with ratchet teeth were also fragile. Some pre-Civil War American watches made by the Boston Watch Co., a

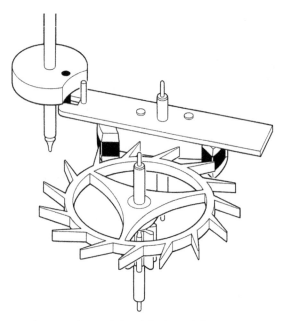

59. A diagram of an English style "right-angle" lever escapement with ratchet tooth escape wheel. In this lever escapement configuration, the relative positions of the balance staff, the lever arbor, and the escape wheel pinion define a right angle, rather than a straight line. Waltham full plate Model 1857 movements of the Civil War period employed right angle escapements, but an attribute that makes the example shown here an "English style" escapement is the ratchet tooth escape wheel. Preferred by most mid-nineteenth-century British watch makers for the theoretical advantage that they minimized frictional losses, ratchet teeth were also fragile. *Image copyright David Penney.*

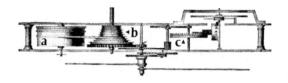

60. Diagram of a verge escapement with contrate wheel with axially oriented teeth ("c," center right) and conical fusee and chain ("b" and "a," left). *Image from commons.wikimedia.org/ wiki/file:pocketwatch_movement.png (modified).*

predecessor of Appleton, Tracy and Co., which used escapement parts imported from Britain, used ratchet toothed escape wheels. Some very early watches made by E. Howard & Co. also used ratchet escape wheel teeth. However, as discussed in REF. 56 and REF. 57, escape wheel tooth shapes evolved at Waltham and at Howard in a roughly parallel trajectory during this period, arriving at the Swiss style club tooth form well before the end of the Civil War.

The "verge" was the almost universal form of escapement used in watches from the earliest examples in the 1600s into the late 1700s. They were still being used in some less expen-

sive watches probably into the 1850s, when they were supplanted in the lower end of the market by watches with cylinder escapements.

Verge watches were notoriously inaccurate. They were so sensitive to the magnitude of the torque delivered to the verge by the wheel train that the use of a fusee to reduce the variation in motive torque over the running period was an absolute necessity. (As the mainspring runs down, the chain wound around the conical fusee pulley unwraps toward the bottom. The moment arm through which the mainspring acts thus continually increases as the driving force decreases, keeping the motive torque approximately constant.) However, a fusee wasn't enough to overcome all the deficiencies of a verge escapement. Fusees were used in most English, and in many Swiss lever escapement watches too.

Pocket chronometers, with the characteristics previously described and shown in **FIGURES 48, 50,** and **54** (see pages 69, 71, and 77), were rare in America and scarce even in Europe. Although helical hairsprings are most prevalent on pocket chronometers, the Jurgensen chronometer watch has a Breguet overcoil hairspring, which is a flat spiral spring of which the last, "terminal" coil that connects to the hairspring stud at the pinning point is bent upward, above the plain of the spiral. Both

61. EH&Co Model 1858 Type C ("Series I") movement, SN 269, with seventeen jewels in screwed-down settings, temperature-compensated bimetallic balance, upright pallets, quick train, and Reed's patented main wheel underneath the barrel plate, with stopwork. This movement exemplifies a scarce variant of the "Series I" out of the First Run (the only run of EH&Co divided-plate keywind movements with more than fifteen jewels). In December of 1859 this watch was destined to be "Howard & Rice" movement SN 119 before it was temporarily taken out of production while a new train plate bearing the "E. Howard & Company" name was made for it. (See REF. 75.) The Type C Model 1858 divided-plate movement is identified by the lack of lenticular cutouts between or along the circumference of the train and barrel plates. The 18-kt. gold case, made by J. M. Harper, a prominent maker of cases for very early Howard watch movements, has a twelve-sided edge, one of the case styles seen in this period.

Breguet hairsprings and helical hairsprings are considered more inherently isochronous than flat spiral springs. During the Civil War, the very highest grade Waltham products, and a very small number of experimental Howard products had Breguet overcoil hairsprings.

The Other American Company: E. Howard & Company (EH&Co)

Apart from the AWCo, the only other American firm to make any significant number of watches before the end of organized hostilities in May 1865 was E. Howard & Co. of Boston. (The Nashua Watch Co. probably completed fewer than a hundred movements before being reabsorbed into the AWCo, and at the Tremont Watch Co. production had scarcely begun when the war ended.) Several AWCo products already have been shown, but EH&Co watches were unique in numerous respects. The EH&Co watches shown in **FIGURES 61–75** all feature visible "Geneva style" stopworks atop their previously mentioned Reed's patented protective main wheels. (The main wheel is that wheel most directly coupled to the mainspring, through which the motive torque is transmitted to the other wheels of the train, terminating in the escapement.) Howard movements also had one of several unique plate designs, and many had unique escapement design elements.

Plate Finish and Other Technical Features

All domestic Civil War period watches will have gilded brass plates and polished and/or blued steelwork. Nickel finish debuted on American watch plates a few years after the Civil War and did not become common until the mid-1870s. Nickel finish turns up a fair amount on Swiss watches before 1865, but was by no means predominant. A variant of a Swiss Lepine calibre Type IV movement with nickel plates is shown in **FIGURE 63**. Type IV movements were produced from approximately 1835

62. The unusual Breguet-style hands and glass enamel dial of EH&Co movement SN 269, with an especially elegant straight, two-line script Howard signature.

63. One version of a Lepine calibre Type IV movement with nickel plates and in-line lever escapement by the well-known Swiss maker Auguste Saltzman, SN 27,865, produced approximately 1850-60. Saltzman's name is marked on the pillar plate between the third and fourth wheel bridges, as well as on the dial. Note the convergent finger bridges for the escape, fourth, and third wheels, which distinguish it from the later Lepine calibre Type V movement style. Saltzman watches of this style might well have been in service during the Civil War. *Image from www.faszination-uhrwerk.de/w/s.html (June 10, 2018).*

64. A more representative EH&Co Series I, Model 1858 Type A, fifteen-jewel movement SN 252, also finished in early 1860, with spun-in plate jewels, solid gold balance, Reed's main wheel, and stopwork. Part of the Reed's main wheel mechanism, which is engraved "Reed's Patent, November 24, 1857," is exposed by the lenticular cutouts in the barrel plate. Like SN 269 (see FIGURES 61 AND 62), the regulator index arm is short and is located atop the balance cock.

to beyond 1860, although the Type V came into production around 1850. A small number of EH&Co movements of the Civil War period had top plates that were ray damaskeened and gold flashed. Damaskeening, used more widely after the war, was a method of plate decoration done with a rotary tool charged with abrasive. Gold flashing was a kind of physical deposition process that seems very occasionally to have been used at EH&Co in the 1860s in place of cyanide bath electro gilding. Gold flashed watch plates had a brighter, more specular appearance than gilded plates.

Incorrect or Anachronistic Features Sometimes Attributed to "Civil War Watches"

Readers should note that there were no "railroad watches," as the term is commonly understood today, in service in the United States during the Civil War. In 1849 the Pennsylvania Railroad began supplying watches to its engineers, but these watches would have been of foreign make and would not have looked like the watches most collectors of railroad watches today imagine. [74] Similarly in 1853 the Bos-

65. The curved signature dial of EH&Co Series I, Model 1858 Type A movement SN 998, finished in 1860.

66. The front of the 18-kt. gold hunting case, made by Baldwin & Co., housing EH&Co movement SN 2,076 (see FIGURE 68, opposite) with clamshell-style decorative motif. The case and movement of this watch have matching serial numbers, an unusual feature for American watches overall, but not quite so unusual for early Howard watches. The exquisite case has lift springs on both the front and rear lids, with a split pusher to activate them separately.

ton & Providence Railroad ordered forty-five watches for use by its conductors from Barraud and Lund of London, through its U.S. distributor, William Bond & Son of Boston, MA. In 1855 the Vermont Central Railroad purchased watches from the same source. [75] However, the first American watches purchased by a railroad company for use on its line were a group of Appleton, Tracy & Co. grade Model 1857 Waltham watches ordered by the Camden and Amboy Railroad in 1863. But the first American watches specifically advertised as having been made for railway service appeared in 1868. These were the Model 1 "B. W. Raymond" full-plate watches produced by the Elgin National Watch Co. of Elgin, IL, whose first watches reached the market in 1867. However, none of these watches have the characteristics that most modern collectors have come to associate with "railroad watches" (e.g., screwed back and bezel cases, lever setting, double-sunk dials with bold, upright Arabic numerals, seventeen

67. The dial of a different EH&Co Series II, Model 1858 Type D movement, SN 1,853, with straight, two-line print-style Howard signature.

68. The movement of EH&Co Model 1858 Type E (Series II) movement SN 2,076, with fifteen jewels, Reed's main wheel (mostly hidden under the barrel plate, bearing the Reed's patent marking), and exposed stopwork.

or more jewels, etc.). The style of watch with the aforementioned characteristics, and which most railroad watch collectors think of as a "railroad watch," did not exist until sometime in the 1880s, at the earliest.

Some Other Characteristics of Civil War Watch Movements

Of American watches, only a few of the very best Waltham movements of the Civil War pe-

riod and a few very early and/or experimental Howard watch movements had anything but flat spiral hairsprings or more than fifteen jewels. Only Howard watches and the upper two grades of AWCo watches ever had stopworks at this time.

Balance wheels on American watches were of three types during the Civil War, in increasing order of sophistication and cost: monometallic steel (see **FIGURE 13** on p. 28), monometallic gold

69. The movement of EH&Co Model 1862-N (Series III) movement SN 4,094, finished on December 14, 1863. (See REF. 64.) This three-quarter-plate movement has Reed's main wheel almost fully exposed and a stopwork in addition to fifteen jewels in screwed-down settings and gold-flashed ray damaskeened plates. The patent marking for Reed's main wheel (also commonly referred to as "Reed's barrel") is engraved on the main wheel itself. In this serial number range, screwed-down jewel settings in the top plate are unusual, and ray damaskeened plates are rare. (Note: damaskeening is an idiosyncratic watch-making term that refers to a manner of decorating watch plates. It bears only a very distant resemblance to the much older decorative process of "damascening" that was applied to objects, such as swords, made of Damascus steel.) The watch case, which was either made and/or retailed by J. M. Harper, has a "pumpkin-style" pendant, which was frequently seen on American watchcases made around the time of the Civil War.

---

alloy (**FIGURE 24** on p. 35 and **FIGURE 64**), and temperature-compensated bimetallic balances (**FIGURES 28, 32, 50, 61, 63, 68, 69,** and **73**). Some very basic foreign watches had monometallic brass balance wheels (**FIGURE 15** on

p. 30). Bimetallic balances consisted of two semicircular arms with free ends. A bimetallic balance is constructed of an inner lamina of steel metallurgically bonded to an outer lamina of brass, which has a higher coefficient of thermal

70. The cuvette of the EH&Co Model 1862 (Series III) watch presented to Woodward, when he was a departing clerk in the Army of the Potomac's Subsistence Department in 1864. The presentation reads, "Presented to Benjamin W. Woodward by his friends in Subsistence Department, Army of the Potomac, October 1, 1864." This is one of only two E. Howard & Co. watches thus far identified by the author bearing a contemporaneous Civil War-related inscription. We do not know what especially meritorious service Benjamin Woodward performed for the Army of the Potomac Commissary, but it clearly must have been significant to have warranted such an expensive parting gift, which would have retailed for close to $200.

expansion than steel. When the temperature increases, differential thermal expansion bends the free ends of both arms inward toward the axis of rotation, thus decreasing the moment of inertia of the wheel. This decrease in rotational inertia is calibrated to approximately offset the decreasing elastic constant of the hairspring, thus maintaining the oscillation frequency of the escapement in a narrower range over the most relevant temperature interval. Compensated balances have rims loaded with screws, which can be added, removed, or moved in and out to adjust timing and poise. (The symmetry of the weight distribution around the balance wheel rim—poise—affects timekeeping when

a movement is not horizontal). On the highest grade watches, these screws were of gold alloy. Many early EH&Co gold balance screws of the Civil War period have no screw slots, and are countersunk.

To reduce friction and wear, watch movements have jewels at many points of contact between moving parts and between some moving parts and other stationary parts. Balance staffs and train wheel arbors often turn in annular jewels that were pierced through the middle with the use of spinning, diamond-charged wires. A lever escapement typically has two jeweled pallets, which periodically stop and release the escape wheel, and a roller jewel

71. Headstone and watch of Benjamin Weston Woodward (1837–1902). Woodward was born in Hector, Schuyler County, NY, and received his MA from Hobart College in 1862. The Schuyler County Draft Registration record of June 1863 lists him as "Lawyer," "Single," and "1 Yr. clerk, Com. Sub. [Commissary of Subsistence] Dept., Army of Potomac." His older brother, Captain (and later, Major) John H. Woodward, was in charge of beef cattle for the Army of the Potomac commissary. Benjamin served as a clerk under John, along with a third brother, Charles. He was admitted to the New York bar in 1865 and acceded to the bench as a Schuyler County judge in 1866, residing in Watkins (now Watkins Glen), NY, where he is now buried. Woodward served for a time on the NY State Supreme Court, while residing in Brooklyn, NY.

BENJAMIN WESTON
WOODWARD
1837 - 1902

◄ **72.** A drawing of Judge Woodward, probably done from a photograph. *Image from History Of Schuyler County New York; With Illustrations And Biographical Sketches of Some Of Its Men and Pioneers, printed in 1879 and partially reproduced in 1976.*

on the roller table, which is the point of contact between the forks of the lever and the balance assembly, which gives impulse to the balance wheel. Balance staffs also typically are capped on both ends by "end stones." End stones, or "cap jewels" on train wheels were rare on American watches in the Civil War period. End stones are sometimes diamond on better watches, because they did not need to be pierced. Jewels and pallet stones are ruby or sapphire on the best watches of the period, which are the same mineral, crystalline alumina, with different impurities. Less expensive American watches of-

73. EH&Co Model 1862-N (Series III) movement SN 5,455, finished on September 19, 1864, with fifteen jewels, stopwork, Reed's patented main wheel, compensated bimetallic balance wheel with unslotted gold screws, and Mershon's patented compound rack and pin micrometer regulator. Mershon's regulator, which incurred a price premium, theoretically enabled finer adjustment of the curb pin positions than a simple regulator, because it reduced the displacement of the curb pins for a given arc length of travel of the index arm.

ten use "rock crystal," often described as chrysolite, but which are actually chrysoberyl, which is crystalline beryllium aluminate $(BeAl_2O_4)$. The cheapest Swiss watches might even have had glass "jewels." A lever watch with fifteen jewels was considered "full jeweled" and is often marked as such on the cuvettes of Swiss watches. Most American watches in this period had seven, eleven, or fifteen jewels, and only the best and most expensive American watches had seventeen, nineteen, or twenty jewels. English jewel counts were mostly conservative as well, although a small number of contemporaneous twenty-three-jewel watches are known

74. The single-sunk enamel dial of EH&Co movement SN 5,455, with script, two-line signature and classic Howard teardrop-style hands with polished tips and bosses. Notice the elegant engraving on the gold bezel of this particular J. M. Harper case.

by makers such as James Hoddell. Mostly only special Swiss watches of the Civil War period, like General Rains's chronograph, have more than fifteen jewels.

Differences in the vibrational frequencies of American watches, and varying provisions for protecting the escapements of American watches, which lacked fusees, from damage in the event of mainspring failures, have already been mentioned in passing. When the Civil War began, Howard watches were the only American watches with the aforemen-

75. The front of the 18-kt. gold three-ounce hunting case of the Benjamin Woodward EH&Co watch, movement SN 5,455.

tioned "quick trains," which beat 18,000 times per hour, or five times per second. All other American and most European watches had escapements that beat 16,200 times per hour, or four and a half times per second. A faster beat makes for more stable performance and reduces the likelihood that the watch would "set" (i.e., stop) if subject to a shock. Quick trains were introduced into Waltham products during the Civil War. Howard watches and some scarce, higher-grade AWCo movements feature one of a few different patented mechanisms (e.g., Reed's main wheel, Fitts's pinion, Fitts's barrel [on smaller size watches, primarily for ladies], and Stratton's barrel) to protect the wheel train and escapement from incurring damage during all-too-common mainspring breakages. How-

ever, most American watches and most foreign watches of the time had simple going barrels with no protection for the wheel train. Most English watches and some Swiss watches incorporated fusees, which obviate the need for other protective measures.

Watch Dials and Hands

Authentic watch dials of the Civil War period were oven-fired, hand-painted enamel with copper backings. They were nearly all either flat, one-piece dials, or "single-sunk" dials, as in **FIGURE 27** (p. 38), meaning that the seconds bit was a separate disk that was cemented slightly below the plane of the main dial. (The only domestic double-sunk dials of the period appear on a small number of the highest-grade Waltham Model 1859 movements, such as in **FIGURE 33** (p. 43). These dials had a separate chapter ring cemented to and surrounding the central disk, which was set slightly below the chapter ring and above the seconds bit. This writer has never seen or heard of a foreign double-sunk dial from the Civil War period, but if they existed, they were rare.)

Roman numerals greatly predominated on watch dials in the Civil War period, although Arabic numeral dials, such as the example shown in **FIGURE 76**, also were known since at least Napoleonic times. Painted metal dials generally came much later.

Foreign watch dials of the Civil War period were mostly enamel as well. However, gold and silver watch dials with raised Roman hour numerals, an older style, were still in use on some foreign watches. An example of such a dial, one that reportedly belonged to Confederate General William Mahone, is shown later

76. An uncommon pre-Civil War example of an Arabic numeral watch dial of the "serpentine" style. This single-sunk AT&Co-signed dial graces an AT&Co grade Model 1859 movement with SN 6,724, finished in December, 1858. (A similar movement with a similar dial, with SN 17,939, manufactured in July 1859 is a second of several known examples noted.) Dials of the same general style also have been seen on contemporaneous E. Howard & Co. watches, but those occurrences are even scarcer. However, serpentine numeral dials grew somewhat more popular in later decades. This dial may be an early unsigned example of Josiah Moorhouse's work. Moorhouse, who was in charge of dial making at the Nashua Watch Co. and subsequently became the dial room foreman at E. Howard & Co., signed the backs of several later serpentine numeral dials extremely similar to this one.

in Chapter 7 (p. 117). Confederate Captain Sally Tompkins, who was in charge of the Robertson Hospital in Richmond, owned an open face watch with a similar dial. (Captain Tompkins was probably the only female commissioned officer in either army during the Civil War. According to the blog of the American Civil War Museum (ACWM), "During the war, Captain

77. A likely Civil War period Swiss watch signed "M. I. Tobias, Liverpool" on the brass dust cover of the otherwise silver case, with a classic patriotic American scene painted on the center of the dial. The dial depicts Lady Liberty with a liberty pole in her left hand, on a seat of crossed cannons and rifles with fixed bayonets, and floating on a cloud. She is placing a laurel on the head of a soldier bearing a US flag with thirteen stars, which was the canonical number of stars for such images, regardless of the actual period of the painting. The "liberty pole" is an iconic symbol that originated in ancient Rome, and was popular even before the American Revolution. Lady Liberty was prominently featured on American silver coins of the Civil War period with a liberty pole in her hand. The pole has a pileus (sometimes called a "liberty cap") at the end of it, which was a kind of hat worn by manumitted slaves in ancient Rome that symbolized their freed status. Despite the English name on the case, the movement is quite clearly Swiss. *Image courtesy of Stefan Osdene, Cambridge Golden Antiques, Cambridge, WI.*

Tompkins' hospital served more than 1,300 soldiers, and achieved the lowest mortality rate of any hospital, losing only 73 men." Her watch, which is in the ACWM's collection, is inscribed "Redeem Time.")

Some foreign watch dials typically found on inexpensive watches featured likenesses of popular figures, or marshal scenes, which were hand painted over the oven-fired enamel. One Swiss watch dial has been seen with a likeness of Union Major General Franz Sigel painted on it. "Little Sigel," as he was affectionately called by his men, commanded the AoP's 11th Corps until June, 1863. The 11th Corps was comprised mostly of recent German immigrants like himself. ("I fights mit Sigel" was a proud boast in the German American community.) [76,77] Another watch dial reported to the author features a portrait of Union Major General Benjamin Butler. Close examination of the military scenes on these painted dials often reveals a general lack of familiarity with the details of American Civil War uniforms or the U.S. flag, and so forth, reflecting that these dials were likely painted by women and girls in Swiss cottages at very low piecework wages. The military uniforms on the figures frequently appear European, and the U.S. flag, when it can clearly be discerned, often has the wrong number of stripes, and typically has only thirteen stars in the canton. These kinds of dials most often turn up on unsigned Swiss movements of indifferent quality in similarly nondescript, inexpensive cases. An example of a Civil War painted dial is shown in **FIGURE 77**.

Some Swiss watch dials depicted camp or marshal scenes. On many such dials, the second hand was removed, rendering the subsidiary seconds dial, or "seconds bit," vestigial and useless. This was a significant functional sacrifice, because the second hand provided the very useful information about whether a watch was still running in noisy environments in which a watch's tick could not easily be detected.

Hand styles vary quite a bit on Civil War period watches. Spade hands are the most common style, though these typically are much narrower than those found on late-nineteenth-century railroad watches. Breguet (a.k.a. "moon") hands, as in **FIGURE 62** (p. 82), turn up on movements of both the AWCo and EH&Co during this period, though EH&Co Breguet hands are rare. EH&Co also occasionally used trident style hands, which are also rare. The great majority of original EH&Co

watch hands of the Civil War period were slender, elongated spades—the so called "tear drop" style—with blued shafts and polished spades and bosses, per **FIGURE 67** (p. 84) and **REF. 78**. The same style of hand was shown on a high-grade Waltham watch in **FIGURE 33** (p. 43). Other hand styles may be seen on foreign watches. Blued steel was standard for watch hands, though many early Boston Watch Co. (BWCo) products and some foreign watches had gold hands.

Watchcases

Case Metal

Cases of the cheapest available foreign watches of the Civil War and pre-Civil War periods were typically brass (sometimes thinly gold-plated) or silver of inferior purity. Vermeil cases, which were gold-plated silver, also were known. Vermeil had more of the heft and feel of solid gold than plated brass, and when unmarked or falsely marked, could be used to deceive. Most other original pre-Civil War and Civil War watchcases were higher-quality silver or gold. American silver cases were most often "coin silver," which is 90% silver and 10% copper. English silver cases, which were hall-marked, were sterling silver, which is 92.5% silver and 7.5% copper. Swiss-made silver cases varied widely in composition and were often of inferior quality with silver-plated cuvettes (see "Case Construction"). American gold cases were most often nominally 18-kt. but could test as low as 16-kt. Fourteen-karat and 12-kt. gold American cases were considerably less common in the Civil War period, but they also did exist. English gold watchcases, always hallmarked with a crown signifying gold, along with a purity mark (expressed in karats or a millesimal fraction), could be 9-kt. (.375), 12-kt. (.500), 15-kt. (.625), 18-kt. (.750), or 22-kt. (.917). (The 12-kt. and 15-kt. marks were replaced by the 14-kt. (.585) mark in 1932.) English gold watchcases typically were well made regardless of the gold purity, but 18-kt. was the predominant purity during the American Civil War. Once again, the term *albata* (also called *silveroid*, *silverode*, and *silverine* in later periods) referred to an alloy of nickel, copper and zinc. The 1864 Robbins & Appleton trade catalog states that cases of such alloy were available, and this writer has seen a few albata cases for Waltham watches that he judges are likely to date to the Civil War period. Albata cases are sometimes, but not most often marked as such. The patent for "gold filling," a process in which two thin sheets of 14-kt. or 10-kt. gold are roll bonded to a thick brass substrate, slightly predates the Civil War. However, gold filled watchcases were uncommon before 1870 and rare before 1866.

Case Styles

A hunting case, which was the most popular Civil War case style, has a front cover that is opened by pushing on a spring-loaded button, or pusher, built into the pendant. (Britten's and DeCarle's horological dictionaries both call this part a "push piece.") The term "hunting case" implies that this case style, with added protection for the crystal and the watch face, is intended for use in rugged environments, such as those encountered while hunting. However, open-face cases, which usually have thicker glass crystals than hunting case watches, also were used in the Civil War period, and presumably

by Civil War soldiers. Simulated "box-hinged" cases and multicolor gold cases were both creatures of the 1880s and 1890s and have nothing to do with the Civil War period. In recent years the nebulous term *double hunter* has become ubiquitous in a portion of the antique watch market. It is used more or less synonymously with the correct, historically accepted term *hunting case*. The superfluous qualifier, "double," does not change the meaning of a "hunter," or more correctly "hunting case"; it only adds confusion to no useful purpose.

Case Construction

All Civil War period watchcases will have both inner and outer rear lids. The inner rear lid, also called a *dust cover*, or *cuvette*, will have at least one key hole for winding, and depending on the model, often a second hole, which is almost always in the center, for setting. American and Swiss watchcases will have hinged inner rear lids, which can be swung up to access the movement. American-made Civil War period cases typically have the hinges for the rear lid offset from, rather than parallel to those for the front lid. On English watchcases, the inner rear lid usually will be fixed in position with no hinge. Instead, the movement itself will be attached to a mounting ring that is in turn attached to the case by a hinge. One accesses the movement of an English "swing-out case" by depressing a catch on the dial side of the watch at 6 o'clock and swinging the movement out on its hinge, at 12 o'clock, to expose the rear of the movement. For this reason, an English watch usually will have a gilded brass dust cover fitted directly to its movement, completely apart from the inner rear lid of the watchcase. (See

"English Watches" on p. 119 and **FIGURES 92–97** starting on p. 119)

Case Decoration

Hand engraving and machine engraving, the latter of which is also commonly called "engine turning" or "guilloche" (two originally distinct terms which have grown together over time in common usage), were standard on silver and gold watchcases of the Civil War period. Engine turning, a kind of engraving pattern seen in **FIGURE 4** (p. 3), **FIGURES 14–17** (p. 29), **FIGURES 22 & 23** (p. 34), and **FIGURE 75** (p. 91), among others, consists of interpenetrating sets of lines, most commonly arcs of circles, and are made with specialized lathes called "rose engines." The engine-turning pattern most often seen on the exterior surfaces of Civil War period watchcases is called *barley-corn*, per **FIGURE 4** (p. 3), **FIGURE 22** (p. 34), and **FIGURE 75** (p. 91). Most engine-turned exterior watchcase surfaces have a raised disk (on the rear lid) or some other feature (commonly a shield or some other hand-engraved decoration, on the front lid) at the center that allows the engine-turning pattern to be terminated at a manageable radius of curvature for the rose engine. Originally smooth polished cases from the Civil War period were much scarcer, and will lack this raised disk. More often than not, surviving Civil War period cases lacking apparent engraving or engine turning are the worn and refinished remnants of originally engine turned or engraved cases. This fact is often revealed either by traces of remaining engine turning, especially around the periphery near the pendant and the hinges, or by a remnant of the aforementioned raised disk at the center

of the rear lid. Other forms of case embellishment, such as black or colored enamel, were rare on American men's watches in this period, but not unheard of.

The edges of Civil War period watchcases were most often "milled." Milling could take several forms, including the dot pattern shown in **FIGURE 29** (p. 40). Reeding, which was the most common form of milling, was one in which closely spaced parallel grooves were machined into a case edge. Milling had both cosmetic and functional aspects. Reeding was used contemporaneously on the edges of gold and silver coinage to discourage shaving. On watchcases, milling improved the holder's grip.

Case Originality Relative to Movements

The cases of Civil War watches typically offer many clues to their likely originality to the movements they house. First, American and Swiss movements will be secured to their cases by one or more case screws, which leave characteristic semicircular marks on a case where the movement was fastened to it. On Waltham Model 1857 full-plate watches, the case screw fastened to the case adjacent to the "top plate," which is the side of the movement that most would call the rear of the watch. The "front" of a watch movement, often called either the "dial plate" or the "pillar plate," though the latter term was by then mostly archaic, is the side to which the dial is attached and where one tells the time. Other American watches, such as Waltham three-quarter-plate movements and some watches made by E. Howard & Co., principally in the serial number range between 1,800 and 3,500, had a case screw (the

Walthams) or two screws (the Howards) that fastened to the case on the underside of the dial plate, though one accesses these screws from the rear of the watch. Most Swiss watches of the period likewise had case screws that fastened to the case from the rear of the dial plate. Most American and Swiss watches of the Civil War period have one case screw, but examples with as many as three also are known. (The odd man out was E. Howard & Co., some of whose movements had provisions for two case screws on the dial plate, and a third case screw on the top plate. Often, the top plate case screw hole was left empty, however.) Any extraneous case screw marks on a watchcase are a clear sign that other movements have been in it. If any parts of a case have different serial numbers, then that case is a marriage of parts originating from different watches, though not all parts of all cases had serial numbers. (Note: movement and case serial numbers are usually not the same, especially on American watches. This is normal. Swiss watch movements and cases of the Civil War period often have no serial number at all.)

When assessing case originality, one should check to see that the movement is a good fit in its case both horizontally and vertically. One should ensure that there is no visible gap be-tween the movement and the case, and that the case screws have a secure purchase on the case lip without need of spacers or shims underneath. Similarly, one should check that the dial has not been ground down along the edge, that the movement locating pin has not been removed to make the dial align properly with the pendant of the current case, nor to make the winding and setting arbors align with the keyholes in the cuvette. Dust covers in particular are a special treasure trove of originality clues. Original key holes should be well centered above their winding arbors, and American watchcases usually have engraved borders around them. One should look closely to be sure that there are no filled holes in the dust cover that have been disguised by being plated over and that no existing hole obliterates any part of the serial number on the underside of the dust cover. (On silver cases, filling material often tarnishes differently than the rest of the dust cover. On both silver and gold cases, the filling material usually has a somewhat different composition than the rest of the dust cover, as it needs to melt at a slightly lower temperature, and this usually leads to subtle color differences as well.)

6

AMERICAN-MADE
CIVIL WAR WATCHES:
GENERAL CONSIDERATIONS

WHILE MOST watches in use in Civil War armies were of foreign make, American watches are emphasized in this book for several reasons. First, the majority of Civil War timepieces with documented provenances, which are the main focus of this book, were presentation pieces, and American watches were heavily favored for such purposes in the Federal armed forces. Obviously, this would not have been true in the Confederate armies, but Confederate presentation watches seem much rarer altogether. (This is probably due to both the reduced availability of new watches within the changing borders of the Confederacy, and the fact that few if any end-of-war presentation gifts were made to Confederate soldiers, when presentation watches were most popular.) Second, American watches of the Civil War period were nearly all sold and used domestically, and a large proportion—perhaps even a majority—likely ended up in a soldier's pocket sometime during the war. The same cannot be said of foreign timepieces unless they were clearly cased in the United States during or before the war (and quite a few were). Third, most American watches can be dated reasonably accurately by their movement serial numbers, whereas English watches usually can be dated only to, at most, their year of production, and only if they were cased in England. Most other foreign watches cannot even be dated that accurately. Thus, when considering watches without specific known provenances, one usually can have greater confidence whether an American watch was both in the US and available for service during the Civil War, than with a foreign watch. Similarly, when considering a watch with a known provenance, the more accurate movement production information can often increase confidence in the authenticity of a dated presentation.

There are two important general points to note about American-made Civil War period watches. First, the majority of American watch movements were manufactured by what were then state-of-the-art mass production methods based on standard models and designs. (This was less true of the much scarcer E. Howard & Co. watch products than the Waltham products, but Howard's production methods were still very innovative compared with those in use by most European makers.)

To be clear, Waltham's production methods were state-of-the-art. Their watches mostly were not. American watch production methods employed automatic machinery to a hitherto-fore unprecedented degree and emulated the interchangeable parts-manufacturing practices pioneered by the Springfield Armory and the New England wooden clock industry. (However, full interchangeability in the finer parts of watches would not be achieved until several decades after the Civil War.) [2] Important choices were made in the design of the watches produced by these methods to facilitate the new mode of production. Conversely, most contemporary English and Swiss watches mostly were still being made by decentralized, semi-industrial (craft) methods and, consequently, exhibited much less standardization. In contrast with Waltham's management, Edward Howard, the founder and CEO of E. Howard & Co. still had one foot in the Old World. Howard saw machine manufacturing as much as a means of perfecting the traditional gentleman's watch as of redefining it. [57] However, his output was comparatively small—only about 7,000 watches by April 1865—and relatively few of these expensive, luxury timepieces likely saw Civil War service.

The second thing to know about American watches is that American watch movements and the cases made for a particular watch model were interchangeable by design. This was not true of contemporary foreign watches. The interchangeability of American watch movements and cases enabled purveyors of American watches to offer customers greater choice and variety in movement and case combinations with a limited inventory. However, this attribute of American watches also poses some unique issues for modern collectors and historians attempting to assess the originality of a particular watchcase to a particular watch movement. To exacerbate this problem, most American watches of the Civil War period were not cased in the watch factory (there are important exceptions), and matching movement and case serial numbers are very much the fortunate exception rather than the rule.

The aforementioned difficulty is somewhat ameliorated by the fact that most of the Civil War era factory production records for the two American watch manufacturers then active still exist. (The exception is the earliest watch production record book of E. Howard & Co. The lowest EH&Co serial number for which the records are known to have survived is SN 3,301, completed in November or December of 1862, although production is believed to have begun at SN 101.) Factory records often make it possible to establish the date of manufacture of at least the movement of an American watch, often to within the month, and sometimes even to the actual day! This is very useful information when evaluating the likely authenticity of dated inscriptions. As mentioned, the same is not true of the great majority of foreign watch movements. (However, as elaborated subsequently, English silver and gold *cases* were date marked with the year of their production.) To find the production date of a Waltham watch movement, one may consult *nawccinfo.nawcc.org* as the most reliable online source. However, note that it is the movement serial number that is relevant. A case serial number seldom provides useful information unless it happens to match the movement serial number.

Dating American Watch Movements

A handful of small, independent American watch makers were active during the Civil War in addition to the two manufacturers. The most

SN Range	Dates	Remarks[A]
1–50	1852	HD&D and Warren Mfg. Co.
51–400	1853	Warren Mfg. Co. & Saml. Curtis
401–1,000	1854	BWCo Product (Saml. Curtis)
1,001–5,000	1857	BWCo Product (DH&D)–BWCo ends May 1857
5,001–10,000	July 1857–May 1858	TB&Co (5 or 6 weeks), then AT&Co[B]
10,001–20,001	May 1858–May 1859	AT&Co; becomes AWCo in January 1859
20,001–30,000	May 1859–Jan. 1860	AWCo (Lincoln elected Nov. 6, 1860; SC secedes, Dec. 20, 1860; CSA formed 1861)
30,001–40,000	Jan. 1860–April 1861	AWCo (Lincoln inaugurated, March 4, 1861; Fort Sumter shelled April 12, 1861)
40,001–50,000	Nov. 1860–July 1862	AWCo (1st Bull Run, July 21, 1861; Peninsula Campaign, Mar–July 1862; Shiloh, Apr. 6–7, 1862; Siege of Corinth, Apr–May, 1862)
50,001–70,000	July 1862–Mar. 1863	AWCo (Antietam, Sep. 17, 1862; Emancipation Proclamation, Sep. 22, 1862; Fredericksburg, Dec. 11–15, 1862)
70,001–90,000	Mar. 1863–Sep. 1863	AWCo (Chancellorsville, Apr–May 1863; Gettysburg, July 1–3 1863; Fall of Vicksburg, July 4, 1863)
90,001–110,000	Sep. 1863–Feb. 1864	AWCo (Chickamauga, Sep. 19–20, 1863)
110,001–130,000	Jan. 1864–Sep. 1864	AWCo (Overland Campaign, March–June, 1864; Battle of Atlanta, July 22, 1864; Siege of Petersburg, June 1864–March 1865)
130,001–150,000	Sep. 1864–Feb. 1865	AWCo (Fall of Atlanta, Sep. 2, 1864)
150,001–158,000	Feb. 1865–Apr. 1865	AWCo (Lee surrenders at Appomattox; Richmond falls, April 2–9, 1865)
158,001–159,000	Apr. 1865–June 1865	AWCo (Lincoln assassinated, Apr. 14, 1865; Last battle of the Civil War: Palmito Ranch, TX, May 13, 1865)

TABLE 6: Approximate correspondences between Waltham (AWCo) watch movement serial numbers and production dates for movements produced during the Civil War Period, based on American Watch Co. production records.

A. Legend: **BWCo**: Boston Watch Co.; **HD&D**: Howard, Dennison & Davis (8-day movements, Nos. 1–17); **DH&D**: Dennison, Howard & Davis; **TB&Co**: Tracy, Baker & Co. (which existed for only 5–6 weeks in 1857); **AT&Co**: Appleton, Tracy & Co.; **AWCo**: American Watch Co.

B. AT&Co reused most BWCo numbers between 1,001 and 2,000. These were marked "C.T. Parker" or "P. S. Bartlett".

SN Range	Dates	Remarks
101–3,300	Dec. 1858–Nov. 1862	Civil War begins at Fort Sumter, 4/12/61 First Bull Run/First Manassas, 7/21/61 Peninsula Campaign, March – July, 1862 Battle of Shiloh, 4/6-7/62 2nd Battle of Bull Run, 8/28-30/62
3,301–3,320	Nov. 1862–Dec. 5, 1862	Battle of Antietam, 9/17/62 Lincoln issues Emancipation Proclamation (EP), 9/22/62 2nd Battle of Corinth, 10/3-4/62
3,331–3,500	Dec. 5, 1862–Feb 9, 1863	Battle of Fredericksburg, 12/11-16/62 Parker's Crossroads, 12/31/62 Battle of Stones River, 12/31/62 – 1/2/63 EP takes effect, 1/1/63
3,501–3,650	Mar. 21, 1863–May 20, 1863	Capture of New Orleans, 4/25/62 – 5/1/62 Battle of Chancellorsville, 4/30/63 to 5/6/63 2nd Battle of Fredericksburg (Marye's Heights), 5/3/63
3,651–4,000	May 20, 1863–Sep. 25, 1863	Production in this range was especially nonsequential; Battle of Gettysburg, 7/1-3/63 Fall of Vicksburg, 7/4/63 Capture of Port Hudson, 7/9/63 Battle of Chickamauga, 9/19-20/63
4,001–4,170	Sep. 25, 1863–Dec. 4, 1863	Chattanooga Campaign, 9/21/63 – 11/25/63
4,171–4,200	Dec. 5, 1863–Apr. 28, 1864	The next two serial number intervals overlap in time Overland Campaign, 3/64–6/64
4,201–4,899	Dec. 4, 1863–May 30, 1864	Sherman's March to the Sea, 12/15/64 – 12/21/64
4,900–5,430	June 7, 1864–Aug. 31, 1864	Siege of Petersburg, 6/64–3/65 Battle of Atlanta, 7/22/64
5,431–5,700	Sep. 16, 1864–Oct. 25, 1864	Fall of Atlanta, 9/2/64
5,701–6,100	Oct. 25, 1864–Jan. 2, 1865	Battle of Nashville, 12/15-16/64
6,101–6,220	Jan. 3, 1865–Feb. 1, 1865	Carolinas Campaign begins
6,221–6,390	Feb. 1, 1865–Feb. 28, 1865	Surrender of Charleston, 2/18/65
6,391–6,755	Feb. 28, 1865–Apr. 1, 1865	Stoneman's Raid Richmond abandoned by CSA, 4/2/65 Lee surrenders at Appomattox, 4/9/65
6,756–6,760	May 10, 1865	These next two serial number intervals overlap in time
6,761–7,000	Apr. 7, 1865–May 13, 1865	Last battle of the Civil War, Palmito Ranch: 5/13/65

notable among these was Charles Fasoldt, who worked in Albany, NY, and all of his watches are horological rarities. However, the only two U.S. watch *manufacturers* selling any significant number of watches during the Civil War were the American Watch Co. (AWCo) of Waltham, MA, and E. Howard & Co. (EH&Co) of Boston. **TABLE 6** and **TABLE 7** provide approximate pre-Civil War and Civil War period production dates for ranges of AWCo and EH&Co watch movement serial numbers, respectively. However, readers must keep in mind that specific movements either were or may have been finished out of sequence, sometimes even by years. Furthermore, higher grade movements, in particular, sometimes took many months, or even longer to sell after they were put into inventory.

Cases for American Watch Movements

The AWCo and its predecessors (principally, AT&Co and the BWCo) made some of their own watchcases. EH&Co did not. Early cases made in Waltham's own case department, circa 1857 to probably sometime in 1860 (though the company name actually changed in early 1859), are marked "A.T.& Co," on the inside of the outer rear lid. (A very rare marking, "T. B. & Co.," for the very short-lived predecessor of AT&Co, called Tracy, Baker & Co., also is known.) Beginning around 1861, Watchcases made in the AWCo's case department typically

78. A typical eagle marking stamped into the interior surface of the front lid of the silver hunting case of a Waltham Appleton, Tracy & Co. grade Model 1859 movement SN 140,138, sold by Robbins & Appleton. Such markings, which emphasized that a case so marked was a proudly American product, were common immediately before and during the Civil War but faded from use soon afterward. In earlier decades, eagle marks also appeared on American gold cases made for some English movements sold in the United States. The exact appearance of eagle markings varies quite a bit among examples. *Image courtesy of Ben Hutcherson.*

are marked "A. W. Co." BWCo cases (which are scarce in silver and rare in gold) are marked "B.W. Co." This marking should not be confused with that found on cases made postwar by the Brooklyn Watch Case Co., which were marked "B.W.C. Co." Many early AWCo movements also were sold in cases bearing the "R. & A." mark of the company's aforementioned principal sales agency, the firm of Robbins & Appleton.

Various other case markings also turn up on

original cases for Civil War period Waltham watches, because probably most AWCo movements were sold uncased to wholesale and retail establishments. It is not unusual to find both American and Swiss watchcases with simulated "hallmarks" somewhat resembling those appearing on English watchcases. Many American watchcases of the Civil War period also had eagles stamped into the inside of a prominent case surface as a patriotic statement, as in **FIGURE 78.**

Watchcases for Howard movements marked "E.H. & Co." were made to order by various case makers for the Howard sales offices in Boston and New York City. They were not made in the Howard factory. Other maker's or retailer's marks that were seen often, or not infrequently on original cases for early Howard watches from the approximate period of the Civil War include the following: [80]

+ **J. M. Harper** ("J. M. H."; often seen)
+ **Palmers & Batchelder** ("P. & B."; this often-seen marking is often mistaken for Peters & Boss)
+ **Baldwin & Co.** ("B & Co."; makers of Baldwin's patented "reversible," hunting-case-to-open-face cases, among other case styles)
+ **Thiery & Serex** ("T. & S."; often seen on very early Howard watchcases, pre-1863)
+ **J. T. Scott & Co.** ("J. T. S. & Co.")
+ **Charles E. Hale & Co.** ("C. E. H. & Co."; often seen, also see next paragraph)
+ **E. Tracy & Co.** ("E. T. & Co."; often seen)
+ **Warren & Spadone** ("W. & S."; often seen)
+ **Cooper & Fellows** ("C. & F.")
+ **Fellows & Co.** ("F. & Co.")
+ **Fellows & Schell** ("F. & S.")
+ **Crosby & Mathewson** ("C. & M.")
+ **"F. M."** (no known attribution)

79. "Dennison, Howard & Davis" "Model 1857" movement, made by the Boston Watch Co. ca. 1855, SN 3,330 with fifteen jewels in screwed-down top plate settings and solid steel balance. Aaron L. Dennison and Edward Howard were principal founders and organizers of the BWCo, whereas David P. Davis took no active role in the running of the watch company. The company produced 4,000 such movements with serial numbers between 1,001 and 4,999. It is likely that at least a few of these DH&D watches made by the BWCo before 1857 saw service in the Civil War.

80. The unsigned, unsunk dial of the pre-Civil War "Dennison, Howard & Davis" watch with movement SN 3,330. The gold hands are typical for these watches and appear original.

+ **C. & A. Pequignot** ("C. & A. P.")
+ **D. T. Warren & Co.** ("D. T. W. & Co.")
+ **Margot Brothers** ("M. B.")
+ **Mathey & Brother** ("M. & B.")
+ **Celestine Jacot & Brother** ("C. J. & Bro.")

Contrary to certain reports in the literature and on the Internet, the "C. E. H. & Co." marking has *nothing to do* with the aforementioned "E. H. & Co." marking. AWCo watches also turn up with cases bearing the "C. E. H. & Co." marking. Still other cases are known bearing both the "E. H. & Co." marking and the actual maker's or retailer's mark, which is never "C. E. H. & Co." Chas. E. Hale & Co was succeeded in business by Wheeler, Parsons & Co. (W. P. & Co.) in 1867.

The reader is cautioned that the preceding list of case makers for EH&Co movements is by no means complete. Cases bearing other makers' or retailers' markings, or *no* such markings at all, can also be original.

American Watch Co. Watches

Predecessor Companies

The American Watch Co. evolved out of a succession of short-lived firms, the most productive of which were the aforementioned Boston Watch Co. (from approximately 1854 to mid-1857) and Appleton, Tracy & Co. (from late 1857 to 1859). Most products of the Boston Watch Co. (BWCo), were engraved "Dennison, Howard & Davis," after its two principal founders, Aaron Lufkin Dennison and Edward Howard. The third name was that of D. P. Davis, Howard's partner in the clock business. With one known exception, these watches had unsigned dials. Examples of BWCo watches with movements marked "Dennison Howard & Davis" and "Samuel Curtis" are shown in **FIGURES 79–82**. Many "Dennison Howard & Davis" movements were sold in cases marked "B. W. Co." (**FIGURE 81**), which were made in the BWCo's own case department. As mentioned, the great preponderance of BWCo-marked cases were coin silver. But the BWCo case of

81. Not all "Dennison, Howard & Davis" movements originally were sold in cases marked "B.W.Co.," as was the example shown here, which was made in the Boston Watch Co.'s own case department. However, such usually inarguably original cases do command a premium among collectors. Nearly all surviving "B. W. Co." cases are coin silver, but this rare example is 18-kt. gold. (The partly obliterated other marking at center cannot be determined with certainty.)

movement SN 3,330 is 18-kt. gold. Many very early BWCo products, such as Samuel Curtis movement SN 375, shown in **FIGURE 82**, were sold in hallmarked English-made, but American-style cases.

AT&Co produced two movement models, both of which continued to be made by the American Watch Co., and which came to be known as the Model's 1857 and 1859. With one exception, each succeeding company in the Waltham lineage began its serial numbers where the preceding firm had ended. The exception is that AT&Co reused perhaps a thousand BWCo serial numbers beginning at around SN 1,001, marked either "C. T. Parker" or "P. S. Bartlett," when they otherwise began production in late 1857 at SN 5,001. To confuse matters further, the AWCo continued to use the AT&Co name as a grade designation on many of its watches throughout the Civil War and beyond. **TABLE 6** (p. 101) shows

82. An even earlier Boston Watch Co. product, movement, SN 375, signed "Samuel Curtis" after an important financial backer of the company. This particular Curtis movement has a rare feature, a Geneva-style stopwork, perhaps the only such stopwork appearing on any known Boston Watch Co. movement. (Even earlier products of this company, marked "Warren Manufacturing Company," the few surviving examples of which are horological treasures, have annular-style stopworks.) Although this movement appears very similar in design to later, so-called "Model 1857" movements made by the BWCo's successor companies, the wheel train is laid out differently. Given that a significant fraction of the Northern adult male population saw service sometime between 1861 and 1865, it is likely that at least a few of these 800 or so "Samuel Curtis" pre-Model 1857 watches would have found their way onto a Civil War battlefield. Like many other of the approximately 800 Curtis movements made by the BWCo circa. 1853, this watch's original sterling silver case was made in England.

that any watch made by the AWCo or one of its several predecessors with a serial number below approximately 160,000 *may* have been made prior to May 1865. (However, it is again stressed that neither the AWCo nor EH&Co produced watch movements in strict serial order, though the AWCo's production practices were considerably more orderly. Thus, some movements with serial numbers greater than 160,000 may date to the Civil War period, and others with serial numbers substantially earlier than SN 160,000 may postdate the war.)

AWCo Watch Models of the Civil War Period

The following men's watch models were manufactured by the Waltham family of companies during and/or prior to the Civil War:

83. A William Ellery grade Waltham Model 1857 movement, SN 67,581 with seven jewels and monometallic steel balance. The watch carried no warranty, and the single-piece, single-plane (i..e, unsunk) Roman numeral dial is unsigned. This movement, which was finished in January 1863, is essentially identical to the Model 1857 movement, SN 67,613, of the watch presented to President Abraham Lincoln by the AWCo. *Image courtesy of Robert McCabe.*

+ **Model 1857**, an 18-size full plate, wound from rear, set from front; Waltham's most abundant workhorse model (e.g., see **FIGURE 83**)

+ **Model 1859** "thin model", an 18-size three-quarter plate, wound from rear, set from rear, advertised as being designed for soldiers (see **FIGURE 84**)

+ **20-size Keywind (20KW) Model**, a.k.a. "Model 1862", a 20-size three-quarter plate, wound from rear, set from rear (see **FIGURE 85**)

+ **16-size Keywind (16KW) Model**, a.k.a. "Model 1860" [sic], a 16-size three-quarter plate, wound from rear, set from rear (see **FIGURE 86**)

It is noted that the "Model 1860" designation, which originated in twentieth-century AWCo trade literature, is inaccurate. The AWCo

84. The Waltham Model 1859 movement of the watch carried by Lt. Colonel John Hodges, Jr. of Salem, MA. This Appleton, Tracy & Co. grade movement SN 31,928, finished in May of 1860, features fifteen jewels in screwed-down top plate settings, a monome-tallic gold alloy balance wheel, and a stopwork (not visible). This movement is an example of Waltham's three-quarter-plate "thin model" that was vigorously promoted to soldiers, although the AT&Co grade example was much pricier than the more modest William Ellery grade.

20-size and 16-size Keywind Models were identical except for size. AWCo movement sizes were based on the Lancashire Gauge, in which a movement with a dial plate diameter of 1⁵/₃₀" is designated as "Size 0," increasing by thirtieths of an inch with each successive num-ber. Hence, 16-, 18-, and 20-size watches had dial plates, or pillar plates, with diameters of 1.7", 1.77", and 1.83", respectively. Both the three-quarter-plate 20-size and 16-size models origi-nated with the short-lived Nashua Watch Co. venture, but only a few 20-size movements were

85. The Appleton, Tracy & Co. grade, 16-size Model 16KW (a.k.a. "Model 1860" [sic]) movement of the watch presented to General John W. Fuller, SN 80,265. It has a monometallic gold alloy balance wheel and a stopwork concealed beneath the top plate. The movement was finished in January of 1864. (This relative imprecision in the production date results because in this instance, only the completion dates for the beginning and end of the production run are available.)

completed at Nashua in 1862 before that undercapitalized startup company was absorbed into the AWCo. The 20-size Keywind model was introduced into the Waltham product line before the 16-size Keywind model, though the exact introduction dates are not known. Only about 2,600 20-size watches were produced, beginning around 1862 and continuing perhaps beyond 1870. An example of a somewhat earlier 10-size ladies' watch movement model (1.5" diameter), the three-quarter-plate Model 1861 designed in Waltham, is shown in **FIGURE 87**.

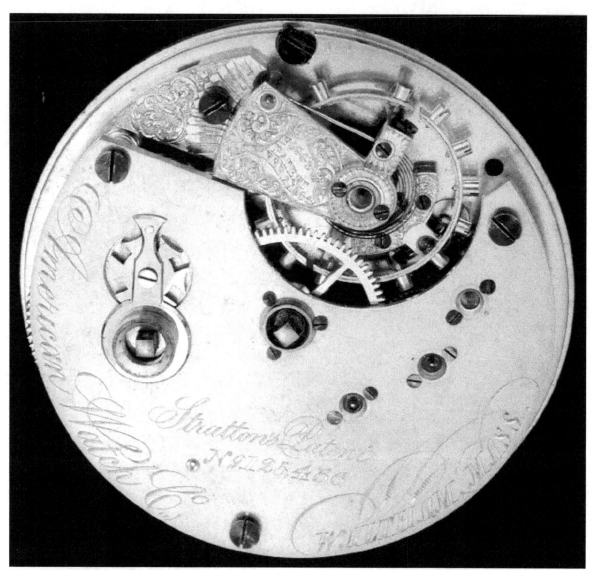

86. A 16-size keywind (Model 16KW) movement of the American Watch Co. grade, SN 125,466, finished between August 1864 and July 1866 (per the NAWCC AWCo serial number lookup utility). This movement was one of the AWCo's highest-quality flagship products and runs of such movements sometimes were completed long after they were begun, as in this case. This particular example, with an exposed stopwork, exhibits two optional features: (1) N. P. Stratton's patented mainspring barrel (indicated on the train plate just above the serial number), which protected the escapement from the damage sometimes resulting from violent mainspring failures; and (2) C. W. Fogg's patented vibrating hairspring stud (indicated on the balance cock in smaller lettering), a form of allegedly isochronous regulator. *Image by Thomas McIntyre, from the Enhanced 2002 NAWCC National Seminar Online Exhibit: web.archive.org/web/20160303230825/http://www.awco.org/seminar2002/*

Representative corresponding Waltham watch dials are shown in **FIGURE 12** (p. 27), **FIGURE 20** (p. 33), and **FIGURE 27** (p. 38); see also **FIGURES 88–91.**

AWCo Watch Grades

The AWCo used various grade designations on its watches. The grade of a watch was announced by the details of the engraving on the watch plate, not by the manner in which the dial was signed, with the exception that the dials of the AWCo's lowest grade watches were *unsigned*. In descending order of quality, Waltham's Civil War era grades were as follows:

+ **American Watch Co.** (where the word "American" is completely spelled out on the watch plate), as in **FIGURE 32** (p. 42) and **FIGURE 86**. This grade name will sometimes be abbreviated here as "AWCo." (Except for one example known to the author, Model 1857 full-plate movements never were made in this highest grade.)

+ **Appleton, Tracy & Co.** (later replaced by the "Amn. Watch Co." grade after the Civil War), as in **FIGURE 24** (p. 35), **FIGURE 28** (p. 39), and **FIGURE 84**. This grade will be abbreviated here as "AT&Co."

+ **P. S. Bartlett**, as in **FIGURE 13** (p. 28) and **FIGURE 87**. (Abbreviated here as "PSB.")

+ **Wm. Ellery**, as in **FIGURE 83**. (These watches typically had unsigned dials)

+ The **Home Watch Co.** grade was not introduced until 1866 and is not discussed further here.

TABLE I (p. 57) shows that different grades of the same Waltham model had different numbers of jewels (they may have had different jewel compositions as well), and offered different balance wheel options. AWCo grade movements always had temperature-compensated bimetallic balance wheels. Early AT&Co grade movements had either bimetallic or monometallic gold alloy balances, but gold balances were phased out over time. The upper two Waltham grades, AWCo and AT&Co, also had stopworks (which were not always visible), and the low-

87. A Waltham Model 1861 10-size (1.5" diameter) ladies' watch movement of the kind that a Civil War nurse might have carried. The watch has fifteen jewels in screwed-down top plate settings with an uncompensated solid gold balance wheel, and it features D. B. Fitts's mainspring barrel, patented on November 30, 1858. This invention shared the same principle and the same purpose as Fitts's patented reversing pinion seen on the men's watch movement in FIG. 28 (p.39), to harmlessly dissipate the shock imparted by a breaking mainspring through reverse motion. (Mid-nineteenth-century metallurgy was still fairly crude, and mainspring failures were a ubiquitous fact of life with which every watch owner, and watch maker, had to contend.) Movement SN 54,033 was finished in February of 1864. *Image courtesy of Stephen Helfant.*

er two grades, PSB and Ellery, did not. Ellery grade movements had monometallic steel or gold alloy balances, whereas PSB grade watches could have any of the three kinds of balance wheels. Similarly, PSB and Ellery grade movements offered no special safety mechanisms to protect the wheel train and escapement from the damage that could occur due to mainspring failures, nor special regulators for more accurate rate adjustment. The William Ellery grade watches had flat, one-piece, unsigned dials. The higher grades had signed dials that were single, or in scarce instances, double-sunk.

Waltham watches of the two highest grades,

88. The dial of Lt. Colonel John Hodges's Appleton, Tracy & Co. grade Model 1859 watch, bearing the name of the American Watch Co. The inner rule on the interior side of the hour chapter simulates a "double-sunk" appearance, as are seen on several American Watch Company grade examples of the same watch model. However, the dial is only single-sunk. The slender 18-size hands exemplify the "Breguet" hand style.

AWCo and AT&Co, were most likely to have been found in a Union officer's pocket. The two lower grades, PSB and Ellery, were the most popular Waltham watches among Union enlisted men. The Bartlett grade was named for Patten Sargeant Bartlett, who until 1864 was foreman of the plate and screw department, and who came from a prominent New England family—his great uncle had signed the Declaration of Independence. The Ellery grade was

89. The dial of the Appleton, Tracy & Co. grade Model 16KW watch presented to "Brigadier" General John W. Fuller. (He actually was a brevet Major General when the watch was presented.)

named for William Ellery (1727–1820), the last signer of the Declaration of Independence from New England to pass away. Ellery had served as a senator from Rhode Island, and he had helped to draft the charter of Brown University. Probably not just coincidentally, William Ellery was a prominent and outspoken early abolitionist. (Several of Brown University's other founders held slaves, but this is true of most of the "Ivies.")

90. The plain, unsigned dial of the William Ellery grade Waltham Model 1857 watch with movement SN 67,581. This flat, one-piece dial has no separate seconds bit, so it has no "sinks." *Image courtesy of Robert McCabe.*

E. Howard & Co. Watches

The other U.S. watch-making firm active during the Civil War, E. Howard & Co., produced relatively small numbers of watches compared with Waltham's production figures, and these were all for the high-end, luxury market. At EH&Co, Edward Howard eccentrically combined in his operations modern manufacturing notions with copious amounts of skilled, traditional craftsmanship. Consequently, early EH&Co watch products were less standardized than contemporary AWCo watches and exhibited greater individual character. That

portion of the Howard factory watch movement production records known to have survived, which is housed at the Smithsonian American History Archives Center, first became available for study in 2001. But even the records now available are terse and chaotic, and they fail to describe many of the movement details important to horologists. These factors, combined with the association of the Howard name with the luxury market, the relative scarcity of surviving examples, their quality, their unique casing requirements, and the absence of public model distinctions or grade designations, have created a mystique around early Howard watches that has magnified their appeal among collectors. The Howard firm, which also claimed succession to the BWCo, [2,56,57,81] did business for a short time under the name "Howard & Rice." [82] Most of these early movements also were signed "Boston Watch Company," before the firm began to sign its watches "E. Howard & Co." on December 10, 1858, per REF. 57 and references therein. The watch movements made by this prestigious clock company often cost more than the gold cases that housed them. Thus, Howard watches typically would have been carried by men of means, and among Civil War combatants, this fact would have most often, but not necessarily always, meant officers.

Originally cased early Howard watches are all significant horological artifacts independent of any connection they may have to Civil War service. However, those Howard watches with movement serial numbers below about 6,500 could conceivably have seen service on a Civil War battlefield. (It is noted that more frequently than with any other kind of American watch, highly original Howard keywind watches sometimes are found with matching movement and case serial numbers.)

Since the Howard firm did not name its watch models in the Civil War period as the Waltham firm did, nor did it designate formal grades for its movement quality levels in that period, modern collectors have devised their own model nomenclatures. In the older, Small-Hackett-Townsend "Series" naming convention, [83] these are the Howard Series I, II, and III. In the Geller model year naming convention of REF. 63, they would be the Models 1858 Types A through E, and Type O divided-plate

91. The single-sunk dial of the 10-size P. S. Bartlett grade Waltham Model 1861 ladies' watch, movement SN 54,033. *Image courtesy of Stephen Helfant.*

keywind; and the three-quarter-plate Model 1862-N. All these movements were both wound and set with a key from the rear. Single hundred-lots of smaller K-size (roughly 14-size), and I-size (10-size) Howard movements also were made, but these likely have little or no significance relative to the Civil War. For a detailed discussion of Howard keywind watch models of the Civil War period, the reader is directed to REF. 57.

If originally cased Howard keywind watches are scarce, those with *bona fide* Civil War provenances are rarities. Many surviving American watch movements, including those made by the EH&Co, have been recased over the years. Non-original cases housing EH&Co movements from the Civil War period are usually among the easier recases to spot. There are two main reasons for this. First, EH&Co used its own unique system of movement sizes. In the EH&Co size system, size A corresponds to a dial plate of 1" in diameter, increasing by six-teenths of an inch with each successive letter of the alphabet. Nearly all Civil War-era EH&Co movements are size N, which is $1^{13}/_{16}$", or about 1.81" in diameter. That diameter is just a hair larger than the 19-size in the Lancashire Gauge system, in between the common AWCo 18-size watches and the much scarcer AWCo 20-size watches. Because Howard movements were all produced in limited numbers, relatively speak-ing, surviving original cases for Howard move-ments are correspondingly scarce, and nearly all surviving original examples already have How-ard movements in them.

Furthermore, more so than most other watches, Howard watch movements originally were cased in gold, and gold cases have fared especially poorly over the years, being soft, and often having been scrapped and melted for their bullion value. Hence, many surviving Howard movements, which outnumber surviving origi-nal Howard movement cases by at least several to one, often find their way into ill-fitting and often modified cases made for movements of other sizes and manufacturers.

The other main reason that recased Howard movements usually are relatively easy to spot is that they are "three-quarter-plate" movements in which the balance wheel turns in a plane in or below the plane of the top plate. This arrange-ment, as illustrated for example in **FIGURE 84**, is in contrast to the "full-plate" movement con-figuration of the Waltham Model 1857 il-lustrated in **FIGURE 83**. In the full-plate con-figuration the balance wheel and its supporting structure, the cock, extend considerably above the plane of the train plate. The full-plate con-figuration thus makes for a thicker movement and a correspondingly thicker watchcase. The profile of a full-plate watchcase, consequently, is generally more domed from edge to center than that of a Howard watchcase. For a com-prehensive review of issues relating to assessing the originality of cases of EH&Co watches, the reader is directed to REF. 80.

7

FOREIGN-MADE WATCHES
USED IN THE CIVIL WAR

OWING TO secessionist passions and the general disruption of North–South commerce, few new American watches likely were purchased within the changing borders of the Confederacy. Some light may be shed on the nature of watches in circulation in at least part of the South by the surviving records of E. Barbier's leading watch repair business in New Orleans for the years 1860 and 1865–66; the records for the intermediate years were destroyed by fire. As reported by J. M. Kinabrew Jr., Barbier had been an apprentice of the "premier clock and watchmaker of New Orleans in the 1860s. Later, [Barbier] took over [his mentor's] business." [84] In 1860 New Orleans, a major international port and the world's largest cotton exporting center, was the most populous city in the South, so the city's watch clientele was not necessarily representative of the South as a whole. Similarly, New Orleans was under Federal occupation after May 1, 1862, so Barbier's customers in 1865 likely would have included Union troops and associated civilians, most of whom would have brought their watches with them when they arrived. Nevertheless, it is worth mentioning that of the thirty-six watches appearing in Barbier's 1860 repair records on which the maker was identified, Kinabrew reports that twenty were English, eleven were Swiss, two were of local make (or, more precisely, probably had local jewelers' names on them), and three were Waltham products; twenty-three watches were of the hunting-case style and thirteen were open face. Of the forty-one watches whose case metal was known, thirty-three were gold and eight were silver, testifying to the affluence of Barbier's clientele. Of the thirty-seven watches whose escapement type was specified, thirty-five had lever (or "anchor") escapements, and two had cylinder escapements, but there was not a single lowly verge watch in the group.

Barbier's post-Civil War records from 1865 to 1866 include 142 English watches (including twenty-two identified as being made in London, and thirty-nine from Liverpool), thirty-five Swiss, twelve American, and six French watches. The same group included 188 hunting-case watches, seventy-two open-face watches, two "double back" (pair cased?) watches, and one "magic bow" watch. (A "magic bow" watch is a hunting-case watch fitted with lift springs on both lids, which are selectively engaged and disengaged by rotating the bow of the case through 180 degrees. The other approach on double spring-loaded cases was to use a split pusher, as in **FIGURE 29**, p. 40) Gold cases outnumber silver by 147 to 102 in Barbier's postwar records, with eleven "composition" (probably nickel alloy) cases. Escapement information is less frequent in this group, but the escapements listed were predominantly detached levers, but as well as thirty cylinder escapements, three duplex escapements, three verges, and two pin levers. The apparent shifts in the distributions of escapement types and makers may reflect the influx of Union personnel into the city that occurred between 1862 and 1865.

Among foreign watches, English products probably enjoyed the best overall reputation in both the North and the South. [2] The Swiss did a very brisk business in all parts of the United States before the war, especially in the bottom end of the watch market, but they exported quality watches to the United States too. Other than these two principal exporting countries, German makers in Glashutte, such as Adolph Lange, Julius Assman, and Moritz Grossman, also exported to the United States, as did Jules Jurgensen of Copenhagen, in Denmark. In Paris, France, the House of Breguet, named for its illustrious founder, Abraham Louis Breguet (1747–1823), also exported some watches to the United States during the Civil War period, as did some less prestigious French makers.

The best English watches mostly were made in London, whereas more English exports to the United States came out of Liverpool, and a few came from Coventry. In an effort to cash in on the superior reputation of English watches in the United States, some Swiss makers even misrepresented their own products as British. The various watch makers of the Tobias family, for example, ware favorite subjects of Swiss counterfeiters. Except for those English watches carrying American retailers' names, English watches of the Civil War period seen in America generally carried the makers' names, the makers' city, and sometimes the maker's address

engraved on their movements. Other than the Tobiases of both London and Liverpool, other British makers who exported significantly to the United States during the Civil War period include Joseph Johnson (Liverpool), Robert Roskell (Liverpool), T. F. Cooper (London), and John Cragg (London).

The big Swiss watch making centers were in Geneva, and in Le Locle, Chaux-de-Fonds, and Neuchatel in the Jura Region. Swiss exporters to the United States in this period were numerous, but the list included D. I. Magnin, Robert Tissot, Patek Philippe et cie, James Courvoisier, Anthony LeCoultre et fil, Charles Jacot, and Auguste Saltzman, among many others. Swiss export watches to the United States during the Civil War period most often had no identifying markings on their movements, though some makers had distinctive movement styles. Most of these Swiss imports carried their makers' identifications on the inner rear lids (cuvettes, dust covers) of their watchcases, often along with other movement details, such as the number and composition of the jewels and/or the type of escapement.

Swiss watches are often the toughest to verify as originating from the Civil War period, because production data for most Swiss makers is scarce or entirely lacking, and there is often no serial number on a Swiss movement to compare with such data, even if it were available. Similarly, the case markings, other than rare, dated inscriptions, usually offer few solid clues to their specific production years. Inferences not infrequently can be made concerning approximate production dates from the movement design or finishing details. For instance, the Lepine calibre Type V movement style exemplified in **FIGURE 100** (p. 124), was widely produced during the Civil War. Thus any of the four styles of Lepine watch that preceded it likely would have existed and conceivably could have seen service during the Civil War as well. References that can provide the years of operation of specific Swiss makers do also exist, [85] although many Swiss watches sold in the United States carry only the names of the American retailer, or even an entirely fictitious American-sounding name. However, it is not usually possible to accurately date a Swiss watch to the Civil War period on such an obscure basis. Collectors should take the increased uncertainty associated with the pedigree of many Swiss watches into consideration when estimating value and authenticity as a Civil War artifact.

English Watches

FIGURES 92–97 exemplify two mid-nineteenth-century English watch movement types: the full-plate and the half-plate configurations. These movements have fusees and dust covers. The dust cover of the full-plate movement is secured with a blued locking spring affixed to the dust cover. The dust cover of the half-plate movement is hinged and is locked in place by a latch on the circumference of the movement.

The full-plate movement shown in **FIGURES 92–95** was made by John Cragg of London, the same maker who signed Jeb Stuart's watch, which sold at Heritage Galleries for $131,450 in December of 2006. The Cragg movement of **FIGURES 92–95** was retailed by the firm of Mitchell & Tyler, whose name appears on both the dust cover and the case. Though this open-face watch, with an elegant and somewhat archaic style gold dial, does not carry the original owner's name, Heritage Gal-

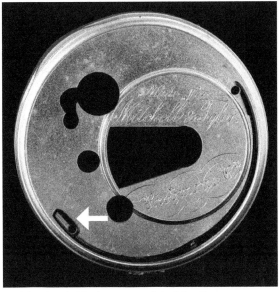

92. The detachable dust cover of the John Cragg movement, which is locked and unlocked by sliding the blued steel spring shown by the arrow a few degrees clockwise to lock, or counterclockwise to unlock. *Image courtesy of Heritage Galleries.*

93. The front of the open-face watch reported to have been owned by Confederate Major General William Mahone, featuring an older style, ornate rose gold dial with raised Roman numerals. The gold wheat link chain in the picture has an eagle's head watch fob attached. Only part of one gold watch hand remains. *Image courtesy of Heritage Galleries.*

94. The high-quality lever fusee full plate movement of the Mahone watch shown in its swung-out position, with diamond end stone, temperature-compensated balance wheel, and at least seventeen jewels, signed, "Jn. Cragg, 8 Northampton Sq., London, 26742." *Image courtesy of Heritage Galleries.*

95. A postwar picture of former General William Mahone (December 1, 1826–October 8, 1895), when he was a railroad executive. Perhaps he is wearing the same watch as pictured in FIG. 93. A brigadier for most of the war, Mahone took part in every campaign of the Army of Northern Virginia, from the Peninsula Campaign all the way to Lee's surrender at Appomattox, except for the Maryland Campaign, when he was recuperating from a shot in the chest suffered at Second Bull Run.

His signature success came during the Battle of the Crater on July 30, 1864, the date of his promotion to Major General. On that day his quick and decisive actions in response to the stunning Federal mine explosion detonated underneath the Confederate lines at Elliott's Salient outside of Petersburg, VA, contained the developing Federal breakthrough and averted what could have been a premature defeat for Lee's Army of Northern Virginia. *Library of Congress Prints and Photographs Division. Brady-Handy Photograph Collection. hdl.loc.gov/loc.pnp/cwpbh.04359*

leries cites a provenance chain back to Confederate Major General William Mahone, who is reported to have owned it during his period of military service. [86] The movement is of high quality, with a temperature-compensated bimetallic balance, a diamond end stone on the balance staff, and jeweling on the center wheel. The second movement style, exemplified by the half-plate movement by the prolific London maker, Morris Tobias, is shown in FIGURES 96–97. This movement, with an uncompensated monometallic steel balance, is of more modest quality than the Cragg watch.

The mercury vapor gilding process used on English watch plates, while more dangerous and unhealthful to workers, produced a generally superior finish to the cyanide bath electrogilding process used on contemporaneous American and Swiss watch plates. The overall finishing standards of English watches made for the U.S. market were perhaps not as high as English finishing standards for the domestic English and European markets, but were still better than the finish most often found on Swiss export watches. Overall, better English watches were finished in a manner at least com-

97. The same movement as FIG. 96, shown here with the dust cover in place. The arrow indicates a second latch that secures the dust cover. *Image courtesy of Keith Richmond.*

96. A Tobias half-plate movement typical of those sold in the United States during and shortly before the Civil War, engraved, "Morris Tobias, 31 Minories, London, SN 2003." The lever fusee movement features a monometallic steel balance wheel with diamond end stone and seventeen jewels. The hinged dust cover is rotated up to expose the balance assembly. The arrow at top indicates the end of the fusee arbor where it protrudes through the top plate. The arrow at lower right indicates the latch that secures the movement in its case, 180 degrees opposite the movement hinge at upper left. *Image courtesy of Keith Richmond.*

parable to, if not better than most American watches. As previously mentioned, most English watches also used fusees (see **FIGURE 60**, p. 80) to improve timekeeping uniformity over the running period. The fusee was a feature that required skilled, specialized labor to produce and, consequently, was eschewed by both American and most Swiss makers (except on obsolescent verge escapement watches, which absolutely required fusees).

Owing to the decentralized, cottage nature of English watch making in the mid-nineteenth-century, little interchangeability exists among most English watch movements and cases of the American Civil War period. This fact makes it much easier most of the time to determine whether a particular English watchcase is original to a particular English watch movement. It is a very handy fact, indeed, because all English silver and gold cases carried at least four "hallmarks" stamped or incused into their surfaces: a maker's mark (two initials); an assay mark or "standard mark," which testifies to the purity of the metal; a town mark, which states where the case was assayed (London, Chester, or Birmingham for watchcases); and most importantly for authenticity determinations, a date mark specifying the year that the case was assayed. A date mark is a letter raised up from within an incused field, and both the calligraphy style of the letter (today, one would call it a font) and the shape of the field are significant in determining the date to which a letter refers. However, readers should beware that

London date mark (changed on May 28)		Chester date mark (changed on August 5)		Birmingham date mark (changed on July 1)	
𝖆	1856	𝕽	1855	A	1849
𝖇	1857	𝕾	1856	…	
𝖈	1858	𝕿	1857	L	1860
𝖉	1859	𝖀	1858	M	1861
𝖊	1860	𝖁	1869	N	1862
𝖋	1861	𝖂	1860	O	1863
𝖌	1862	𝖃	1861	P	1864
𝖍	1863	𝖄	1862	Q	1865
𝖎	1864	𝖅	1863		
𝖐	1865	𝖆	1864		
		𝖇	1865		

Sovereign head duty mark

Sterling silver mark (after approx. 1820)

Gold mark

London guild mark (leopard's head)

Chester guild mark after 1800 (three wheat sheaves)

98. The four, and sometimes five, markings found incused into all silver and gold English watchcases seen during the American Civil War. Date marks for London, Chester, and Birmingham are seen starting at top-left. Guild or town marks for London and Chester are at left. (The Birmingham town mark is an anchor.) At top-right is the sovereign head duty mark; below it the post-1820 "standard mark" for sterling silver, a lion passant with head parallel to its body; below that the gold mark. Gold marks often were accompanied by a millesimal fraction inside an octagonal field, indicating the purity. *Images from Priestly, Philip T., Watch Case Makers of England, NAWCC 1994.*

the date mark did not change on January 1 of the year in question. In addition, London, Chester, and Birmingham date marks are not the same. During the Civil War period the London date mark changed on May 28, the Chester date mark changed on August 5, and the Birmingham date mark changed on July 1. [87] Thus, for example, a case assayed at London in April of 1863 would have the 1862/63 date mark, and a case assayed at London in June of 1863 would carry the 1863/64 mark. Some English watchcases also carried a fifth mark, a "Sovereign head" duty mark, indicating that taxes were

paid on the case. These marks are illustrated in **FIGURE 98**. As mentioned, BWCo watch movement SN 375, marked "Samuel Curtis," resides in an original purpose-made English hallmarked silver case. The interior lid of this case is shown in **FIGURE 99**.

The guild mark or town mark, the assay mark, the date mark, and when present, the duty mark, will be stamped on the interior case surfaces. The maker's two initials may be found on an interior lid surface and/or the exterior of the case near the pendant. (All of these marks are collectively referred to as "hallmarks.") More information concerning English markings on sterling silver and gold objects may be found in the definitive reference on English watchcases, *British Watchcase Gold & Silver Marks 1670 to 1970: A History of Watchcase Makers and Registers of Their Marks from Original Assay Office Records in England, Ireland, and Scotland,* an NAWCC publication by the late Philip Priestley, Ref. 88.

Watch movement production data do exist for a few better-known English makers, but by and large, English movement and case serial numbers, which often match, cannot establish a production date. This is especially so, because many English watches made for the U.S. market were private label products that revealed only the American retailer's name. However, one can find many mid-nineteenth-century English watch makers in various well-known lists, such as *Watchmakers and Clockmakers of the World,* by G. H. Baillie, [88] or the previously mentioned Loomes, *Watchmakers & Clockmakers of the World, Volume 2,* [46] which updated Baillie's work. These sources can provide approximate (or even exact) dates for many watch-making enterprises' periods in business and their locations. Priestley's previously mentioned text has much of this same kind of information for English watchcase makers. As a rule, the date mark on the case of an English watch is usually the single most valuable datum informing the likelihood that an English watch could have been available for use during the Civil War, assuming the watch was in America at that time.

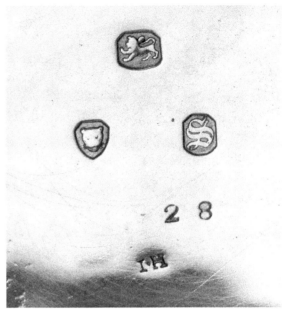

99. Many early Boston Watch Co. products like "Samuel Curtis" SN 375 originally were sold in English cases. Shown here is a segment of the interior of the rear lid of the sterling silver case of Samuel Curtis movement SN 375, showing the London town mark, a leopard's face in a shield. The London town mark is accompanied by the sterling silver "lion passant" assay mark. This mark shows the lion's head facing left, parallel to its body, distinguishing it from the earlier used "lion passant guardant," where the head faces front, at right angles to the body. The initials of the case maker, James Hammon (where the letter "J" is always rendered as an "I," [sic]), also appear. Hammon's mark appears on several other known apparently original surviving Curtis watchcases. Finally, the London date mark for 1853 is seen, a Gothic "S" in an octagonal field. (The letter "S" in a similar, but not identical style, is also used for the 1856 Chester date mark, but the surrounding field is shaped differently.) Note that the leopard's head has no crown, because the case was hallmarked after 1821.

Swiss and Other Foreign Watches

Many Swiss watch movements were sold in the United States in American-made cases. American-cased Swiss watches can often afford greater confidence that they may have seen service, or at least, that they existed in the right time and place to have seen service during

100. The approximately 18-size Lepine calibre Type V watch movement with right-angle lever (sometimes referred to as a "side lever") escapement of the gold watch presented to Colonel George W. Gallup of the 14th Kentucky Infantry in 1863. This watch and its illustrious owner are discussed at greater length in Chapter 9 (p.135). The Type V variety of the Lepine calibre movement design, which is distinguished by its straight barrel bridge and three parallel, nonconvergent train wheel finger bridges, was widely produced by Swiss makers beginning around 1850, continuing through the Civil War period. The prominent center wheel bridge with a curved section partly encircling the third wheel is characteristic of all the later Lepine calibre styles, not just Type V. Part of the watchcase is also visible. Like two of the other American watchcases previously shown, the American case of this Swiss watch movement has a spherical pendant that is visible in the image.

101. This movement style was used on some Swiss watches made during the Civil War but was perhaps most closely associated with the Danish watchmaker, Jules Jurgensen, of Copenhagen, who used it on many of his watches in the same period. The design's most distinctive characteristic is the curved center wheel bridge that wraps around the balance cock. *Image courtesy of Keith Richmond.*

the American Civil War. Swiss movement construction often provides additional clues. Apart from Swiss movements deliberately made to look American, there were a few general styles of Swiss watches that were most prevalent during the Civil War, all of which carried individual train wheels in separate bridges, or "finger bridges." The most prevalent of these was the Lepine calibre Type V, an example of which is shown in **FIGURE 100.** The Type V Lepine calibre variety is distinguished from earlier Lepine

102. The dial, chain and fob of the watch identified to First Sgt. Samuel H. Croyle of the 78th PA Infantry, Company G, by Chopard Fils. The silver fob identifies Sgt. Croyle as the owner. Also shown is the chain, made of links of freshwater clamshell, which may have come from Stones River. *Image courtesy of Michael Kraus, Soldiers & Sailors Hall & Museum, Pittsburgh, PA.*

103. The movement of Sgt. Croyle's heirloom watch by Chopard Fils, with traditional pierced balance cock and verge escapement with fusee, shown in the swung-out position of its swing-out case.

105. A close-up of the rear of Sgt. Croyle's watch fob, engraved: "Siege of Nashville, Lavergne, Stone River, Dug Gap, Chickamauga, Chattanooga, Campaign Ga."

104. A close-up of the front of Sgt. Croyle's watch fob, engraved: "1ˢᵀ Sergᵗ Samˡ H. Croyle, Co. G, 78ᵀᴴ Reg.ᵗ PA Vol. Inf."

types by a straight barrel bridge, and the fact that the three train wheel finger bridges are oriented nearly in parallel, rather than converging toward the center of the movement.

Another generic Swiss movement style of the Civil War period, with no particular name, is shown in **FIGURE 101**. The movements of Swiss watches, including those shown in **FIGURE 100** and **FIGURE 101**, generally had going barrels rather than fusees, and the better ones had detached lever escapements. Most Swiss watches of the Civil War period were set and wound from the rear. Dials of Swiss watches made for the American market often

106. First Sergeant Samuel H. Croyle, 78th PA Infantry. Croyle, born in 1836, was recruited in Armstrong County PA, and was mustered in at Pittsburgh on October 12, 1861. He served three years with the regiment, mustering out with the rest of Company G on November 4, 1864. Croyle passed away in Pittsburgh in July, 1911 and is buried at the Soldier's Home Cemetery in Dayton, OH.

The 78th PA's most severe trial came during the Battle of Stones River near Murfreesboro, TN, on December 31, 1862 to January 2, 1863. On the first day of the battle, their beleaguered division was at one point assaulted on three sides, as neighboring federal units had been driven back. Yet on the final day, after having already taken considerable losses and then bloodily repelling a fierce renewed confederate assault at dawn, the 78th PA and six other regiments of Negley's division spontaneously charged, driving the rebels before them, and capturing a battery and the flag of the 26th TN Infantry. At sunset, the whole rebel line retreated, leaving behind about four hundred men who were taken prisoners.

The 78th PA had gone into the battle with 540 men and suffered 149 dead and wounded and thirty-nine men taken prisoner. Total casualties on all sides in the battle were 24,645 out of 78,400 engaged: 12,906 on the Union side and 11,739 on the Confederate side, or 31.4% of all troops, the highest percentage of any major engagement in the war. The Union Army's repulse of two Confederate attacks at Stones River, and the subsequent Confederate withdrawal boosted Union morale after the recent defeat at the Battle of Fredericksburg, and it permanently dashed Confederate aspirations for control of Middle Tennessee. The timely Union victory at Stones River also lent Lincoln's Emancipation Proclamation, which took effect on January 1, 1863, greater credibility.

were unsigned, like the movements. Other Civil War period Swiss watches carried only an American retailer's name on the movement, the dial, or both.

Some less-expensive Swiss movements had cylinder escapements, and many older heirloom movements with verge escapements and fusees, such as that by "Chopard Fils" shown in **FIGURES 102–105**, were still in use during the Civil War. The Chopard Fils watch, in a silver swing-out case, is identified to Sergeant Samuel H. Croyle of the 78th PA Volunteer Infantry. It is a relatively thin, open-face watch with a traditional pierced balance cock. Baillie [88] lists several Chopards making watches in Switzerland in the late eighteenth century, so a Chopard Fils watch might be expected to have been made from one to a few decades later than that. More than a few heirloom watches like this one certainly accompanied a family's son to war.

The 78th PA also fought in several other major battles and campaigns in the western theatre, among them Chickamauga, Resaca, Missionary Ridge, and Nashville, as well as the Tullahoma and Atlanta Campaigns—losing 267 men in all during service. *Image courtesy of Michael Kraus, Soldiers & Sailors Hall & Museum, Pittsburgh, PA.*

8

ASSESSING DESIRABILITY AND AUTHENTICITY OF CIVIL WAR TIMEPIECES

THOSE IN the antiquarian horological collecting community who, like the author, live in the nation whose survival once hinged on the outcome of the Civil War, may for a time become the privileged custodians of some of the timekeeping artifacts that saw service in that great conflict, or which were given as grateful tributes and tokens to comrades in arms at its conclusion. The previous section provided information for assessing the likelihood that an item offered for consideration may be authentic. Excluded from that discussion were watches, even those with documented provenances, which either were made or that came into the possession of an individual of historical significance substantially after their role in the Civil War had ended. Hence, only those watches that were made or that could have been made (if the exact production date cannot be established) either before, during, or at the immediate conclusion of the Civil War were covered. We now turn to a discussion of the factors that affect the desirability of Civil War timepieces and to the means of assessing the veracity of putative provenances.

Attributes of Civil War Watches Affecting General Desirability

First and foremost, authenticity is the key attribute that horologists and Civil War relic collectors seek in an artifact. Strictly speaking, authenticity, or "originality," of either a watch or a provenance can only be disproven, never proven. Nevertheless, there are Civil War period timepieces the totality of whose characteristics affords ample confidence that a putative provenance is very likely authentic, even without a diary entry or photographic evidence to confirm it. The guidelines provided herein are intended to give kindred spirits to the author who cherish these artifacts as he does the tools to make informed judgments concerning these questions.

Following this paragraph is a list of key, strictly horological attributes of watches dated to the Civil War period affecting their desirability as collectibles. The relative importance of these attributes is a highly subjective matter, although one or two (e.g., gold content) have a large and at least partly quantifiable effect on monetary value. These same considerations also apply to Civil War timepieces identified to specific individuals. However, in the latter case, they are joined by numerous additional considerations associated with the various aspects of the provenance. These new considerations are discussed separately. The following positive attributes increase the value of an artifact as a horological collectible. Civil War artifact collectors have different, but overlapping priorities.

+ Possesses all original parts, or (in American watches) factory parts otherwise indistinguishable from original parts
+ Is in good running order and a reasonable state of overall preservation, with no major dings, dents, dial cracks, corrosion, rust, or unsightly blemishes
+ Is a well-finished and/or high-grade movement
+ Is a scarce and/or desirable movement variety (e.g., Howard divided-plate keywinds, American Watch Co. grade Walthams, or pocket chronometers, per the preceding sections)
+ Has a substantial solid gold case (more often found among watches carried by officers), preferably eighteen karat, as opposed to silver, albata, or brass.
+ For cases other than gold, a case of solid coin silver (90% pure), sterling silver (92.5% pure), or vermeil (gold-plated silver), as opposed to a low-purity silver case (usually Swiss) with a silver-plated inner rear lid, an albata case, or a gold- or silver-plated brass case.

Authenticity of Provenances

Issues of authenticity are more complex for watches with inscriptions indicating provenances. For watches of unspecified provenance, authenticity issues boil down to only two: (1) whether the parts of the watch that are present all began life together; and (2) if so, whether it can be determined how likely it is that the watch in question could have seen service during the Civil War. But for watches with specified provenances, additional questions arise. One will wish to know whether the inscriptions or other evidence documenting the provenance are authentic, and if so, whether the owner likely carried this watch either on campaign, or while performing his or her other war-related duties.

Attributes of Provenances Affecting Interest and Desirability

Documentation of a Civil War provenance of a watch can exist as information appearing on the watch itself, by written letters or other documents accompanying the watch from the original owner, and/or by the attribution of heirs of the original owner. Period documents must surely exist, which tie specific watches— either by make and serial number or by an inscription actually quoted in the document—to specific owners, but this writer has never seen one. The closest example to such a case known to the author is the aforementioned inscribed presentation watch carried by Sergeant William H. Shaw of the 37th MA Infantry. The gift of the watch to Shaw by his company is mentioned in Shaw's surviving diary. Possible kinds of corroborating documents might be probate records, other inventories of effects of deceased persons, wills, sales receipts, or repair records, but if and only if they happen to uniquely identify a particular watch in some way (e.g., by movement and case serial numbers). Conversely, putative provenances based on the attributions of heirs of the original owner to an ancestor who served in the Civil War are relatively common, but are probably the least reliable sources for attribution. This is so, usually because of human fallibility and a tendency toward grandiose delusions (especially about one's ancestors), rather than fraudulent intent.

The most romantic fantasies completely devoid of fact often attach to family heirlooms, increasing with each new generation further removed from the alleged historical connection. For example, online catalogs of certain museums with significant holdings of artifacts reputed to be from the Civil War include multiple examples of watches that were clearly made decades after the Civil War but are described as having been carried by identified Civil War combatants. This information presumably came from the combatants' descendants and is often not necessarily entirely "incorrect." A Civil War veteran actually may have owned one of the watches in question sometime long after the Civil War, but the watch clearly had nothing else to do with the Civil War. Of course, as family lore tends to ripen into fantasy in the vineyard of ignorance watered by wishful thinking, the fiction becomes fact that if grandpa or great-grandpa was a Civil War veteran, then any surviving watch he might have touched must have been *the* watch, if any, that he carried during the Civil War. In extreme cases, even an "old" watch that the veteran's direct descendant may have owned may retroactively acquire the same imagined status.

Provenances Documented by Information Appearing on a Watch

Most often, credible evidence identifying timepieces to specific American Civil War combatants or other persons of Civil War significance (e.g., civilian personalities with a Civil War connection) takes the form of engraving on

the watchcase. Such information can also appear inscribed on a personalized watch dial (see **FIGURE 33**, p. 43), but such instances are less common. The following list gives possible attributes of watch inscriptions, some of which are obvious, which, in the author's opinion, tend to make a provenance more desirable, once its legitimacy has been accepted. This list also is subjective, but it is in line with the thinking of probably most serious collectors of identified historical artifacts generally. The common principle behind all the desirable suprahorological attributes of provenance watches discussed here is that three basic ingredients contribute to the desirability of a provenance:

- the strength of the connection of the owner or recipient of the watch to historical events,
- the importance of the owner's role in those significant historical events, and
- the proximity to, and the specific role, if any, of the watch in those events.

Note that many of the more specific potential attributes in the following lists, some of which relate exclusively to inscriptions, are either mutually exclusive or partly redundant. Thus, the list is not simply a "checklist" of desirable features of an inscription.

Desirable Characteristics of the Owner

- An officer—the higher in rank, the better—rather than an enlisted man (other than a "famous" enlisted man, such as a Medal of Honor winner)
- A man who served in one or more distinguished or famous combat units
- A man who is mentioned in a regimental his-

tory or general Civil War history, especially for some laudable service

+ A man who has a surviving diary or letters (not very common, but not rare) and photographs (common)

+ A man who is personally well known to Civil War history buffs (this is rare!)

+ A man who served in one or more especially important battles, the most magical association being with the Battle of Gettysburg

+ The more extensive and distinguished an individual's combat service record, the better, other things being equal

Desirable Circumstances of the Inscription

+ Gives not only the owner's name, but, if a soldier, his rank and unit

+ Appears on a watch made during or before the owner's period of combat service, so that he may have carried it on campaign. This fact may be documented either by a movement serial number on an American watch, or the case date mark, if an English case of either gold or silver.

+ Names one or more battles or locations of the owner during campaigns

+ Was presented to the owner by his unit, his commanding officer, a famous individual (e.g., the president), his fellow officers, or his men (if he was an officer) on a specified date

Other Desirable Suprahorological Attributes of an Identified Provenance Watch

+ A fully documented, unbroken provenance chain to the present date (extremely uncom-

mon)

+ Is documented to have been carried by the owner on campaign (uncommon)

+ Is documented to have been on the owner's person when he was wounded or killed in action (very uncommon)

+ One or more pictures exist of the owner in uniform (common)

+ A picture exists of the owner in uniform with the specific watch (very uncommon)

+ Documents exist that were written by or to the owner (scarce), especially but not only if they mention the watch (very uncommon)

+ A detailed receipt exists for the watch (extremely uncommon)

+ A regimental history available for one or more units in which the owner served (common)

+ Watches with credible documentation of Confederate provenances are scarcer, on average, than Union provenance watches

Other Attributes of Inscriptions

Ex Post Facto Inscriptions

Ex post facto inscriptions made long after the Civil War, especially when added by someone other than a Civil War participant, are reasonably commonplace. They often read something like the following: "My grandpa, John Smith, carried this watch during the . . ." In this writer's opinion, these kinds of inscriptions are the least desirable for a few reasons. First, the fact that a Civil War participant at some time owned a watch does not prove that he carried it or that it even necessarily existed at the time of the Civil War. Second, by virtue of the *ex post facto* inscription, the watch is no longer, if it ever was, exactly the watch that was carried by Grandpa John during the Civil War. And

107. The inscribed interior front case lid and dust cover of a silver watchcase belonging to Lt. Ward Frothingham of the 22nd and 59th Massachusetts Infantries. The inscription reads, "Shot through the left shoulder by a minie ball at the Battle of Gaines Mills, June 27th 1862. Shot through the right leg by a musket ball at the Battle of Pegram's Farm, Sept. 30th 1864." The "minie ball," named for Claude-Etienne Minié, was actually a tapered conical bullet, not a spherical "ball," which was fired by a rifled musket. Lt. Frothingham would have reported to Lt. Colonel Hodges during the Overland Campaign. The case houses Waltham William Ellery grade seven-jewel Model 1859 movement SN 95,698, finished in November or December 1863. *Image courtesy of Heritage Galleries.*

108. The front of the elaborately engraved case of the Ward Frothingham watch. "Gettysburg," "Gaines Mill," "Wilderness," "Spotsylvania," "Laurel Hill" (part of the Battle of Spotsylvania), "North Anna," "Shady Grove" (a.k.a. Totopotomoy Creek), "Cold Harbor," "Petersburg," and "Richmond" are some of the battles and significant places listed on the exterior of the case. *Image courtesy of Heritage Galleries.*

109. The photogenic and justifiably proud Lt. Ward Frothingham, 22nd and 59th Massachusetts Infantry. *Image from the Library of Congress.*

third, information recalled long after the events documented is more likely to be inaccurate. A possible middle category—more desirable than the examples just described but somewhat less desirable, in this writer's opinion, than presentations made during or immediately after the Civil War itself—are presentations made to officers of Civil War veterans associations, such as the Grand Army of the Republic (GAR). Still other much less desirable inscriptions take the form of presentations to Civil War veterans made for reasons having nothing directly to do with the Civil War by parties not associated with the recipient's war service.

Engraving Styles

Authentic inscriptions could either have been professionally done or made by the owner himself. Both kinds of inscriptions have their charms. Professionally done engraving is often pleasing and impressive to look at, and examples from the Civil War period frequently involve multiple different character styles in combination, as was also often the case with contemporaneous print advertising.

FIGURE 107 and **FIGURE 108** document a silver watchcase with especially striking and elaborate personalizing engraving clearly added at the request of its owner, the proud lieutenant shown in **FIGURE 109**. The engraving he had added lists numerous battles in which

110. The miniature diary of an unidentified soldier in the Army of the Potomac during the Overland Campaign of May–June 1864, scratched into the interior of the rear lid of the silver case of a P. S. Bartlett grade Model 1857 Waltham watch. (See REF. 90.) The diary reads (spellings from original): "Camped at Cedar Mt. Jan 1st to May 4, 1864; Crossed Rapid Ann [Rapidan River] At 12 M[idnight]; Battle of Wilderness 5th 6th 7th; Todd's Tavern 8th Ny River 9th 10th 11th 12th 13th; Spottsylvania C. H. N. [Courthouse North] 14th to 20th; Crossed North Anna [River] Mon. 23d; Battle same evening at 6 o'clock; Crossed Pamunkey [River] 28th noon; Battle Tollapotam[o]y [Creek] 30th & 31st"

he, and very possibly the watch, were involved. The movement of the watch is a seven-jewel William Ellery grade Model 1859, SN 95,698, finished November–December 1863. Ward Frothingham enlisted as a Corporal in the 22nd Massachusetts Infantry on October 2, 1861, and was wounded and captured at Gaines Mills on June 27, 1862. He was discharged for disability as a result of the wound and debilitation caused by prison October 2, 1862. Frothingham subsequently recovered and then was com-

missioned in the 59th Massachusetts Veteran Volunteer Infantry as a Second Lieutenant on April 23, 1864. He was then wounded again at Pegram's Farm, September 30, 1864, and was discharged June 24, 1865. In the 59th Massachusetts, Frothingham's commanding officer was the previously mentioned Lieutenant Colonel John Hodges Jr. from sometime in May 1864 up until Hodges's death on July 30, 1864. Frothingham's watch sold in November 2008 for $7,767 at Heritage Auction Galleries in the

John Henry Kurtz Collection Sale, as part of a grouping of more than twenty of Frothingham's other war service-related items. As the auction lot description of the watch suggests, the Lieutenant "was clearly a rather flamboyant personality and a 'fighter,' who took great pride in his military service as is evidenced by … the material in the Kurtz sale …"

Self-made inscriptions added on campaign, sometimes referred to as "trench art" when sufficiently embellished, can be marvelous historical artifacts too. The unembellished inscription shown in **FIGURE 110** features a miniature diary of the owner's movements and whereabouts during the Overland Campaign for the month of May 1864. [89] The diary breaks off just as the especially bloody Battle of Cold Harbor, which saw between 12,000 and 15,000 Union casualties, was commencing on May 31. Several lines of the miniature diary list multiple dates at the same location in succession, rather than as a range, suggesting that the diary was compiled in real time as history was unfolding, rather than after the fact.

The Pluses and Minuses of Evidence of Use

The degree of wear, or lack thereof, on a watch of Civil War significance can impact desirability in contradictory ways. In most other instances, watch collectors prefer examples that most closely resemble the pristine state of a watch that had just left the factory or the retail shop. However, when much or even most of the interest in a timepiece hinges on its connection to a historical event or its possible use by a participant in that event, then evidence that a watch may actually have been used, and not merely possessed, by its original owner could be construed to enhance that historical connection, and thus the watch's appeal. The same point was made in amusing fashion by John Metcalf, a past NAWCC conservator, who once joked that no one would have congratulated him for taking the Shroud of Turin to the dry cleaners. Specifically, for evidence of historical provenances on watchcases, old scratches running through the bottoms of engraving grooves testify that the engraving is not recent. Few if any watches that were carried on campaign by Civil War combatants have survived in pristine condition. Thus, at least some evidence of careful use is reassuring. Of course, the idea of damage as a desirable authenticating attribute and witness to history can be taken too far. A Civil War relic hunter who walks old campgrounds and battlefields with a metal detector hunting for spent bullets and stray cannonballs might well delight at finding a pocket watch remnant on a battlefield with a bullet hole in it. However, such a sight would make most horologists, including the author, wince.

9

OUTSTANDING EXAMPLES OF CIVIL WAR WATCHES: THE MEN, THEIR UNITS, AND THEIR BATTLES

IN THE final section of this book the interesting Civil War provenances of several of the watches previously shown are discussed in greater depth. It was the owners, their times, and their deeds that make these watches truly special pieces of history, so it is entirely fitting that their legacies are refreshed here for a new generation of admirers.

Lt. Col. John Hodges Jr.

December 8, 1841–July 30, 1864; Salem Zouaves, 19th, 50th, and 59th Massachusetts Volunteer Infantry

In 1860, at the age of seventeen, John Hodges, Jr. of Salem Massachusetts was enrolled as a student at Harvard University when he acquired the watch pictured in **FIGURE 78** (p. 103), **FIGURE 84** (p. 108), and **FIGURE 88** (p. 112), and also in **FIGURES 111–113**. It is a fifteen-jewel AT&Co grade Model 1859 Waltham watch in a silver hunting case marked "A. T. & Co." Upon President Lincoln's initial call for troops, young Hodges answered the call and enlisted as a private in the Salem Zouaves, also known as the Salem Light Infantry. The Salem Zouaves were a ninety-day enlistment unit that saw no actual fighting but did help to rescue the USS *Constitution* ("Old Ironsides") from its dock at the US Naval Academy in Annapolis, MD, where it was threatened with capture by secessionists. [90] The Salem Zouaves were later consolidated into the 8th Massachusetts Infantry Regiment as Company I.

For context, it must be understood that the Federal army was expanding explosively at this time, from fewer than 16,000 remaining men in April 1861 to over 600,000 men by late 1862. So any surviving soldier who showed ability and commitment was apt to rise like a rocket through the ranks. Thus, upon the expiration of his short enlistment in the Salem Zouaves, Hodges was commissioned as a First Lieutenant in the 19th MA Infantry. The 19th MA served garrison duty in and around the capitol during Hodges's time with it. Hodges personally saw no action at that time, on account of becoming incapacitated with fever and severe dysentery in the swamps around the capitol. Hodges was discharged, but thereafter he recovered and was commissioned as a major in the 50th MA, which saw considerable action in Louisiana during the Siege of Port Hudson. Due to attrition in the officers' ranks there, Hodges, then barely twenty years old, found himself in command of not one, but two regiments in that assignment, for a time making him, in his own words, "an acting brigadier general." [91] Hodges

111. Cuvette of Lt. Colonel John Hodges's Waltham Model 1859 watch, engraved, "John Hodges, Jr., Salem, Mass." Given that the movement was finished in May of 1860 and that the case is marked "A. T. & Co.," it is likely that young John Hodges either acquired or was given this watch just prior to the beginning of his military service, when he was still a student at Harvard. (The predecessor firm of AT&Co legally became the American Watch Co. in January of 1859, but the AWCo continued to sell off its existing inventory of "A. T. & Co."-marked watchcases for at least many months thereafter.) Because the cuvette lists no military rank, it is also possible that Hodges acquired the watch in his first few months of military service, before being commissioned as a lieutenant.

returned to Massachusetts, and with undiminished patriotism and zeal he soon accepted a commission as the Lieutenant Colonel of the 59th MA Infantry (a.k.a. the "MA 4th Veteran Infantry") in early 1864.

The 59th Massachusetts—950 men strong—headed south with the Army of the Potomac (AoP) and newly promoted Lieutenant General Ulysses S. Grant on the Overland Campaign

of May–June 1864. The Overland Campaign was the bloodiest and most sustained period of fighting of the entire Civil War. The AoP and Robert E. Lee's Army of Northern Virginia (AoNV) were in almost constant contact for the entire campaign, fighting seven major engagements and countless skirmishes. In one seven-week period the AoP alone lost between 75,000 and 85,000 men, killed, wounded,

112. The front of the trim, engine-turned coin silver case of Lt. Hodges's watch, which was made in AT&Co's own case department. These movements were thinner than Waltham's full-plate Model 1857 watches and were advertised as such, perhaps because the manufacturer thought that the reduced bulk might especially appeal to soldiers.

113. The "A. T. & Co." marking on the interior of the front case lid of Lt. Colonel Hodges's silver watch.

captured, sickened, or died of disease, out of an initial strength of 120,000. [92] (Confederate losses were somewhat less, but even more irreplaceable.) It was the critical and costly Overland Campaign in which General Grant deprived Lee's AoNV of its freedom of maneuver and confined it to a grim siege and near certain fate around Richmond. During this time, the 59th MA saw hard fighting at the Wilderness, and under Hodges's command, at Spotsylvania, North Anna, and Cold Harbor, three of the bloodiest and most terrifying battles of the war. By the time the 59th MA reached Pe-

tersburg, VA, in June of 1864, they were down to 250 men. Lt. Colonel Hodges had been in command of the unit for nearly the entire campaign, because their Colonel, Jacob P. Gould, first had taken sick and then was elevated to brigade command after his recovery. On June 17, 1864, outside of Petersburg, Hodges's oldest brother, Captain Thorndike Deland Hodges, relates that John's men hesitated when ordered to charge a rebel battery, having just seen another Federal unit bloodily repulsed from the same line. He wrote:

… a force of veterans was ordered to charge a battery, and the 59th was to support them. Three several times they saw them march up with firm step and three several times they saw them waver and fall back under a tremendous fire from the Rebel Works,—a sight which might well have caused an older regiment to falter. At this juncture Colonel Hodges received the order to advance with his regiment. For a moment they hesitated, and but for a moment, it was a critical moment. Colonel Hodges saw it, and dashing toward the color sergeant, caught the colors from his

114. A *carte de visite* photograph of a group of recruits of the Salem Zouaves, 8th MA Infantry, Company J, including Private Hodges, sitting on the ground. *Image courtesy of Massachusetts Commandery of the Military Order of the Loyal Legion of the United States* (MOLLUS).

115. An 1861 recruitment poster for the Salem Zouaves. *Image courtesy of Heritage Galleries.*

hand, and without uttering a word, advanced towards the battery. The effect was magical. A sergeant rushed forward and, waving his cap over his head, shouted, 'Look at your Colonel with the colors. Come on, boys! Come on!' A charge, and the battery was carried. [93]

On July 30, 1864, the Union IX Corps' First Division, First Brigade, including the 59th Massachusetts Infantry with John Hodges in command, led the Federal assault on Confederate defensive lines in front of Petersburg during the Battle of the Crater, part of the Siege of Petersburg. Pennsylvania coal miners had dug a tunnel underneath a fort at an exposed point known as Elliot's Salient and detonated a huge explosion, blowing a gaping hole in the Confederate defensive line there. But the hole was a deep, steep-sided crater, and the Federal assault was poorly organized and improperly equipped. If the assault had been competently organized by the AoP's general staff, it might have ended the war nine months early; instead, it was a debacle in which thousands of Union soldiers, including many African Americans, became trapped in the crater and lost their lives. (The commanding general of Hodges' division was discovered behind the lines drunk during the battle and was subsequently subject to a court of inquiry.) [94] Lt. Col. John Hodges Jr. was among the 3,798 Union casualties that day. While leaning against the side of the cra-

117. A *carte de visite* of Thorndike Deland Hodges (1836–1900), John Jr.'s older brother, in civilian clothes, likely taken after the war. Thorndike received the letter enclosing John's watch and wrote John's five-page eulogy appearing in the Harvard Memorial Biographies. Thorndike was himself a Harvard graduate who became a practicing attorney in Haverhill, MA, but enlisted as a private in the 35th Massachusetts Infantry, Company F in August 1862 and was soon promoted to Sergeant and later to Lieutenant. He fought with the 25th MA at South Mountain, Antietam, and Fredericksburg, before accepting a commission as a Captain in the 1st North Carolina Colored Volunteers (35th USCT). After the war Thorndike served briefly in 1868–69 as a Massachusetts state legislator. One would like to imagine that the watch on the end of Thorndike's chain in the image was none other than his late brother John's. *Image courtesy of Massachusetts Commandery of the Military Order of the Loyal Legion of the United States* (MOLLUS).

116. A *carte de visite* of John Hodges Jr. in uniform. In the black-and-white image, it cannot be determined whether the oak leaves on his shoulder boards were gold or silver, so it is not known whether he was still a major or already a Lieutenant Colonel at the time. *Image courtesy of Massachusetts Commandery of the Military Order of the Loyal Legion of the United States* (MOLLUS).

ter nursing a fresh wound, he was killed by shrapnel from a Confederate shell. The rebels retook the crater and buried many Union dead, including John Hodges, in a mass grave underneath their rebuilt works.

However, before the Federals retreated, a few of John Hodges's effects were recovered by the men who were with him when he fell.

Volume 2 of the *Harvard Memorial Biographies* (HMB) includes five pages covering the career and death of Lt. Colonel John Hodges Jr. (**FIGURES 114–116**), who left his studies

"... As the colored troops passed, the Johnnies ranged their batteries so as to throw their shells into the crater of the fort, and some twenty exploded there within half as many minutes. On the explosion of a shell some ten or twelve feet from us, while sitting in the position I have described, a piece of shell struck him on the back of the head, killing him instantly.

"He did not fall, as he was supported by me on one side and the bank on the other. I spoke to a soldier to assist me, and he laid him down carefully, examined his pockets, found his watch, some papers, and a pencil, which I herewith enclose. The man took a blanket, after laying him in an easy position, with one hand by his side, the other across his breast, and covered him up, where I left him, and where I doubt not he was buried, as the enemy afterward took the fort, and buried all the dead in the fort in reconstructing."

This surmise was afterwards ascertained to be correct ...

118. An excerpt from a page of Volume 2 of the Harvard Memorial Biographies, part of Thorndike Hodges's testimonial to his brother, John Hodges, describing John's death and the recovery of his watch.

119. A reconstructed obituary of a beloved animal, the deceased Lt. Colonel Hodges's horse Fanny, from a local newspaper in Salem, MA. The fact that the death of his horse made the local paper eighteen years after John's death is very likely a reflection of the high esteem in which John Hodges Jr. and his family were regarded in the town. ▶

at Harvard to join the First Defenders. The HMB memorial to John was contributed by Thorndike Hodges (**FIGURE 117**), who had been a captain in the First North Carolina Colored Volunteers (a.k.a. the 35th US Colored Troops, a Federal unit of freedmen with white officers). In his HMB contribution, excerpted in **FIGURE 118**, Thorndike quotes from a letter he received at the time of John's death, informing him that, "... a piece of shell struck him on the back of his head, killing him instantly. ... I spoke to a soldier to assist me, and he laid him

AN INTERESTING ANIMAL.

Fanny, the famous mare, belonging to the late Lt. Col. John Hodges, Jr., died in Salem, Monday evening, Dec. 4, about thirty years of age.

The members of the Fiftieth and Fifty-ninth Massachusetts Regiments will remember her, as she accompanied her late master (then Major) with the Fiftieth to Port Hudson, in their nine months campaign, and afterward, with the Fifty-ninth into Virginia.

Fanny carried her master through the battle of the Wilderness and swam the North Anna River with him on her back. She was never wounded and, after Lt. Col. Hodges' death, at Petersburg, July 30, 1864, was returned to his family in Salem. She was useful until her final illness, which was quite short, and retained her high spirits and graceful carriage to the last.

Salem. Dec. 6. 1882.

down carefully, examined his pockets, found his watch, some papers, and a pencil, which I herewith enclose." Thus is recorded the fact that Lt. Colonel Hodges—barely twenty-two years old—had the watch pictured here in his pocket when he made the ultimate sacrifice for Constitution and country.

It is interesting that Lt. Colonel Hodges's horse Fanny fared better than her master and that the local press in Salem thought to record the fact. She survived the war and went home to Salem, living to a ripe old age of approximately thirty years, as attested by the animal's obituary in a local news article reproduced in **FIGURE 119.**

First Lt. James A. Sage

1836–1913;
25th Michigan Volunteer Infantry

The Watch

A P. S. Bartlett grade Waltham Model 1857 movement, SN 42,888, finished between June 1 and July 31, 1862, was presented to Sergeant James A. Sage, pictured in **FIGURE 120** and **FIGURE 121,** by his company. The movement has seven "rock crystal" jewels and a solid steel balance. It is in a handsome, engine-turned four-ounce coin silver hunting case (see **FIGURES 11–14,** p. 26) with elegant interior decoration on the front lid. The dust cover is engraved, "Co B 25th MI [Infantry], to J. A. Sage, 1862." The April 2, 1864, retail watch advertisement in *Harper's Weekly* (see **FIGURE 46,** p. 50), offered watches exactly like this for $47, presumably a favorable price, given that it was being advertised.

120. Lt. James A. Sage, 25th Michigan Infantry. *Image from The Charles Woodruff Papers in The Bentley Historical Library of the University of Michigan.*

James Sage's Life and Service

James A. Sage was born on March 20, 1836, in New York State. When the 25th Michigan Infantry was formed in September of 1862, Sage, then age twenty-six, was enlisted as a sergeant in Company B, consisting primarily of men from Otisco, MI, the town where Sage then resided. The company presented James with a practical gift: a watch. It was neither the least expensive watch nor even the least expensive American watch they could have given him.

121. Retired Lt. Sage's tombstone and a late civilian life image of him. *Image from the Find-A-Grave website.*

After an earlier promotion to 2nd Lieutenant, Sergeant Sage was promoted to 1st Lieutenant in command of Company B on April 7, 1864. He served in that capacity until August 6, 1864, when he was wounded in the thigh at Utoy Creek, during the fighting around Atlanta, causing him to be discharged on November 30, 1864. The wound ended his military career but not his life. After serving stints as both a supervisor and a registrar of deeds in Otisco, MI, between 1876 and 1881, in 1904 he moved to southern Georgia, along with a group of other Union Army veterans, to help found the town of St. George on the Florida border.

Sage's migration to a place where he had once fought against the local population was in response to a campaign by a Northern publisher to seed Northern free labor ideals throughout the South, one of several such initiatives in the South at the time. [95] Sage served in St. George as the town's first treasurer, but eventually retired to the National Soldiers Home in Johnson City, TN, where he died on May 20, 1913, at the age of seventy-seven.

25th Michigan Infantry

Lt. Sage's unit, the 25th Michigan Volunteer Infantry, had a distinguished record, which is

Dates	Remarks
Sep. 22, 1862	Mustered into service, Kalamazoo, MI (Sgt. James A. Sage assigned to Co. B)
Sep. 22–Dec. 9, 1862	Duty at Louisville, KY
Dec. 12, 1862–Jan. 2, 1863	Operations against General John Hunt Morgan (CSA Cavalry)
Mar. 26–Apr. 26, 1863	Operations against Pegram's forces in Kentucky
July 4, 1863	Battle of Tebb's Bend (a.k.a. Battle of Green River) in Taylor County, 7/4/63
Nov. 24, 1863	Repulse of Wheeler's attack on Kingston, TN, 11/24/63
	Sgt. Sage promoted to 1st Lt., assumes command of Co. B
May 4–Sep. 8, 1864	Atlanta Campaign, GA (under fire for 58 days!)
May 14 & 15, 1864	Battle of Resaca, GA
June 27, 1864	Battle of Kennesaw Mountain, GA
July 22, 1864	Battle of Atlanta
July 22–Aug. 25, 1864	Siege of Atlanta
Aug. 5–7, 1864	Battle of Utoy Creek, near Atlanta (Lt. Sage wounded, August 6, 1864)
Aug. 31–Sep. 1, 1864	Battle of Jonesboro, GA
Nov. 30, 1864	Battle of Franklin, TN (Lt. Sage discharged, same day)
Dec. 15–16, 1864	Battle of Nashville, TN
Jan.–Mar. 1865	Carolinas Campaign
June 24, 1865	Mustered out of Service, Salisbury, NC (Three officers and 175 enlisted men killed, mortally wounded, or died of disease)

TABLE 8: Service summary of James A. Sage and the 25th MI Volunteer Infantry. Sources include the 1860 and 1880 U.S. Census data on James A. Sage, Smyrna, MI; the *Find-a-Grave* website; an obituary for James A. Sage in the *Ionia Standard*, published May 23, 1913; Lt. Sage's enlistment, service and pension records; the website *www.charltoncountyarchives.org/saintgeorgehisto.html*, for the history of St. George, GA; the *www.civilwarchives.com* website; and most especially, the 25th Michigan Infantry Regimental History preserved at the University of Michigan.

summarized in **TABLE 8.** Not nearly as famous as the 24th MI, which was part of the famed Iron Brigade of the Army of the Potomac, the 25th MI, nevertheless, earned its own significant laurels on July 4, 1863. As it happened, the nation's eyes were turned in different directions on that day. The Battle of Gettysburg had just ended the day before, and on the very same day of July 4, CSA Lt. General John C. Pemberton was surrendering the key Confederate strong-

122. Colonel Orlando Hurley Moore, C.O. of the 25th Michigan Infantry. *Image from kvm.kvcc.edu/civilwar/2012/02/26/25th-michigan-regiment/*

hold on the critical Mississippi River, in Vicksburg, MS, to Union Major General Ulysses S. Grant. Yet on July 4, 1863, still another equally dramatic if smaller scene was unfolding on the bank of the Green River at Tebb's Bend, near the towns of Munfordville and Columbia, KY. There about 200 to 260 men of the 25th MI Infantry were dug in along the riverbank near a wooden bridge. They were attacked by a force of Confederate cavalry of nearly 2,500 men supported by artillery under Brigadier General John Hunt Morgan, "the Thunderbolt of the Confederacy," [96] but the stubborn Michiganders won the day.

In 1861 President Lincoln wrote to a friend, O. H. Browning, a fellow Kentucky native and attorney, that "I think to lose Kentucky is nearly the same as to lose the whole game. Kentucky gone, we cannot hold Missouri, nor, as I think, Maryland. These all against us, and the job on our hands is too large for us. We would as well consent to separation at once, including the surrender of this capitol." [97] He was speaking not only of the loyalty of Kentucky's people but of the strategic location of the state itself. What was true in 1861 remained just as true in 1863. Thus, it was a matter of great concern when for three weeks in July of 1863, J. H. Morgan's most ambitious raid of the war attempted to terrorize local defensive forces in Kentucky, southern Indiana, and Ohio, threatening Northern supply and communication lines and endeavoring to force the Northern army to detach many thousands of troops to counter his threat.

On June 11, 1863, Brigadier General Morgan and about 2,500 Confederate cavalrymen, mostly Kentuckians, two three-inch Parrott guns, and two twelve-pound howitzers, had ridden west from Sparta in middle Tennessee, intending to divert the attention of the Union Army of the Ohio from Southern forces in the state. On the night of July 2 they crossed the Cumberland River—swollen by recent rains—and advanced into Kentucky, camping between Campbellsville and Columbia. Morgan aimed to cross the Green River at Tebb's Bend the next day. A wooden bridge there was guarded by five companies of from 200 to 260 men of the 25th Michigan Infantry—the number varies depending on the source—led by Colonel Orlando Hurley Moore (July 13, 1827–October 31, 1890) (**FIGURE 122**). Morgan's first major objective was Louisville and its warehouses full of supplies awaiting shipment on the L&N [Louisville and Nashville] Rail-

123. A period illustration of the Battle of Tebb's Bend, from page 131 of the 1895 British book *Illustrated Battles of the Nineteenth Century, Volume 2.* The illustration may well be inaccurate, however, because Morgan's men made most if not all of their eight assaults dismounted.

124. The regimental flag of the 25th Michigan Infantry. *Image from seekingmichigan.contentdm.oclc.org/cdm/singleitem/collection/p15147coll5/id/124/rec/12*

125. A road marker near the site of the Battle of Tebb's Bend. *Image courtesy of William J. Bechmann III.*

126. An explanatory plaque near the battleground, relating Morgan's confident surrender demand and Moore's courageous refusal. *Image courtesy of William J. Bechmann III.*

road. Moore erected earthworks in the woods near the valuable bridge, which was a rarity in that part of the state. The Battle of Tebb's Bend (**FIGURES 123–126**) was fought for control of the bridge. The nearest rail line ended at Lebanon, twenty miles north of Campbellsville. Thus, supplies for southeast Kentucky and northeast Tennessee were carried over this road and bridge. The mail stage route ran over the same road, which also connected the large Federal military camps at Lebanon and Columbia. Moore's earthworks were guarded by a line of abatis of felled trees and several forward rifle pits. His force protected the easiest route for Morgan into Louisville.

Colonel Moore, who had no artillery, planned meticulously to receive the Confederate assault. Abandoning his stockade and his encampment north of the Green River, he concentrated his entire small force in a temporary fortified position on a narrow neck of land east of the bridge, a knoll in the Tebb's Bend of the river. Historian Joe Brent relates the following:

> The only access to the bend was through the Narrows, an opening only 100 yards wide flanked on both sides by the river. This land gave a decided advantage to the defenders. Here the land '… drops precipitously on the north side of the ridge 150 feet into the river.' Confederate Col. Basil Duke, Morgan's brother-in-law and right-hand man, later described it as 'one of the strongest natural positions I ever saw.' … Moore formed up his untried troops and told them, 'Don't be afraid, my boys. Be quiet, men. Let your guns speak for themselves. No shouting. No colors are to fly so the enemy will not know our numbers … We can take on thousands.' Moore's final preparations included getting the local citizenry out of harm's way. The Michigan troops rode to the houses located within what they feared would be the battlefield and urged the inhabitants to flee. [98]

Morgan divided his force, sending the bulk of his cavalry, guided by local men who knew the area well, over the fords west of Tebb's Bend to flank the small garrison, cut off their avenue of retreat, and isolate them from reinforcements from the larger Union base at Lebanon. At sunrise on July 4, Union pickets opened fire on approaching enemy cavalrymen. Soon, Morgan's artillery answered, wounding two Union soldiers in the rifle pits. About 7:00 AM Morgan called a cease-fire and sent forward three officers under a flag of truce, demanding that Moore surrender, wishing to avoid further bloodshed. Then, as Joe Brent relates:

> It was Independence Day and Moore answered Morgan's demand saying, 'Present my compliments to General Morgan, and say to him that, this being the fourth day of July, I cannot entertain his proposition.' Moore['s] … force numbered only about 260 men [a slightly larger number than cited in other sources]; with only about 170 on the field [the reason for the ambiguity]. The remainder were deployed at the fords and at the bridge; some were serving as teamsters and hospital stewards. Morgan's cavalry and artillery totaled 800 to 1,000, not including the two regiments held in reserve. Moore was outnumbered 4 or 5 to 1 [again, not including Morgan's nearly 1,500 reserves]. When Col. Robert Alston, who delivered Morgan's demand for surrender, pointed out the Confederate advantage, Moore replied, 'I have a duty to perform to my country, and the presence of this day supports me in my decision; therefore I cannot reconsider my reply to General Morgan.'

Confederate trooper J. T. Tucker later wrote that when he learned that Moore had refused to surrender, "I knew then that it was a fight to the death." [99] Morgan sent forward two dismounted regiments under Col. Adam R. Johnson, about four hundred troopers, who easily overran the advanced rifle pits. However, the attack stalled under heavy fire from Federals concealed behind the abatis. Morgan then sent in the 5th Kentucky Cavalry from Col. Basil W. Duke's brigade to support Johnson. Over a three-hour period Morgan pushed forward a total of eight separate attacks, with each one being repulsed, including the flanking column. Finally acknowledging that he could not seize the fortifications, Morgan sent another delegation under a flag of truce to Colonel Moore to

127. The interior of the front lid of the 18-kt. gold hunting case presented to General Copeland. Camp Copeland was a recruit collection and training base that was named in General Copeland's honor. It was located in current-day Braddock, PA, just outside of Pittsburgh.

request permission to collect his wounded and bury his dead. Moore magnanimously consented, and Morgan then withdrew southward along the bluffs of the Green River.

Morgan lost thirty-five killed and forty-five wounded in the battle, whereas Moore counted six killed and twenty-three wounded among the 25th Michigan. But among Morgan's casualties were twenty-four experienced officers, who were a special focus of the Michigan marksmen. From that day on, the 25th MI was known within the Federal Army of the Cumberland as the "Green River Boys." [100] Historian James A. Ramage called the Battle of Tebb's Bend, "one of the most outstanding victories in the Civil War." [101] A reporter from the *Louisville Times* wrote that "the Battle of Tebb's Bend was evidently one of the finest planned and best fought battles of the war." Major Generals George L. Hartsuff and Ambrose E. Burnside wrote commendations. After hearing Col. George T. Wood describe the battle and his

opinion that Moore and his men had "saved the city of Louisville from sack and pillage by the rebel hordes," the Kentucky House of Representatives acknowledged Colonel Moore and the 25th MI in two complimentary joint resolutions. The Battle of Tebb's Bend (A.K.A. the Battle of Green River Bridge) was reenacted on its 150th anniversary in 2013.

Brigadier General Joseph Tarr Copeland
Michigan Cavalry Brigade and C. O. of Camp Copeland (near Pittsburgh)

The Watch

A gold Waltham pocket watch that was presented to Federal Brigadier General Joseph Tarr Copeland is shown in **FIGURES 127–130**. AT&Co grade Model 1857 movement SN 107,296, finished in February 1864, with fifteen jewels, compensated balance and stopworks, was presented in an 18-kt. gold, engine-turned hunting case bearing the retailer's trademark of J. R. Reed & Co., a prominent Pittsburgh area jeweler of the period. The presentation engraved on the interior of the rear lid reads: "Presented to J. T. Copeland Brig. Gen. Vols. [Brigadier General of Volunteers] by the Officers of Camp Copeland, 1864." Copeland is pictured in an earlier, colonel's uniform in **FIGURE 131**.

According to the 1864 Robbins & Appleton trade catalog, such a watch movement, sans the gold case weighing about three ounces, would have wholesaled for a price between $38 and $43, depending on its level of adjustment. The retail price of the complete gold watch was

128. AT&Co grade Model 1857 movement, SN 107,296, finished in February 1864, with fifteen jewels in screwed-down top plate settings, compensated balance, and stopworks. The movement would have wholesaled for between $38 and $43, depending on the level of adjustment, and the case would have contained from $40 to $45 in gold. *Image courtesy of Jones & Horan Auctioneers.*

likely something in excess of $100, which was something like a month's salary, not counting expense allowances, for a typical Union colonel, or even a brigadier general. While this watch was presented to Copeland by the officers of Camp Copeland, a large recruit collection and training base renamed in his honor in what today is Braddock, PA, the general is best known as the original commanding officer of the Michigan Cavalry Brigade, the famed "Wolverines." This illustrious connection was significantly burnished by his brigade's achievements very shortly after Copeland was relieved of command on account of age. This deserved credit likely explains the high esteem in which Copeland was held by his subordinates at the

129. The single-sunk enamel dial and blued spade hands of General Copeland's Waltham watch. *Image courtesy of Jones & Horan Auctioneers.*

base named in his honor. Today, two Braddock, PA, streets, Copeland Street and the intersecting Copeland Avenue, mark part of the former boundary of Camp Copeland.

The Man

Joseph Tarr Copeland was born in Newcastle, ME, on May 6, 1813, the eldest of eleven siblings. As summarized in **TABLE 9** (p. 152), Copeland's long personal career includes stints as an attorney, a Michigan state senator, a Michigan State Supreme Court Justice, a businessman (having operated a sawmill in Michigan for a time), and having served as a colonel in the Maine militia before the Civil War. His law career touched that of Daniel Webster, who had served as a congressional representative from both New Hampshire and Massachusetts, a U.S. senator from Massachusetts, and as a Secretary of State for three presidents. Copeland's

130. The engine-turned exterior of the front lid of General Copeland's gold watch, with the original watch key. *Image courtesy of Jones & Horan Auctioneers.*

131. Colonel Joseph Tarr Copeland, probably between August and December 1862. *Image from www.generalsandbrevets.com/ngc/copeland.htm*

career even briefly may have touched that of President Andrew Jackson, who it is rumored, had dispatched Copeland on a "secret mission" [102] to the Michigan Territory.

When the Civil War broke out, Copeland volunteered for service at the age of forty-seven, and because of his prior experience as an officer in the Maine Militia, he was commissioned as a Lieutenant Colonel in command of the 1st Michigan Cavalry, then only a battalion, on August 22, 1861. When the 5th Michigan Cavalry regiment was formed in August 1862, Copeland was made its colonel and commanding officer. In December 1862 the 5th MI Cavalry was consolidated with the 6th and 7th MI Cavalry regiments into the "Michigan Cavalry Brigade," and Colonel Copeland was promoted to brigadier general to command the unit that became known as the "Wolverines." Shortly thereafter, the 1st MI Cavalry, now a full regiment, and the 2nd U.S. artillery were added to the brigade. Though the Wolverines ultimately would achieve fame under a different com-

mander, Copeland can claim much of the credit for their training and fighting spirit. He had led the 1st MI Cavalry in its first engagement at the Battle of First Kernstown on March 23, 1862. In that battle, Stonewall Jackson's only tactical defeat, his unit's aggressive advance netted perhaps as many as three hundred Confederate prisoners. Historian Russell H. Beatie wrote:

When the Confederates broke, he [Copeland] unleashed his men … in pursuit. Stone walls and fences did not dissipate the enthusiasm of the horsemen when Copeland gave the order to charge. Between two and three

132. Street signs in current-day Braddock, PA indicating the intersection of Copeland Avenue and Copeland Street, which once comprised part of the boundary of Camp Copeland.

133. "The Castle" was the name given to General Copeland's sprawling Georgian Revival mansion on Orchard Lake, near Pontiac, MI. This picture was taken during the time when it was the home of the Orchard Lake Military Academy. *Image from www.loc.gov/item/2016801494/*

hundred retreating Rebels fell prisoner to them. [103]

With the support of Michigan Governor Austin Blair, Copeland also shares the credit for having had the foresight to arrange for two regiments of the Wolverines, which he trained to fight as mounted infantry, to become among the first Federal units to be equipped with repeating rifles. This was accomplished despite stiff resistance from the hidebound Federal ordnance department, which adhered to an outdated military doctrine and at the time staunchly resisted the issuance of repeating weapons. The seven-shot Spencer repeating rifle, a critical force multiplier, undoubtedly was a factor in the MI Cavalry Brigade's outstanding subsequent effectiveness, including at Gettysburg. (The shorter barreled repeating carbines were not yet available when Copeland equipped his regiment.)

General Copeland's last and least rewarding assignment was as commandant of the Federal camp for Confederate prisoners of war in Alton, IL. All Civil War prison camps—North and South—were dismal places with high rates

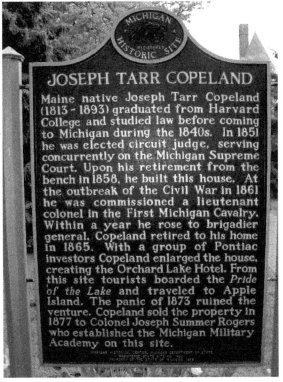

134. The historical marker that currently stands in front of The Castle. *Image from tinyurl.com/ycbv3wnb*

Dates	Remarks
May 6, 1813	Born in Newcastle, ME, the eldest of 11 children
	Attended Harvard Law School Studied law with Daniel Webster in Boston, MA Unknown "Secret Mission" to Michigan for President Andrew Jackson [102]
1834	Service in Maine Militia begins, rising to the rank of colonel in 1839
1835–1838	Justice of the Peace
1837	Postmaster, North New Portland, ME
1839	Involved in the "Aroostook War," a bloodless boundary dispute between New Brunswick and Maine that was resolved by a compromise negotiated by Daniel Webster
1844–1851	Moved to St. Clair, MI, where he operated a sawmill and practiced law from 1844; Served in various municipal offices around St. Clair 1848–51; MI State Senator from St. Clair 1850–51
1852–57	14th MI State Supreme Court Justice
Aug. 22, 1861	Commissioned Lt. Colonel, 1st MI Cavalry Battalion
Aug. 14, 1862	Promoted Colonel, 5th MI Cavalry
Dec. 1862	Promoted Brigadier General, MI Cavalry Brigade
Mar. 23, 1862	Battle of First Kernstown, Winchester, VA

TABLE 9: General Joseph Tarr Copeland life and career summary. Sources include Michigan Supreme Court Historical Society *www.micourthistory.org/justices/joseph-copeland/*; Beatie, Russell H. *The Army of the Potomac: Birth of Command, November 1860–September 1861* Boston, MA: Da Capo Press, 2002; the *Find-a-Grave* website; and Lt. Colonel

of death and disease, and some were horrific. The Alton "camp" had been a prison before the war, and its structures provided some shelter from the winter cold and summer heat. But the site was poorly located, too close to the Mississippi River, it had no potable water on-site, and sanitation was poor. To make matters worse, many Confederate prisoners arrived already in undernourished and underclothed condition, and the prison was greatly overcrowded, making bad circumstances worse. Even the death rate due to disease among Union soldiers in the field was high, and Confederate POWs certainly fared no better. The worst period at Alton, when a smallpox epidemic ravaged the prison population in the winter of 1862 and spring of 1863, had already ended before Copeland arrived.

Postwar, General Copeland returned to his elaborate Georgian Revival mansion, "The Castle" (**FIGURE 133** and **FIGURE 134**), situated on Orchard Lake, near Pontiac, MI. This structure became, in turn, a hotel and resort, the now defunct Michigan Military Academy, and St. Mary's Women's College, which it remains to the current day. Joseph Copeland

Dates	Remarks
June–July 1863	Surveillance of AoNV near Gettysburg, PA
June 29, 1863	Reassigned
July 3, 1863	MI Cavalry Brigade (which Copeland trained and equipped, but now under command of the newly promoted Brig. Gen. George Custer), is heavily engaged on the East Cavalry Field, near Gettysburg, PA
	Assigned to command of a recruit collection and training camp near Annapolis, MD
July 18, 1863	Assigned to command of a similar camp at Braddock Field, near Pittsburgh, PA, renamed "Camp Copeland"; receives watch from fellow officers
April 1864	Relieved and reassigned
	Commandant of Alton Prison Camp, Alton, IL, last military assignment
Nov. 8, 1865	Resigned his commission and returned to his residence, an extensive Gothic Revival structure, known locally as "the Castle," on Orchard Lake in W. Bloomfield near Pontiac. (It becomes, in succession, a hotel, the Michigan Military Academy, and St. Mary's Catholic Women's College, which it remains at present.)
1878	Justice of the Peace, Orange Park, FL
May 6, 1893	Dies on his 80th birthday The MI Cavalry Brigade, consisting of the 1st, 5th, 6th, and 7th MI Cavalry regiments, and the 2nd U.S. Artillery, sustained greater casualties during the Battle of Gettysburg than any other Federal cavalry unit there engaged

Copeland's report of the 1st MI Cavalry Battalion's action at First Kernstown in, *The War of the Rebellion: v.1–53* [serial no. 1–111] Formal reports; and a source discussing General Copeland's assignments at Annapolis, Camp Copeland (in Braddock, PA), and Alton Prison camp: *www.gdg.org/Research/People/Buford/witt3.html*

moved to Orange Park, FL, in 1877, one year after the town's founding, to become its first Justice of the Peace. He died on May 6, 1893, on his eightieth birthday.

The Michigan Cavalry Brigade and the East Cavalry Field, Gettysburg, July 3, 1863

The Michigan Cavalry Brigade, one of whose regimental flags is shown in **FIGURE 135**, saw its finest hour on July 3, 1863, at a place now known as the East Cavalry Field, outside of Gettysburg. On June 29, 1863, a messenger from the Army of the Potomac (AoP) headquarters had reached General Copeland, who was in the field dogging the flank of Robert E. Lee's Army of Northern Virginia (AoNV) as it penetrated deeper into Pennsylvania. (The Wolverines had just passed through Gettysburg, PA.) Part of a larger shake-up in the AoP general staff, the message from Major General George Meade, who had just replaced Joe Hooker as AoP commanding general, relieved General Copeland, then fifty years old, of command of the Wolverines because of his advanced age. On that day Copeland was replaced by a newly

135. Flag of the Michigan 6th Cavalry Regiment, one of the constituent regiments of the Michigan Cavalry Brigade—the "Wolverines." The flag is adorned with the names of several battles in which the regiment participated. *Image from michiganradio.org/post/flags-help-us-remember-service-and-sacrifice-civil-war-soldiers*

136. A later picture of George Armstrong Custer, the succeeding commander of the Michigan Wolverines Cavalry Brigade on July 3, 1863, after he received his second star. *Image from the Library of Congress.*

137. An earlier picture of Custer (at right) as a line officer, taken at Fair Oaks, VA, in 1862. He is sitting beside his ex-classmate and friend Confederate Lieutenant James Barroll Washington, a POW, who was an aide to General Joseph E. Johnston. It was common for Confederate officers to bring slaves to war with them, as was apparently the case here. The young man's name was not recorded. Custer had a deserved reputation for bravery and audacity, which served him well on the East Cavalry Field, but he was never accused of an overabundance of wisdom. Ironically, his greatest fame came as the result of the day his luck ran out, at the Little Bighorn, on June 26, 1876. George's far less well-known younger brother, brevet Lieutenant Colonel Thomas Ward Custer, who was one of only fourteen men in the history of the U.S. armed forces to receive two Medals of Honor for independent actions, perished there along with him. *Image from the Library of Congress.*

promoted former captain, impetuous twenty-three-year-old Brigadier General George Armstrong Custer (**FIGURE 136** and **FIGURE 137**). The Battle of Gettysburg began two days later on July 1. It was Custer, not Copeland, who led the unit whom Copeland had done much to train and equip to its greatest glory on the third and final day of that historic engagement. On July 3 Confederate cavalry commander Major General James Ewell Brown ("Jeb") Stuart with 6,000 men and fourteen guns, attempted to swing around the Federal rear. His goals were to secure Corps commander Lt. General Ewell's flank, to cut off the Union army's escape in anticipation of Pickett's frontal assault succeeding, and, if the opportunity presented itself, to strike the Union army in the rear. Standing in Stuart's way were one brigade of Union Brigadier General David Gregg's cavalry division under Colonel John McIntosh and the Michigan Wolverines, together totaling 2,500 men and ten guns. (Colonel McIntosh was a Unionist originally from Florida, whose brother James had made a different choice. The eponymous Confederate Brigadier General James McIntosh, of McIntosh's Cavalry Brigade, had fallen at the Battle of Pea Ridge in March 1862. The tragically divided McIntosh family was far from unique. Jeb Stuart's father-in-law, Brigadier General Philip St. George Cooke, commanded a Union cavalry brigade, and his command crossed paths with Stuart's at least once during the war.)

The Confederate and Union cavalry units met about three miles to the east of where Confederate Colonel Porter Alexander's cannon bombardment was beginning to fall on the Union center and artillery positions. Alexander's barrage was meant to neutralize the Federal artillery and weaken the Federal center in advance of Pickett's Charge, Lee's costly gamble to snatch an improbable victory from imminent defeat. Dismounted fighting had continued around the Rummel farm for about two hours, as the men of the 5th Michigan Cavalry with their deadly repeating rifles held off their rebel assailants. Then Stuart spotted a seam between the two distinct Federal lines of McIntosh's brigade and Custer's Wolverines. He ordered the 1st Virginia Cavalry of Fitzhugh Lee's brigade to make a mounted charge at the gap. McIntosh tried to deploy his reserve, the Purnell Legion, but discovered that Gregg had moved the Maryland men off to guard the flank. He then realized that he had nothing to plug the gap and that the Confederate charge would hit the seam between his brigade and Custer's, splitting them apart and opening the

way to the road intersection—and the Federal Ammunition Reserve beyond!

Custer had only one of his unengaged Wolverine regiments up, the 7th Michigan, when around 1:00 PM Custer and Gregg both saw rebel cavalry under Fitzhugh Lee pouring through the Union skirmish line at the Rummel farm. Turning to Gregg, the senior Union officer on the field, Custer asked, "Do you want me to charge?" Gregg responded affirmatively. Turning to his Michiganders, Custer issued his now famous cry, "Come on, you Wolverines!", and led the 7th MI forward, as illustrated in **FIGURE 138**. Stephen Sears (REF. 44, page 461) relates:

> The two regiments collided along one of farmer Rummel's fence lines. An astonished Union skirmisher watched the 7th Michigan, 'apparently without any attempt to change direction, dash itself upon a high staked and railed fence, squadron after squadron breaking on the struggling mass in front, like the waves of the sea upon a rocky shore, until all were mixed in one confused and tangled mass.' Troopers of both sides, many unhorsed by the collision, struggled at point-blank range with carbines, revolvers and sabers. Custer's horse was hit and he took another from one of his men [reportedly a bugler]. … Enough Yankees managed to break down the fence and spur through to send the Virginians into retreat. Now Stuart countered. Elements from all three of his brigades, hastily thrown into the spreading fight, were enough to drive back the Yankee pursuit.

As the retreating Michiganders were streaming past John McIntosh's Pennsylvanians, the Colonel cried, "For God's sake men, if you are

138. "Come on you Wolverines!" by Don Troiani. An artist's impression of one of two heroic Wolverine Cavalry charges on the East Cavalry Field, near Gettysburg, July 3, 1863. *Image used with permission of Don Troiani.*

ever going to stand, stand now, for you are on your own free soil!" [104] A brief pause ensued. Then as General David Gregg wrote, "… there appeared emerging from the woods a large force advancing in fine style. It was evident that a grand charge was intended." [105] Stuart sent the bulk of Wade Hampton's brigade, accelerating in formation from a walk to a gallop, sabers held forward, eliciting "murmurs of admiration" from the Union men. Union horse artillery batteries punished the rebel formation with shell and canister, but the Confederates moved quickly, closing up the gaps torn by the guns and maintaining their momentum. This occurred just as the last of Custer's regiments was arriving on the scene. Once again Custer cried, "Come on, you Wolverines!" as he and Colonel Charles H. Town led the 1st Michigan Cavalry, General Copeland's original unit (which was outnumbered five to one!) into the melee.

The fight on the East Cavalry Field was pos-sibly the only occasion in the entire Civil War in which large, tightly packed formations of horsemen charged right at one another and collided with sabers swinging and revolvers blazing. A trooper from one of Gregg's Pennsylvania regiments recalled:

> As the two columns approached each other the pace of each increased, when suddenly a crash, like the falling of timber, betokened the crisis. So sudden and violent was the collision that many of the horses were turned end over end and crushed their riders beneath them. [106]

Part of the 3rd Pennsylvania that was positioned alongside the 1st New Jersey near the Rummel farm turned and opened a raking fire on the flank of the charging Confederates. Captain William E. Miller's squadron watched from the woods. Miller turned to Lieutenant William Brooke-Rawle and asked, "I have been ordered to hold this position, but if you will back me up in case I am court-martialed for disobedience, I will order a charge." [106] Brooke-Rawle agreed, and Miller's squadron fired a volley, drew sabers, and struck the left flank of Fitzhugh Lee's Confederate cavalry brigade, cutting off a portion of it. Captain James H. Hart's squadron of the 1st New Jersey, holding the flank with Miller's men, also charged from the Low Dutch Road, falling in on Miller's left. The sudden and furious Union counterattack broke the momentum of Lee's charge, and the Virginians fled in the face of the determined flank attacks.

"Then it was steel to steel," recounted Capt. James H. Kidd of the 6th Michigan, "For minutes, and for minutes that seemed like years, the gray column stood and staggered before the blow, then yielded and fled. [Colonel Russell A.] Alger [5th MI Cavalry] and McIntosh had pierced its flanks, but Town's impetuous charge in front went through it like a wedge splitting it in twain, and scattering the Confederate horsemen in disorderly rout back to the woods from whence they came."

Miller's and Hart's men swept clear through the rear of Fitzhugh Lee's charging column to a rail fence and then turned and swept back through the gray mass a second time. Rather than court-martialing Miller for disobedience, General Gregg heartily endorsed the Medal of Honor Miller received years later. Wade Hampton, who was perhaps South Carolina's wealthiest slaveholder (and one of its cruelest [107]), received a serious saber wound to the head. Custer lost his second horse of the day. Stuart's assault had been stymied both by the courageous charge of the outnumbered 1st MI men and by two small groups of Federals, each numbering fewer than a hundred men, led by audacious minor officers on their own

initiatives. The enterprising flanking attacks surprised the Confederates and sowed confusion and fear of envelopment, precipitating a panicked retreat. Historian Eric Wittenberg, wrote:

> These flanking attacks and the severe flanking fire of the Northern gunners did much to take the steam out of the rolling Confederate juggernaut. When Miller's charge crashed into their flank, the surprised Virginians of Fitz Lee's brigade believed that a much larger force had hit them—and many broke and ran. [108]

The desperate fight on the East Cavalry Field lasted less than three hours. The Union suffered 251 casualties, 219 of them from the Michigan Brigade, the greatest number of casualties among all the Union cavalry brigades engaged at Gettysburg. Stuart's Confederates suffered 181 casualties, fewer than the Federals, but Confederate aims were thoroughly thwarted by an inferior Union force.

Lt. Brooke-Rawle, who produced one of the most detailed eyewitness accounts of the action on the East Cavalry Field, later wrote:

> We cavalrymen have always [believed] that we saved the day at the most critical moment of the battle of Gettysburg-the greatest battle and the turning point of the War of the Rebellion. Had Stuart succeeded in his well-laid plan, and, with his large force of cavalry, struck the Army of the Potomac in the rear of its line of battle, simultaneously with Pickett's magnificent and furious assault on its front, when our infantry had all it could do to hold on to the line of Cemetery Ridge, and but little more was needed to make the assault a success, the merest tyro in the art

of war can readily tell what the result would be; fortunately for the Army of the Potomac, fortunately for our country, and the cause of human liberty, he failed. Thank God that he did fail, and that, with His divine assistance, the good fight fought here brought victory to our arms!

General David M. Gregg noted, "General Stuart had in view the accomplishment of certain purposes, his plans were disarranged by being compelled to enter into a fierce encounter with a smaller force of Union troops. His was to do, ours to prevent. Could he have reached the rear of our army with his force of perhaps six thousand bold and tried troopers, disastrous consequences might have resulted." [109]

Thereafter, the Wolverines, whom Copeland first led, equipped, and trained, took part in all the remaining campaigns of the AoP, including the blood-soaked Overland Campaign (May–June 1864), the Richmond–Petersburg Campaign (June 1864–March 1865), and the climactic Appomattox Campaign (March–April 1865). On May 11, 1864, a Wolverine shot and mortally wounded their arch nemesis, J. E. B. Stuart [110], with his revolver during the Battle of Yellow Tavern, six miles north of Richmond.

Brevet Brigadier General George Washington Gallup
Previously Colonel of the 14th Kentucky (Mounted) Infantry [111]

The Watch

Shown in **FIGURE 100** (p. 124) and in **FIGURES 139–142** is a Swiss, approximately 18-size, watch with an unsigned fifteen-jewel Lepine calibre Type V movement with right-angle lever escapement and going barrel, in a triple-backed 18-kt. gold hunting case. The quality case, which is likely of American make, has an extra rear lid, shown in **FIGURE 140**, with a fixture for capturing a picture. One may surmise that this extra inner lid once held a picture of the owner's wife, given how much he wrote to her while he was away on military service. The cuvette bears two inscriptions, shown in **FIGURE 139**, as follow:

> Presented to Col. Geo. W. Gallup by the Officers & Soldiers of the 14th Reg.ᵗ KY V. [Volunteer] Inf., May 1, 1863

and

> Gen.ˡ G. W. Gallup to his son G. F. [Gideon Frederick] Gallup, May 15, 1873.

The second presentation, from General Gallup, pictured in **FIGURE 143** and **FIGURE 144**, to his son, Gideon Frederick, a Catlettsburg, KY, attorney, reflects the general's postwar brevet promotion to brigadier by order of President Andrew Johnson in 1867.

As mentioned, more than one of Colonel Gallup's surviving letters refers to his watch, suggesting that Gallup had kept it with him for the previous, very eventful year in Kentucky. But as he prepared to join General Sherman's Atlanta Campaign for what he could easily have foreseen to be a period of hard, sustained fighting, he sent the watch home for safekeeping. In one of two letters dated May 18, 1864, he writes to his wife, "Dear Beck, I do not know what to do with my watch. If Nichols would carry it, it would be safest with him. Your watch [his wife's, the surviving case of which

139. The cuvette of George Washington Gallup's watch, bearing two presentations.

is shown in **FIGURE 145**] cost $181.35 and your chain $100.00. The watch is warranted by Wilson & McGrun for two years. ..."

The colonel's watch is clearly precious to him, not only because of its monetary value but because of the significance of how it came to him. Other letters home glow with fond sen-timents toward his men of the 14th Kentucky Infantry and the cause for which they fought. To wit, that written on June 20, 1863:

Do not be uneasy about me. Our men are brave and trustworthy, knowing their cause is just, that they fight for an outraged country, for her noble and free institutions, [and] her time-honored and glorious old flag. They will brave danger and death and dear will be the victory. ... So content yourself, my dear wife, knowing that brave arms and noble hearts surround me.

If ever I fall upon the battlefield, let it be among my noble boys, men who I love next to you and my dear children.

A public speech with such strong patriotic sentiments might not seem unusual in any time, but in a personal letter to one's wife, it strikes one as extraordinary. Such was the mood of the country in those tumultuous days. The colonel's affection for his men appears to have been requited. On September 8, 1864, he wrote Rebecca that "I arrived today from Atlanta and joined my regiment and brigade ... The boys (so much like children to me) broke ranks to run and shake hands with me. I do not know how I could leave them for any length of time."

In another letter to his wife on June 12, 1864, Gallup once again mentioned his watch, a gift and token of esteem from the unit he loved, because its safety was clearly much on his mind. He wrote, "How do you like your watch? [the one he had purchased for his wife] I think you had better let Nichols have mine or let sister Francis keep it ... ."

The Man and His Unit, the 14th Kentucky Infantry

George Washington Gallup's life and career are summarized in **TABLE 10**. A native of New York, he moved to Ohio around 1845, where he taught school and studied law. In 1850 he moved to Louisa in eastern Kentucky, at the confluence of the Tug and Levisa Forks of the

140. An unusual extra interior rear lid on George Gallup's watch, between the outer lid and the cuvette, with a frame for capturing an image. The maker's or retailer's mark "A. S." is seen above some fake hallmarks. Fictitious hallmarks were not uncommon in the Civil War period, even on cases of legitimate purity like this one. *Image by Brad Sawyer.*

141. The front lid of the 18-kt gold Gallup watch. The pumpkin-style pendant is a distinctly American feature. It is clear that this watch was carried for some time, as Gallup's letters also suggest. On a watch with a distinguished provenance like this one, signs of careful use can actually add to its appeal.

142. The unsigned, single-sunk Roman numeral dial of the Gallup watch, typical of Swiss movements of its type. The solid gold hour and minute hands, although both are period appropriate, don't quite match, indicating that at least one of them is a replacement. However, one or both may have been replaced during Colonel Gallup's use of the watch during the war, in which case the current hands may both, nevertheless, be part of the watch's significant history.

143. Colonel George Washington Gallup, C.O. of the 14th Kentucky Infantry and Commander of the Eastern Kentucky Military District. *Image courtesy of Roger D. Hunt and Jack R. Brown, Brevet Brigadier Generals in Blue (Olde Soldier Books, Inc., 1990)*

Big Sandy River. There he met and studied law with Laban T. Moore (January 13, 1829–November 9, 1892). Moore later represented the 9th Congressional District of Kentucky in the House of Representatives as a member of the Whig Party from 1859 to 1861 and served in the Kentucky State Senate beginning in 1881. Gallup received his law license in 1850 at the age of twenty-three and went into partnership with Moore, marrying Moore's sister, Rebecca Apple Moore, in 1851. In 1860 Gallup purchased a hotel, known for a while thereafter as the Gallup Hotel, in Louisa, which served transiting steamboat and stagecoach passengers.

The state of Kentucky, a slave state bordering the free states of Ohio, Indiana, and Illinois, was bitterly divided as national disunion

loomed in 1860. Moore and Gallup were both ardent Unionists opposed to secession, and the town of Louisa, with a population at that time of 258, became an outpost of staunch Unionist sentiment within the state. Not long after armed hostilities began, in September 1861, Moore, with Gallup's help organized the 14th Kentucky Infantry, a mounted infantry unit much like the Confederate 1st Kentucky Mounted Rifles. The 14th KY operated in and around eastern Kentucky for much of the war, to as late as early 1864 (**FIGURE 146**). Moore became the original colonel of the regiment, and Gallup was its first quartermaster. Their first engagements occurred on November 8 and 9, 1861, at Ivy Mountain, and on January 10, 1862, at Middle Creek. In both battles, rebel

Dates	Remarks
Oct. 28, 1828	Born in Albany, NY
	Attended NY Central Academy, McGrawville
1845–49	To Ohio, taught school, and studied law at Burlington Academy
1850	To Louisa, KY; studied law under Laban T. Moore
1850	Obtained law license, went into partnership with Moore, and married Moore's sister, Rebecca
Sep. 1861	14th KY Infantry organized at Louisa, with L. T. Moore as Colonel and Gallup as Quartermaster
Dec. 1861	14th KY moved to Catlettsburg, KY
	Action at Middle Creek, along with three companies of the 14th KY
1862	Promoted to Lt. Colonel
	Served with Gen. George Morgan at Cumberland Gap against Gen. Carter L. Stevenson
Jan. 1863	Promoted to Colonel
Aug. 1863–May 1864	Commander, Military District of Eastern KY, based in Louisa
Feb. 15, 1864	14th and 39th KY surround and defeat Col. M. J. Furguson's 16th VA Cavalry, Laurel Creek, Wayne County, WV
Apr. 14, 1864	14th and 39th KY surround and defeat Col. Ezekiel F. Clay's 1st KY Cavalry, Puncheon Creek, Magoffin County, KY
May 1864	Joined Sherman's Command; Sherman's Atlanta Campaign
June 22, 1864	14th KY plays key role in Union victory at Battle of Kolb's Farm
	Brigade Command, 1st Brigade, 2nd Div., XXIII Army Corps[A]
	(14th KY saw action in all the battles of the Atlanta Campaign; lost 157 killed and wounded)
1865	Col. Gallup Returns to Louisa, KY, and Resumes Law Practice
1867	Breveted to Brigadier General by President Andrew Johnson
	"Prominently connected with the building of the C. & O. RR and the Big Sandy RR"[B]
1880	Postmaster Catlettsburg, KY
Dec. 31, 1880	Died, aged 52

TABLE 10: Life and career summary for George Washington Gallup. Compiled from REFS. 111–114 plus (A) *freepages. rootsweb.com/~us14thkyinfantry/military/obit/gallup.html* and (B) *History of the Upper Ohio Valley*, Brant & Fuller, pub.s, 1891:750.

144. G. W. Gallup in civilian clothing. *Image from FindAGrave.com.*

145. The case of the smaller watch that General Gallup gave to his wife and mentioned frequently in his letters. It likely once held a Swiss movement as well. The inscription, "Presented by Col. G. W. Gallup to his wife Rebecca," is unusually formal for a spousal gift. *Image by Brad Sawyer.*

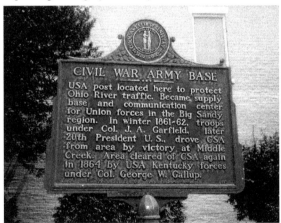

146. Historical marker in Louisa, KY, commemorating the 14th Kentucky's actions against Confederate forces in Eastern Kentucky, including at Middle Creek in 1861–2 and on to mid-1864. In 1864 construction was begun of a fort commanding a high point of the local topography. It was alternately known as "Fort Bishop," "Fort Gallup," or simply as "Fort Hill." *Image from waymarking.com/waymarks/wm1yvz_civil_war_army_base_catlettsburg_ky (June 10, 2018.)*

forces attempting to recruit volunteers in Kentucky were either hastened or dislodged back to Virginia.

Gallup, by then a Lieutenant Colonel, and the 14th Kentucky next were assigned to Union Brigadier General George W. Morgan (not to be confused with Confederate Cavalry General John Hunt Morgan), when George Morgan moved against the rebels holding the Cumberland Gap, near the junction of Kentucky, Virginia, and Tennessee. George Morgan, who described Gallup as "a soldier of rare merit," [112] defeated Carter L. Stevenson's Confederates and chased off the defenders on June 18, 1862. He held the gap with his four brigades of infantry, including the 14th Kentucky Infantry regiment, augmented by artillery placed on the heights, until September, when Braxton Bragg's invading army cut off his supply line and forced him to withdraw. Morgan's troops were at one point nearly surrounded in Cumberland Gap by a superior rebel force. Morgan desired to draw the Confederate commander on the scene, Major General Carter L. Stevenson, into a fight. (The 14th Kentucky and Stevenson's division met once again at Kolb's Farm in Georgia two years later.) For his part, Stevenson figured that time was on his side. An unnamed officer in Morgan's command sent a long letter to the *New York Times*, dated August 27, 1863, although the sender expressed doubt it would ever get through. The letter, which subsequently was published on September 19, described the Federals' predicament at the Gap and their audacious response. Part of it reads:

> Gen. Stevenson, with his rebel division, is on our south front, for now that we are surrounded by the enemy, we have no rear. Our indomitable and gallant commander, Gen. G.W. Morgan, has used every stratagem to draw him into a fight; but he [Stevenson] is too good an officer to risk a battle where he believes that he is sure of the desired result without the loss of a man, by simply starving us out. The enemy considers our immediate capture so certain, that he has published everywhere that he has already ten thousand prisoners at Cumberland Gap. But he should remember the old adage of the chickens. We took this great military stronghold from Gen. Stevenson, and he now desires to return the compliment; but he will fail; for we will be neither starved nor beaten. He is paying us the compliment to fortify his own position to await the processes of hunger upon us. But our hardy and determined soldiers, though occasionally on short allowance, are full of health and courage, and laugh at the threats of the foe.

> In order to tempt the enemy into a fight, Gen. Morgan sent out, on yesterday, a for-

aging train four miles from the Gap, under the convoy, apparently, of only the Thirty-third Indiana, and the Provost-Guard, under **Lieut.-Col. Gallup**. But at the same time, our Commander had the brigades of Baird and De Courcey masked by the forest, ready for action should the enemy come out from his camp, which is located in a strong position. The foraging wagons were loaded in sight of the enemy and driven away; and, after remaining in the open field from 8 o'clock in the morning till 5 in the evening, to coax up a fight, our forces were signaled to return for the night. But before doing so, our troops were instructed to form line, faced to the enemy, and play 'Dixie,' and then march into their headquarters to the tune of 'The girl I left behind me.'

Gallup's choice of the popular tune, "The girl I left behind [me]," which would have been instantly recognizable by the rebels even without sung words, was a clever taunt. It was clear to all who "the girl" was whom the Federals had "left behind" as they turned their backs on their foes and returned unmolested to their base.

George Morgan's 8,000 men then executed a skillful retreat in the face of Bragg's greatly superior enemy force, marching two hundred miles in sixteen days, despite persistent interference from Confederate Colonel John Hunt Morgan's pursuing cavalry. [113] Gallup played a special role in the withdrawal, successfully burning and destroying the Union's valuable stores at the Gap before retreating, right under the noses of Confederate scouts and without giving away Morgan's plan to retreat. Historian Christopher Kolakowski [114] relates:

> Late in the afternoon, a group of Confeder-

ates was seen approaching the Federal picket line. Fearful that the evacuation had been given away, George Morgan sent for the post provost marshal, **Lt. Colonel George Gallup**, and a party to meet them under a flag of truce. The two delegations conferred between the lines, and it soon developed that the Confederates were on a scouting mission. Gallup engaged them in a conversation when suddenly flames blazed up from the gap. Someone had prematurely set fire to one of the warehouses in the valley.

It was a bad moment for the whole garrison. Suspicious, one of the Confederates asked Gallup, 'Why Colonel, what does that mean? It looks like an evacuation.' Without skipping a beat, Gallup replied, 'Not much. Morgan has cut away the timber obstructing the range of his guns, and he is now burning away the brush on the mountainside.' … shortly thereafter, both parties returned to their lines. That explanation seemed to suffice …

At 8 PM, the garrison formed up and set off toward Manchester. … By 10 PM the post was almost deserted, save for 200 picked men commanded by [Lt.] Colonel Gallup. His detachment set fire to the various buildings in the gap; one participant later noted that 'the little valley, encircled by the mountains at the foot of the gap was one sea of flame.'

At this point the Confederates became very suspicious and began to probe the Union position. Gallup's pickets held them at bay. After midnight, the area rocked with explosions as engineers blew up the forts and the powder magazine. [The chief engineer] Craighill's charges successfully blocked the south road into the gap. … As dawn approached, Gallup's detachment marched out amid what George Morgan later reported was, 'the explosion of mines and magazines and lighted

by blazes of the storehouses of the commissary and quartermaster.' After more than four weeks of siege, the 7th Division had evacuated Cumberland Gap.

Gallup's quick thinking and cool-headed leadership at Cumberland Gap enabled the 7th Division's successful retreat and deprived the rebellion of a wealth of supplies that the Union was forced to abandon. He took command of the 14th Kentucky as its colonel in January 1863 and received the watch shown as a token of his men's esteem the following May. With Gallup at its helm, the most intense chapter of the 14th Kentucky's combat history still lay ahead of it. The regiment's service history is summarized in **TABLE II**.

In August of 1863 Colonel Gallup acceded to command of the Military District of Eastern Kentucky, making his base in Louisa, from which he engaged with rebel threats to the region. In early 1864 Gallup and his regiment attacked and defeated two Confederate mounted units in succession: Colonel M. J. Ferguson's 16th Virginia Cavalry, at Laurel Creek, Wayne County, KY, on February 15; and Colonel Ezekiel F. Clay's previously mentioned 1st Kentucky Mounted Rifles, at Puncheon Creek, Magoffin County, KY, on April 14. (Some Internet sources confuse Clay's 1st Kentucky Mounted Rifles, a unit that moved on horseback and fought dismounted with infantry weapons of rifled muskets and bayonets, with the 1st Kentucky Cavalry. The 1st Kentucky Cavalry was a completely different Confederate unit with a different commander, and which fought with carbines when on foot and with revolvers and sabers when mounted.) At the Battle of Puncheon Creek (a.k.a. Half Mountain), Colonel

Date(s)	Battle
Nov. 8 & 9, 1861	Ivy Mountain, KY
Jan. 10, 1862	Middle Creek, KY
Feb. 12, 1864	Laurel Creek, WV
Apr. 13 & 14, 1864	Salyersville, KY
Apr. 14, 1864	Half Mile/ Puncheon Creek, WV
May 25 & 26, 1864	New Hope Church, GA
June 9–July 3, 1864	Fighting at Marietta, GA
June 22, 1864	Kolb's Farm, GA
June 27, 1864	Kennesaw, GA
July 20, 1864	Peachtree Creek, GA
July 22, 1864	Atlanta, GA
Aug. 31–Sep. 1, 1864	Jonesboro, GA
Nov. 4 & 5, 1864	Johnsonville, TN

TABLE II: List of battles of the 14th Kentucky Infantry. In total, 201 officers and men were killed or died of disease. (Compiled from REFS. 111–114.)

Gallup led a combined force of eight hundred men consisting of the 14th and 39th Kentucky Infantry. There the speed and tenacity of his pursuit surprised Clay's six hundred Confederates in their camp along the Licking River, near Salyersville. In a four-hour engagement, during which Clay was wounded and captured, total Confederate losses were sixty killed and wounded, sixty captured, and two hundred horses and all of Clay's unit's tents and other equipment. Union casualties were only one killed and four wounded, a fact that may go a long way to explain one basis for Gallup's men's apparent affection for him. Colonel Gallup wrote to his wife the day of the battle, from "Headquarters, Battlefield on Half Mountain, Licking River, April 14, 1864, 3 PM":

147. Kolb's Farm Historical Plaque. *Image from georgiainfo. galileo.usg.edu/topics/historical_markers/county/cobb/battle-of-kolbs-farm2 (June 10, 2018).*

Dear Beck,

We were attacked yesterday at Paintsville and whipped the rebels. We have followed them to this place, 13 miles above Salyersville and are now fighting. The battle is warm, the rebels fight desperately, but must give way.

[unintelligible] PM … The rebels are in full retreat, we have killed some 20 or 30, captured 50 (Col. Clay among them, who is wounded, right eye shot out.) … A complete rout … We are masters of the field! I will return to Paintsville in the morning.

Your Husband

The following month, the 14th Kentucky became part of Major General William Tecumseh Sherman's command, as the general prepared his historic drive into Georgia, Atlanta Campaign and the March to the Sea.

The 14th Kentucky saw action in essentially every major battle of the Atlanta Campaign (May 7–September 2, 1864), suffering in that period 157 killed and wounded. Their most arduous service was rendered during the action at Kolb's Farm, Cobb County, GA, near Marietta, on June 22, 1864 (**FIGURE 147**). This battle was one of several positional struggles between Sherman's troops and Confederate General Joseph E. Johnston's Army of Tennessee, as Sherman pushed relentlessly toward Atlanta. Sherman's army was divided into four unequal parts. He moved Joe Hooker's XX Corps and elements of the XXIII Corps, to which the 14th Kentucky was attached, into position south of the Powder Springs Road to threaten the right flank of the strong Confederate defensive line between Big and Little Kennesaw Mountains farther north. Johnston's command was divided into three corps. Anticipating Sherman's flanking move, Johnston struck first with the corps commanded by Lt. General John Bell Hood.

Major General Carter L. Stevenson's division led Hood's assault, but it immediately encountered fierce resistance from a strong Federal skirmish line consisting of the 14th Kentucky and 123rd New York Infantry regiments. Hood eventually moved forward with his entire corps, pushing the Kentuckians and New Yorkers aside, but the Federal skirmishers had slowed Hood's offensive considerably and inflicted sufficient casualties on two of Stevenson's brigades to put them out of action for the remainder of the battle. (One of these damaged Confederate brigades was commanded by Brigadier General Edmund Pettus, after whom an infamous bridge subsequently was named in Selma, AL.) On June 22, Colonel Gallup wrote:

My Dear Wife,
Today has been a hard one for the 14th KY. At 12 o'clock I was ordered to advance my regiment to envelop the enemy's line of battle. I marched one mile to the front and captured the enemy's picket line, 45 in number, when General Clayborn [Cleburne—he actually

148. A modern photograph of the former home of Gideon Frederick Gallup, Esquire, General Gallup's son to whom the General presented his cherished watch in 1873. The two men resided at the same address at the time of George's death. *Image from the Find-A-Grave website, June 10, 2018.*

faced Stevenson] attacked me with his brigades and after a stubborn fight we retreated ½ a mile, fighting as we went. Then I found cover under the crest of a ridge and held the enemy until our artillery came up. Killed 104 and wounded 250, took 45 prisoners, and I lost, out of 700 men, 77 killed and wounded, a large loss. The boys are brave. General[s] Hooker, Thomas [of Chickamauga fame], McPherson and Sherman complimented this regiment and say it is the best in the 23rd Corps.

I am worn and weary, have not eaten anything since yesterday morning and I cannot write much. Lieut. Osborn, son of Walter, was killed. Lieut. Burgess, arm shot off. Capt. Gardner wounded. Ensign [color bearer] Jordan Oty killed. … Love to all.—Your Husband.

The commendations from the commanding generals Gallup mentioned were lavish. Major General Harrison Haskell, Gallup's division commander, issued the following message:

Headquarters Second Division, 23rd Army Corps, Army of the Ohio, June 23, 1864, Marietta Road, the General Commanding this division desires to draw attention to divisions, brigades and regiments, officers and men, to the conduct, undaunted courage and bravery of this Fourteenth Regiment, Kentucky Volunteers, now assembled, Colonel George W. Gallup, his officers and men, who are now present before you, who held back and checked the advance of the enemy's attack in Marietta Road in column of companies front and artillery in sections moving and deployed to left of road, ... This noble regiment alone and determined met the advance, which had much superior numbers, with such effect, repulsed the head of their column, deliberately firing at less than forty yards into their forward line, before the second deployed line came up the inclined ground to where the front line of attack fell and received from the Fourteenth Regiment a second firing which struck them with terrible effect, creating a panic or confusion. ... [The 14th KY's] resistance and valor held the enemy back until our fortifications and positions were secure ..., while alone and undaunted the Fourteenth Regiment Kentucky Volunteers retired and brought their casualties with them inside our fortifications. For this noble example set, and worthy to be emulated, for such worthy conduct in the face of and against infantry and artillery of superior numbers, for this great achievement, the General commanding this division returns his thanks with his proud admiration of Colonel G. W. Gallup, his officers and the Fourteenth Regiment of Soldiers.

Colonel Gallup returned to Louisa after the war but subsequently moved to Catlettsburg, where he served as the local postmaster until the day of his death on December 31, 1880. One of his sons, Gideon Frederick Gallup to whom George gave his watch in 1873, followed his father into the law profession, and in the last years of George's life, George's address was the same as Gideon's. Gideon's Catlettsburg home is shown in **FIGURE 148**.

Brevet Major General John Wallace Fuller
C.O. of "Fuller's Ohio Brigade," prev. Colonel of the 27th OH Infantry

The Watch

Shown in **FIGURE 85** (p. 109), **FIGURE 89** (p. 113), and **FIGURE 149** is a fifteen-jewel Appleton, Tracy & Co. grade 16-size key-wind watch movement, SN 80,265 with solid gold balance wheel, finished in January of 1864, in an 18-kt. engine-turned hunting case with no maker's mark. According to the 1864 Robbins & Appleton trade catalog reproduced in **REF. 62**, the uncased movement would have wholesaled for about $40, and the heavy 18-kt. case would have contained about another $40–50 worth of gold, so this watch would have cost the men who presented it to Gen. Fuller well over $100.

The cuvette is engraved "Presented to Brig. Gen.l J. W. [John Wallace] Fuller by the Officers and Enlisted Men of the 27th Reg.t Ohio Vet. [Veteran] Inf. Vol.s [Volunteers], July 20, 1865." General Fuller is pictured in his brigadier's uniform in **FIGURE 150** and in civilian clothing in **FIGURE 151**. The proud reference in the presentation to "Veteran Infantry" likely indicates that in 1864, the remaining men of the 27th Ohio Infantry had largely reenlisted in the same unit when their original three-year obligations had been completed.

149. The cuvette of Major General John Wallace Fuller's 18-kt. gold watch, with a presentation from the men of his original regiment. Fuller was actually a brevet Major General at the time he received the watch, but his admiring men of the 27th Ohio Regiment had always known him as first their colonel and then their brigade commander.

General John Wallace Fuller and His Ohio Brigade

General Fuller's life, career, and military service are summarized in **TABLE 12**. Arriving in New York from England at the age of six, John Wallace Fuller became one of over half a million immigrants from many countries (England, Ireland, Germany, France, Portugal, Italy, Hungary), whose service and sacrifices were instrumental in saving the Union. By the 1850s Fuller had become a successful bookseller and

publisher, first in Utica, NY, where he served as the city treasurer from 1852 to 1854, and then in Toledo, OH. But when the rebels fired on Fort Sumter, he heard his adopted country's call. In Toledo Fuller organized the 27th Ohio Infantry regiment and became its commander, a colonel, in August of 1861. The regiment saw hard fighting throughout 1862, beginning with the battles of New Madrid and Island Number 10 along the Mississippi River in Missouri and Tennessee. In the early fall of 1862 Fuller

150. Brigadier General John Wallace Fuller. *Image from ironbrigadier.com/2014/07/13/general-john-w-fullers-report-divisions-action-battle-atlanta/ (June 10, 2018).*

151. A later image of retired Major General Fuller in civilian life. *Image from generalsandbrevets.com/ngf/fuller.htm.link (June 10, 2018).*

was given command of the brigade that would become associated with his name, consisting of the 27th, 39th, 43rd, and 63rd Ohio Infantry regiments. In 1862 he led the Ohioans in their fierce struggle at the Battle of Second Corinth in Mississippi, one of their most severe tests, and at Parker's Crossroads in Tennessee, surprising the South's irregular cavalry genius, Nathan Bedford Forrest, on the last day of that same year.

After a year spent primarily on garrison duty in 1863, in January 1864 Fuller was promoted to Brigadier General, commanding the 4th Division, XVII Corps, Army of the Tennessee. He led that division, which included his namesake brigade, in the Atlanta Campaign and through the March to the Sea and Carolinas Campaign. For distinguished service, he was breveted a Major General of U.S. Volunteers on March 13, 1865, before resigning his commission on August 15. After the war Fuller resumed his publishing career and was appointed in 1874 by President Grant as U.S. Collector of Customs in the Port of Toledo on Lake Erie.

Service Highlights

Second Battle of Corinth, Mississippi, October 3-4, 1862

Corinth, MS, dubbed "the Crossroads of the Confederacy," was situated at the junction of

Dates	Remarks
July 28, 1827	Born Harston, Cambridgeshire, England
1833	Immigrated to Oneida County, NY
1852–54	Treasurer of Utica, NY; Officer in NY State Militia
late 1850s	Book Seller & Publisher, Toledo, OH
Aug. 1861	Commissioned Colonel, 27th OH Infantry
Mar. 14, 1862	Battle of New Madrid, MO
Feb.–Apr. 1862	Battle of Island No. 10, MO & TN
Aug. or Sep. 1862	Given Command of "Fuller's Ohio Brigade," in Army of the Mississippi
Sep. 19, 1862	Battle of Iuka, MS
Oct. 4, 1862	Second Battle of Corinth, MS
Dec. 31, 1862	Surprised N. B. Forrest at Parkers Crossroads, TN
1863	Garrison Duty
Jan. 5, 1864	Promoted to Brigadier General
Mar. 1864	Captured Decatur, AL
July 1864	Hard Fighting against J. B. Hood at Ruff's Mill and Nickajack Creek, GA
July 22, 1864	Division Command, Opened the Battle of Atlanta, GA; Repelling a Surprise Attack
Nov.–Dec. 1864	Commanded 1st Division, XVII Corps, Sherman's March to the Sea, GA
1865	Carolinas Campaign
Mar. 13, 1865	Breveted to Major General
July 20, 1865	Watch Presented by Officers & Enlisted Men of the 27th OH
Aug. 15, 1865	Resigned
1874	Appointed by Pres. Grant as Customs Collector, Port of Toledo
1878	Reappointed Customs Collector, Port of Toledo
Mar. 12, 1891	Died, Toledo, OH

TABLE 12: John Wallace Fuller and Fuller's Ohio Brigade, Life and Service Summary. Sources include information from Smith, Charles H. [Major, US Army Retired, 27th OH Volunteer Infantry, Brigade Historian] *The History of Fuller's Ohio Brigade, 1861–1865; Its Great March, with Roster, Portraits, Battle Maps and Biographies* A. J. Watt Press, 1909; the *Find-a-Grave* website at *www.findagrave.com/cgi-bin/fg.cgi?page=gr&GRid=5893554* and *The Twentieth Century Biographical Dictionary of Notable Americans*, Johnson, Rossiter and Brown, Howard ed.s, Harvard 1904:1897.

Other battles of Fuller & his Brigade include the Siege of Corinth (MS), Resaca (GA), Dallas (GA), New Hope Church (GA), Allatoona (GA), Kennesaw Mtn. (GA), Jonesboro (GA), Lovejoy's Station (GA), and Bentonville (NC).

THE DEFENSE OF BATTERY ROBINETT. FROM A WAR-TIME SKETCH.

152. The defense of Battery Robinett (Second Battle of Corinth, October 4, 19862), from a wartime sketch. *Image from flickr.com/photos/britishlibrary/11189202483 (June 10, 2018).*

two vital rail lines, the Mobile and Ohio Railroad and the Memphis and Charleston Railroad. Before his capture of the city earlier that year, Union Major General Henry Halleck opined that "Richmond and Corinth are now the great strategic points of the war, and our success at these points should be insured at all hazards." [115] He also understood that the capture of Corinth by Union forces would threaten the security of Chattanooga and challenge Confederate control of areas in Tennessee west of Corinth.

Corinth fell into Union hands on May 29, 1862, when Union forces under Halleck forced the outnumbered Confederate defenders to abandon the town after a siege. Union forces under Major General Ulysses S. Grant took control, and the town became Grant's base of operations for campaigns directed at the Mississippi River Valley, especially the crucial Confederate stronghold at Vicksburg, MS. In late 1862 the defense of the city was the responsibility of Union Major General William Rose-crans.

The Confederates were determined to get Corinth back. Two previously separate Confederate armies combined under Major General Earl Van Dorn and moved to retake the town. On October 3, 1862, rebel forces drove Union troops from their outer defenses, a ring of rifle pits that the rebels themselves had dug during the siege earlier that year. But on the following day Union resistance stiffened. The Federals had placed an artillery battery consisting of three twenty-pound Parrott rifles under the command of 2nd Lieutenant Henry C. Robinett atop the middle of a small fortified hill, College Hill, on their inner defensive line. Fuller's brigade was assigned to defend the position, a redan (an arrow-shaped embankment) protected by a five foot ditch. Along with the adjacent batteries on the same hill, "Battery Robinett" became the object of determined rebel assaults on October 4 (**FIGURE 152**). At around 11:00 AM, Confederate Brigadier General Dabney Maury's division of three brigades came straight at the Union center with everything they had. The fighting in front of Battery Robinett was savage, and Maury's command was ultimately thrown back with heavy losses after some initial success. Major Charles Smith of the 27th Ohio, who became the historian of Fuller's Ohio Brigade (FOB), wrote:

[… A large] force of Arkansas, Texas, Alabama and Mississippi troops, … their columns five lines deep, emerged from the woods [which were only about two hundred yards in front of the fort] in full view and rushed forward with desperate charge upon [the FOB]. Their columns moved in almost unbroken lines, their battle flags flaunting in the clear sunlight. [116]

Sixteen-year-old Private J. A. McKinstry of the 42ⁿᵈ Alabama Infantry, Company D, also lived to describe the attack on Battery Robinett. [117] He later wrote:

> In front of us was the most obstructive abatis [felled trees with the branches facing toward the enemy] that it was my misfortune to encounter …, the forts belched destruction into our ranks; yet our men did not waver or halt … when about half through the abatis, Robinett changed shells for grape and canister on us. Our yells grew fainter and our men fell faster, but at last we reached the unobstructed ground in front of the fort …

A Union soldier, Cloyd Bryner of the 47ᵗʰ Illinois Infantry, remembered:

> Grape and canister tore terrible lanes through the Confederate ranks … but the determined men of Arkansas, Texas and Mississippi never faltered. … Upon the advancing lines the 47ᵗʰ was pouring a deadly enfilading fire with telling effect, the guns of Robinett were double charged and the redoubt was a circle of flame. Magnificently mounted and bearing the Confederate colors aloft, Colonel Rogers of Texas led the line of gray, led them to the very edge of the ditch which he was in the act of leaping when the Ohio Brigade arose and delivered a murderous fire, before which the Confederates recoiled … [118]

The aftermath of Colonel Rogers's gallant charge can be seen in **FIGURE 153**. Major Smith's narrative continued:

> When the enemy had reached a distance of a few yards from the position occupied by [the FOB], the 27ᵗʰ, 43ʳᵈ and 63ʳᵈ Regiments rose en masse and simultaneously delivered a tre-

153. Photo of Confederate dead of the 2ⁿᵈ Texas Infantry before the parapet at Battery Robinett, October 5, 1862. Shown at left is the body of Colonel William P. Rogers, the unit's Commanding Officer. *Image from The Photographic History of The Civil War in Ten Volumes: Volume Two, Two Years Of Grim War. New York, NY: The Review of Reviews Co., 1911:150.*

> mendous volley of musketry fire and went at them.
>
> …
>
> In the meantime the assailants tumbled behind shelter of stumps and fallen trees and fired point blank into the Union lines, exchanging shot with the brigade at twenty paces. Thus the two contending forces continued murdering each other until the enemy, gathering in their number and strength, rushed their columns up to the Union lines. Reaching the muzzles of the guns in Battery Robinett, the defenders and assailants began clubbing each other with their muskets [and, according to other accounts, with cannon ramrods].

Major Smith next reports—and other accounts confirm—that the FOB's gun barrels got so hot and so choked with spent powder that many could no longer be used. In addition, he continued:

> The Union batteries were obliged to cease fir-

ing because of the close proximity of the contending forces. The fighting was thus desperate and matters looked precarious. The Forty Third [Regiment] had suffered severely, losing nearly one fourth of its men.

...

[After several other officers were wounded or killed] The command of the regiment fell to Lieutenant Colonel Swayne who changed front under a withering fire that would have tried the mettle of any regiment that ever saw a battlefield, and every rebel who showed his head above the parapet of Battery Robinett or attempted to enter the embrasure was either killed or wounded.

The Sixty Third [Regiment, which] had occupied an exposed position, had suffered a loss of forty eight percent of all those engaged. All of their officers except three had been killed or wounded while the remnant stood to their work with greatest determination.

...

The right companies of the Twenty Seventh Ohio were firing incessantly. Being screened and protected by fallen trees, they did fearful execution upon the ranks of the enemy. The left of that regiment ... was fully exposed, with a road in front upon which the enemy came en masse. Companies B, G, and K had lost half of their number killed or wounded, including all of the commissioned officers of Company G. The company was therefore left in command of Charles H. Smith, the Orderly Sergeant [and future major].

In the savage fighting the Confederates temporarily seized the parapet and drove the defenders from their guns. Lieutenant Robinett and thirteen of his twenty-six men in his battery were casualties. In desperation Captain George Williams fired two shells from nearby Battery Williams into the masses of Confederates swarming into Battery Robinett, stalling their attack just long enough for the remnants of the FOB to stem their advance. A fierce hand-to-hand struggle ensued. "Oh we were butchered like dogs," lamented a Confederate Lieutenant Labruzan, "The dead lay piled from three to seven deep; for a hundred feet the bodies lay so close it was almost impossible to walk between them." [115]

Having run low on ammunition, or otherwise unable to shoot, Fuller's regiments were forced to withdraw a short distance and temporarily concede the hilltop fort. But then, with the support of a fresh regiment, the 11th Missouri, which had been held in reserve, all fixed bayonets and charged back up the hill, driving the rebels from the position and capturing the flag of the 9th Texas Infantry. [116]

The FOB's gallant stand at Battery Robinett was a key factor in the Union victory at Second Corinth. After the battle, a captured rebel lieutenant is known to have remarked, "You licked us good today, but we gave you the best we had in the ranch." [116] The commanding Union General, William Rosecrans, rode up to the FOB's position, dismounted, and looked at the ghastly pile of dead, gray mixed with blue, in front of the FOB's recaptured fort. As widely reported, he stood before the men and said, "I know that I stand in the presence of brave men and I take my hat off to you. I know this from what I have heard and from what I have seen at a distance, and also from these piles of dead I see along your front, and I thank you in our country's name for your great valor." [119]

Union General William T. Sherman wrote

that after the Second Battle of Corinth, "In Memphis I could see its effects upon the citizens, and they openly admitted that their cause had sustained a death-blow." [120]

Parker's Crossroads, Tennessee, December 31, 1862

An extraordinary and unorthodox Confederate, Nathan Bedford Forrest (**FIGURE 154**), rose through the ranks from private to Lieutenant General. Forrest was called the "Wizard of the Saddle." [121] General William T. Sherman called him "that devil Forrest." He was, in Ulysses S. Grant's estimation, "the most remarkable man our civil war produced on either side." Forrest remains today as controversial as he was remarkable. Before the war he made his fortune in large part as a slave catcher and slave trader. He also bore at least some culpability, and perhaps more than some, as the commanding officer at the scene, for an infamous massacre of black Federal troops and white Unionist prisoners at Fort Pillow, TN, in April 1864. Along with former Confederate General John B. Gordon, Forrest played a prominent early role in the original and extremely violent Ku Klux Klan after the war. (Both men would become perennial favorites of organizations, such as the Daughters of the Confederacy, who erected Confederate monuments all over the South.) Forrest also ran a prison camp, where he profited from the contract prison labor system, which was a form of postwar continuation of the prewar slave labor system sans only the name. Yet Forrest's many adoring admirers will hasten to cite supposedly mitigating circumstances or even exonerating facts for all of the aforementioned charges, so the controversy and the hagiography surrounding him contin-

154. Confederate General Nathan Bedford Forrest, the extraordinary and controversial "Wizard of the Saddle." He was surprised and sent running at Parker's Crossroads, but he escaped to fight another day. He appears to have been at least a Major General in this image. *Image from the Library of Congress (Digital ID: PPMSCD 00082).*

ues. Perhaps the only fact about Forrest about which there is virtually no dispute is that he was a brilliant military tactician and a daring and extremely effective cavalry commander. For this reason, combined with his meteoric rise through the Confederate ranks from private to Lieutenant General, admirers continue to see him as a romantic figure.

Forrest rarely lost an engagement with the Federal army, which is what makes the events at Parker's Crossroads, on December 31, 1862, in Henderson County, TN, especially noteworthy. But even in adversity, his tactical skill and resourcefulness was abundantly evident. As then Brigadier General Forrest's expedition into West Tennessee neared its conclusion in late 1862, Union Brigadier General Jeremiah C.

Sullivan, commanding the brigades of Colonels Cyrus L. Dunham and John W. Fuller, endeavored to stop Forrest from withdrawing across the Tennessee River. Dunham encountered Forrest first, and Forrest got the upper hand in the engagement, getting around Dunham's flanks and rear. Dunham had just rejected Forrest's unconditional surrender demand and was preparing to receive another attack on his position when Fuller's brigade appeared. Fuller's men attacked Forrest from the rear, surprising his horse holders, some of whom fled right past the general during the Ohioans' assault. (When a cavalry unit fought dismounted, roughly every fourth man was assigned to hold the horses.) Faced with enemies in both front and rear, Forrest's calm solution was to "Charge 'em both ways." [122] The Confederates briefly reversed front, stalled Fuller's advance, then rushed past Dunham's demoralized force and withdrew south to Lexington, TN.

While Forrest's now famous "attack in both directions" averted a greater disaster and allowed him to make it back across the Tennessee River, the fact remains that Fuller's surprise attack cost Forrest three hundred men, 350 horses, and six of his own cannons plus one he had captured. That loss likely amounted to his entire artillery complement and at least half a regiment of troops. Thus, while failing to capture the Saddle Wizard or prevent his escape, John Fuller could still rightly claim that he was probably the only Federal commander to surprise Forrest in an engagement and send him running. The FOB historian, Major Smith, wrote of the battle:

> Some hundreds of the enemy who had dismounted and had been fighting as infantry, had left their horses in the orchard and yard near Parker's house. These four hundred horses [a somewhat larger but still very plausible number than some others have reported] and several pieces of artillery were the first trophies that fell into our hands, and more than three hundred of their riders, unable to get away, surrendered themselves as prisoners. A small train of wagons which the enemy had gained possession of was recaptured in the road a short distance south of Parker's house, and one at least of the guns belonging to Colonel Dunham's command was retaken from the enemy on the road. The dead bodies of our artillerists lying close to this gun attested the fidelity and bravery with which the men of the 7th Wisconsin Battery stood at their posts until their last round of ammunition was exhausted.
>
> Among the prisoners who surrendered were several officers of prominence: Lt. Colonel Cox and Major Strange (Forrest's Adjutant General), who together with the Captain commanding Forrest's bodyguard, were unhorsed by a volley from the 27th Ohio when riding off the field with their general, and Colonel Black, who afterward escaped in citizen's clothes … [reminiscent of Jefferson Davis' less successful attempted escape from Federal troops a few years later] [106]

The historical plaque commemorating the events at Parker's Crossroads on December 31, 1862, is shown in **FIGURE 155**. Fuller's small victory over Forrest on that day was an added morale boost for the Union after the costly defeat at Fredericksburg two weeks earlier, but at the time it was overshadowed by greater events. For on the same day, the far more sanguinary Battle of Stones River (December 31, 1862 to January 2, 1863) had commenced. That battle, which had the highest total casualty percentage among all forces engaged of any major clash of the war, thwarted Confederate aspirations to control Middle Tennessee. Both the large and the smaller Union victories, however incomplete, were a much needed morale boost after the defeat at Fredericksburg earlier in December, and they lent greater credibility and impetus to Lincoln's Emancipation Proclamation, which came into effect on January 1.

Battle of Atlanta, Georgia, July 22, 1864

The Prussian general, Carl von Clausewitz, famously made the point that warfare was ultimately an instrument of politics. [123] The great political issue before Northern voters in the presidential election of November 1864 was whether to stay the course and win the war on Northern terms with Abraham Lincoln, or to elect George B. McClellan, who wished to end the war immediately by allowing the seceded states to reenter the Union on terms preserving the institution of slavery. In mid-August of 1864 Northern morale was strained. As mentioned, the Army of the Potomac, commanded by Major General George G. Meade but supervised by overall U.S. Army commander, Lieutenant General Ulysses S. Grant, had suffered between 75,000 and 85,000 casualties in one seven-week period, out of an initial strength of 120,000 men. The disastrous assaults at Cold Harbor (May 31–June 12), which Grant later came to consider his biggest mistake of the war, and the debacle of the Battle of the Crater (July 30), were fresh memories, and Grant was being excoriated in the Northern antiwar press as a "butcher." While the Confederate fortifications around Richmond and the key rail junction at Petersburg continued to seem impreg-

155. Parker's Crossroads historical plaque in Henderson County, TN. *Image from hmdb.org/marker.asp?marker=118580 (June 10, 2018).*

nable, far from the front Northern enlistment had fallen off and the deeply unpopular Federal Conscription Act continued to roil unrest and resentment. Thus, the Battle of Atlanta on July 22, 1864, and the subsequent Union capture of that major Southern city after a siege on September 2, boosted Northern prospects at a crucial moment, renewing confidence that the end of the Confederacy—and of slavery—was in sight. Lincoln won reelection in a landslide, capturing 55.1% of the popular vote and 212 of 233 Electoral College votes.

July 22, 1864 saw General Fuller in command of the 4th Division, 16th Corps in the Army of the Tennessee under Major General James B. McPherson. Fuller's division was positioned on the left of the Union lines around Atlanta. The division consisted of two brigades, the FOB and another, under Colonel John W. Sprague. General McPherson ordered the 16th Corps to reinforce their position on the left, anticipating an attack from the Confederate commanding general, John Bell Hood. Two of Hood's divisions indeed attacked at that location. Major General William H. T. Walker's division came against Fuller. Sprague's brigade had been deployed a few miles away at Decatur, GA, so Fuller had only his Ohio Brigade with him to face Walker's assault. Sprague's brigade had its own hands full that day. They successfully defended the Union supply trains against a much larger Confederate force. (For his actions at Decatur, Sprague was promoted to Brigadier General, and years after the war ended, he received the Medal of Honor for his service on that day.)

Fuller too would perform his most heroic personal service of the war that same day. The following is excerpted from the FOB historian's account of his own brigade's actions:

> About one o'clock in the afternoon the enemy had arrived at a point on the left and rear of the Union Army, and were well in position. [The enemy] advanced and struck the Union pickets, being enabled under cover of the forest to approach quite near before he was discovered. Indeed his skirmish line had got into the field in the rear of General Giles A. Smith's division of the Seventeenth Corps unseen. … Suddenly on the left and rear came the sound of firing. It startled the soldiers and instinctively the danger of a flank movement flashed upon their minds. Instantly they grasped their muskets. Orders were anticipated and every man fell into line. … Orders to move were received in a moment, to meet the impending danger on the left. The movement was on the double-quick for a distance of half a mile, then faced to the South, formed quickly into line of battle, at right angles with the Seventeenth Corps and as quickly as it takes to tell it, the battle was on and raging with great fury. Connection with the Seventeenth Corps on the right of this new position was not complete. A gap of one half a mile or more was left unoccupied by Union troops. It was over this space and the unused road that General Fuller's command had just marched and on which General McPherson, commander of the Army of Tennessee, was riding when he was ambushed and killed. [General McPherson] had passed our troops who cheered him vociferously, had bowed his head in acknowledgment with his usual genial smile, and had ridden on unconscious of his danger to his death.
>
> The Fourth Division [i.e., Fuller's Division] moved quickly for position to save our trains or to avoid a worse disaster. The Second Division was separated from the Fourth Division by a transverse ravine. The right of the rebel line had struck our left flank while in motion. The rebels attacked boldly and repeatedly but met an equally fierce resistance and on that bloody ground the battle raged from a little after noon till night.
>
> When the enemy advanced, the men were lying on the ground. No orders could keep them down. They rose to their feet, took deliberate aim and discharged their pieces.
>
> As soon as the 27th and 39th [Ohio] Regiments were halted, Company A of the 27th Ohio, commanded by First Lieutenant Charles H. Smith [the FOB historian] … was by order thrown forward as skirmishers to cover the field in front. … They were under a terrific fire from the enemy who had formed in masses at the edge of the dense wood, and who advanced their whole line upon the field, four deep, their bullets pattering upon the ground like rain-drops. The skirmishers held them at bay until the order was given for the 27th and the 39th to charge. The two regiments sprang from the ground and rushed upon the enemy. Then came the impact of the two opposing forces—a battle waged in the open field, with no protection of earthworks on either side—a battle, the most sanguinary of

the war.

The flags of the 27th and 39th Ohio and of the Confederate regiments were placed side by side, and the two opposing forces fought with desperation and bitterness to gain the mastery, until the Confederate lines were broken and driven back into cover of the woods. In the meantime a large body of the enemy had passed through the open space to the rear, so that Fuller's Division was actually surrounded on the front, right flank and rear.

General Fuller … brought up part of a reserve regiment, the splendid 64th Illinois, who struck the enemy, which had passed the rear, unawares, and pushed him back. At the same time, the 27th and 39th made a half wheel and commenced firing into their flank, compelling them to retreat in confusion from the field, for a second time. The two [FOB] regiments followed them to the timber, but again the enemy reformed their lines under command of [Major] General [William H. T.] Walker, who was killed while urging his men, almost at the instant of their forward movement. He fell in front of the firing line of the 27th Ohio Company A. The two regiments now lay flat upon the ground, firing at the advancing enemy. At this moment, General Fuller seized the flag of the 27th, raised it aloft, and the two regiments moved forward with a great shout and drove the enemy back in final defeat. [106]

The scene that Major Smith describes was one in which the FOB met and repelled a surprise attack on one flank, only to be flanked and nearly taken from the rear by a second Confederate column that had found a gap between them and the Union Second Division. Fuller successfully wheeled two of his regiments in the face of heavy enemy fire—an extremely difficult maneuver—then personally took up the flag of the 27th Ohio from the regiment's color sergeant and led a countercharge that broke the back of the Confederate assault. General Fuller's own report of the day's fighting reads in part as follows:

It was near 1 o'clock when skirmishing was heard in our rear, and General Dodge [the XVI Corps commander], then dining in my tent, said he had been informed that the enemy's cavalry had been seen in that direction, and ordered me to place a regiment in position to cover our trains. The regiment was sent for, but within four or five minutes after General Dodge left me the skirmishing was so heavy that I ordered out the entire brigade at a double-quick. Three regiments were formed in line in the field in rear of our trains, with our backs toward Atlanta, and my left near the right of the Second Division, which had just arrived, … the Eighteenth Missouri being held in reserve. Skirmishers thrown out to cover our front had scarcely crossed the field when they were driven back by the enemy's line of battle, and my command became at once warmly engaged.

The enemy advanced into the open field, halted, and opened fire upon us. But he seemed surprised to find himself facing our infantry in line of battle, for their steady fire, aided by the guns of the Fourteenth Ohio Battery, which held an enfilading position on my left, soon caused him to go back under cover of the woods. I then ordered the regiments to lie down behind the crest of the ridge, and, seeing the enemy was preparing to again advance, directed Colonels McDowell, Thirty-ninth Ohio, and Churchill, Twenty-seventh Ohio, to wait until the enemy should march half way across the field, and then to rise, fire a volley, and charge. Bayonets were immediately fixed to carry out this order, but for some reason the regiments did not wait, as I had ordered, but charged as soon as the enemy's line had again emerged from the woods. This movement was executed too soon to give us very many prisoners, the woods covering their retreat, but it so thoroughly routed that portion of the enemy's line which was in front of these regiments, and sent them back in such confusion, that his supports retired also, and no enemy afterward showed himself on that part of the field. All who were not shot, or did not run away, of the Sixty-Sixth Georgia Infantry were captured by the Thirty-ninth Ohio, including the colonel, the adjutant, and 1 captain.

Immediately after this charge I discovered that such of the enemy's line as overlapped our right flank was marching past the right of the Twenty-seventh [Ohio] Regiment on toward Atlanta, which now lay in our rear. His supports followed closely, halted, and some rebel regiments marching in columns doubled on the center, changed direction to their right, and marched straight for the flank of those regiments which had just made the charge described. Seeing this, I ordered these regiments to change front to face this new enemy. To accomplish this we were obliged to throw back the right rapidly; a very hot fire during this hazardous but necessary maneuver rendered it impossible to keep the line well dressed, and for a moment it seemed as if these veteran regiments would be routed. The Twenty-seventh [Ohio] especially, occupying the right and obliged to make the movement on a run, when reaching the ground, where it was to halt and face about, was in confusion and looked like defeat. There was not a moment to lose, and the din of the battle was too great to hear orders, so the colors were moved out from the confused mass toward the ap-

proaching enemy, and my sword indicated where the line should be reformed. The men of the Twenty-seventh [Ohio], noting this movement of their colors, and instantly comprehending what was required, with a great shout came up on either side in less time than I can write. The Thirty-ninth [Ohio] instantly formed on their left, bayonets were brought down to a charge, our men advanced, and the rebels, now distant less than a hundred yards, came to a right-about, and ran back into the woods.

While the movements just described were occurring, some rebel regiments which had outflanked the Twenty-seventh Ohio, and were marching toward our rear, were stopped by the fire of the Sixty-fourth Illinois and the Eighteenth Missouri. Colonel Sheldon, of the Eighteenth, rapidly changed the direction of his line, so as to give his men a raking fire on the enemy. These rebels were partly covered by a piece of rail fence, but soon began to break, when a general officer (supposed to be General Walker) rode out from the woods, and swinging his hat made a great effort to urge forward his troops. The next moment his horse went back riderless, and so sharp was the fire of our men that the enemy disappeared almost immediately, and nobody seemed to heed the cry of their officers to 'bring off the general.' The slaughter here may be judged from the report of Colonel Sheldon, who found as many as 13 dead rebels in a single fence corner. … Very soon, the rebels having reformed under cover of the woods, returned to the fence at the edge of the field, and reopened a heavy fire upon us. I ordered the Sixty-fourth Illinois to move to the right, then advance into the woods, and, if possible, get a flank fire on this line. This proved a heavier job than one regiment could accomplish. They drove back the rebels temporarily;

THE BATTLE OF ATLANTA JULY 22 1864 —FULLER'S DIVISION RALLYING AFTER BEING FORCED BACK BY THE CONFEDERATES.

156. An 1886 illustration by noted artist James E. Taylor of General Fuller rallying his Ohio Brigade during the Battle of Atlanta on July 22, 1864. Fuller is portrayed at the center of the image with the colors of the 27th Ohio in his left hand and a sword in his right. *Image from battleofatlanta.digitalscholarship.emory.edu/tour/the-battle-of-atlanta/7/ (June 10, 2018).*

they captured and sent to the rear 40 prisoners; they took a stand of colors; and their valor rescued the body of McPherson, whence it was borne to the rear; but after a hard fight, in which they lost several officers and more than 50 men, they were driven out of the woods pell-mell. Yet our line in the field, now lying down and partially covered by the crest of a ridge, aided by the Fourteenth [Ohio] Battery, which threw shells incessantly over our men into the rebel ranks, made it so hot that the enemy was eventually compelled to withdraw. [124]

In Fuller's own account, he modestly glosses over his own act of valor in personally taking up

the colors of the 27th Ohio and leading a charge when defeat threatened, an account confirmed by independent sources. But his bold action on that day is memorialized in a well-known 1886 illustration, **FIGURE 156**, drawn by James E. Taylor. Taylor's drawing shows the general raising the 27th's colors aloft and rallying his brigade. In large part because of this superlative performance, Fuller was brevetted to Major General the following March.

It is no mean feat to have led men into harm's way time and again over an extended period and at the end of it to be both respected and liked by the men one led. John W. Fuller's watch attests that he accomplished precisely that feat during the greatest and most formative struggle of the United States. As Major Charles H. Smith, who rose within the FOB from the enlisted ranks, attests in the FOB's regimental history, "the splendid record of the Ohio Brigade and the honorable place it oc-cupies in the history of our country is due in large measure to the fact that it was the good fortune of the organization to have for its commander a most thorough and accomplished officer—a commander in whose skill, judgment, and bravery every man in the Brigade had the utmost confidence." [116]

FINAL THOUGHTS

In this book I have endeavored to provide a reason for why horologists should respect and cherish timepieces carried by Civil War combatants as precious pieces of history, even if the horological attributes alone of the artifacts in question would not warrant special attention. I also have endeavored to give persons already devoted to the collecting and preservation of Civil War artifacts the information they need to make informed judgments about the nature and likely authenticity of Civil War timepieces. It is my hope that in the process I have managed to transfer a fraction of the awe and reverence I feel for these artifacts to my readers. This book is my small contribution toward ensuring that the individuals who carried these watches will continue to have their stories told and that their courageous deeds, which were so essential to the survival of the American Democracy, will live on in the national memory. Readers with additional information to share or comments to offer are encouraged to contact me either through the NAWCC message board, or through my website, *ClintGeller.com*.

ACKNOWLEDGMENTS

I am indebted to many people for their kind assistance and encouragement in the development, review and production of this book. For scholarly review I sincerely thank Shoshana Bee Burris, Pat Young, Colonel Albert Mackey (US Air Force, retired), Michael Kraus (Curator, Soldiers & Sailors Hall & Museum, Pittsburgh, PA), Jerry Treiman, and Craig Risch (FNAWCC). For production assistance I heartily thank Editorial Director Christiane Odyniec, Copy Editor Freda Conner, Proofreader Gillian Radel, Saul Bottcher of *indiebooklauncher.com*, my photographers Laura Magone and William Fuller, and my cover photo editor, Mary Korey. I thank my friend Charlie Talbert for help with researching provenances. For kindly providing photos for the book or for making their collections available to me for photographing, I greatly appreciate the help of Heritage Galleries, John Cote, Craig Risch (FNAWCC), James Bollman, Bob McCabe, Keith Richmond, Dr. Russell Schuh, William Bechmann III, Ben Hutcherson, Dr. Tom McIntyre, and Dr. Stephen Helfant, and the Division of Political History, National Museum of American History of the Smithsonian Institution. I thank Major William T. Carr (Air National Guard, retired) for sharing his knowledge of Civil War uniforms. I offer a special thank you to my friend Don Barrett for all of his varied help in my collecting endeavors culminating in the publication of this book. For advice and encouragement in this project I thank my friend of many years, Commander William (Bill) Locke (U.S. Navy, retired). I acknowledge NAWCC Chapter 174 Pocket Horology, whose bequest to the National Association of Watch and Clock Collectors underwrote the publication of this book. For encouragement, suggestions, and other miscellaneous help, I thank my many internet friends on the NAWCC message board and the Civil War Talk website, and especially Mike Serpa of the CWT for his kind proof reading of the text, and Thomas Elmore of the CWT for providing invaluable input from soldiers' letters and diaries. Finally, my wonderful wife, Maria, has my heartfelt gratitude for her inexhaustible patience during my labors on this book.

APPENDIX

"The fact that Slavery is the sole, undeniable cause of this infamous rebellion, that it is a war of, by, and for Slavery, is as plain as the noon-day sun."

—The Wisconsin Volunteer, newspaper of the 13th Wisconsin Infantry Regiment, February 6, 1862, Leavenworth, Kansas

The Background to the War

In retrospect the Civil War may seem like it was virtually inevitable. A succession of crises and increasingly unpopular and desperate compromises that were meant to defuse them ultimately failed to avert the widely foreseen tragedy. A leading Southern statesman, John C. Calhoun of South Carolina, the "Apostle of Slavery," [125] who in his long public career had served as a congressman, vice president, secretary of state, secretary of war, and finally a senator from South Carolina, prophesied in 1850 that a civil war would ensue between North and South over the future of slavery. [126] In a speech read for the dying Calhoun by a colleague, James Mason, on the floor of the Senate, he predicted:

> I fix [the war's] probable occurrence within twelve years or three presidential terms. You and others of your age will probably live to see it; I shall not. The mode by which it will be done is not so clear; it may be brought about in a manner that no one now foresees. But the probability is, it will explode in a presidential election.

The seeds of the crisis were present even at the nation's founding, a consequence of the irreducible contradiction between the institution of hereditary chattel slavery and the most fundamental tenets of liberal democracy. As a noted later commentator, John Jay Chapman, wrote, "There was never any moment in our history when slavery was not a sleeping serpent. It lay coiled up under the table during the deliberations of the Constitutional Convention [in 1787]." [127]

Through the first half of the nineteenth century the American nation rapidly expanded both demographically and geographically. Population increases, from just under four million persons in 1790 (of whom 17.8% were in bondage), to 39.4 million persons in 1860 (of whom 12.6% were slaves), were augmented by both the voluntary ingress of hopeful immigrants seeking a better life and until 1808, by the international slave trade. Geographic expansion occurred in great gulps: in the Louisiana Purchase from France in 1803 (827,000 square miles); in the acquisition of Florida from Spain in 1819–21 (65,750 square miles); in the 1845 annexation of Texas, whose boundaries were disputed but which was a larger territory than the current State of Texas, which is 268,000 square miles; in the settling of the boundaries of the Oregon Territory by treaty with Great Britain in 1846 (286,541 square miles); and in the "Mexican Cession" of 1848 that followed the Mexican War (529,000 square miles). These rapid expansions ultimately undermined and destabilized the uneasy compromises on which the nation's fragile unity had depended, as new territories became first political and ultimately, literal battlegrounds over the boundaries of Slavery.

The first national census, taken in 1790, informs us that the total slave population of the United States—both Southern and Northern—was just under 700,000 people. Although they could not vote, slaves were counted in the census because the House Congressional delegations of all states were inflated by a number proportional to three-fifths of their slave populations. (The "Three Fifths Clause" of the U.S. Constitution (Article I, Section 2), was the first of many onerous compromises made to slaveholding interests on the way to disunion.) New Jersey became the last of the Northern states to enact a gradual abolition of slavery in 1804. [128] However, the importation of slaves into the United States was not banned until January 1, 1808, which was the earliest date allowed by Article I Section 9 of the U.S. Constitution for any Federal action banning the international slave trade. (The exact date set forth in Article I was the subject of an early Southern secession threat. [129]) After this date, interstate sales of slaves from Northern to Southern states continued and even accelerated. By the eve of the Civil War in 1860, 3,954,000 people were living in bondage in fifteen Southern and Border South states, the District of Columbia, and the Federal territories. A handful of slaves were still being held in the "free" states as well.

Viewed as property, these millions of human beings represented an economic resource worth "$3.5 billion in 1860 dollars—more than the value of America's railroads, banks, factories or ships." [130] While slaves grew corn and

wheat as well, and some even worked in mines or in other industries, the most economically important products of slave labor were in five cash crops: cotton and sugar cane in the bulk of the Lower South; cotton and tobacco in the Middle South, tobacco and (mostly well before 1860) indigo in the Border South; and along the South Carolina littoral, often adjacent to malarial swamps that took a terrible toll on the slave laborers, it was rice. "King Cotton" in particular was critical to the textile industries of both England and New England. Cotton was the most critical raw material of the mid-nineteenth-century industrial revolution, analogous to what petroleum would later become in the twentieth century. And in 1860, three-quarters of the world's supply of cotton was produced in the American South! [131]

Owing to the extremely lucrative nature of slave agriculture for its beneficiaries, the antebellum South remained a largely agrarian, mostly preindustrial economy controlled by reactionary slaveholding interests even as the North was rapidly industrializing. Large slaveholders were hostile to the economic and social changes associated with industrial development, because they feared that these changes would undermine their own control by promoting the emergence of a large, educated, and politically powerful urban middle class not tied directly to Slavery. Southern planters thus generally opposed the national improvements and infrastructural investments promoting these developments and the national tariffs created to finance them—tariffs that also raised the cost of the manufactured goods planters had to purchase from outside their region.

In the early Republic a combination of the Three Fifths Clause [132] and occasional Southern secession threats exercised an outsized Southern influence on national politics, especially in matters touching on Slavery. Historian William W. Freehling noted that even by 1860 the slave states, with only 29% of the nation's eligible voters, still controlled 38% of House seats, 47% of Senate seats, and roughly four-tenths of the Presidential Electoral College. [133] Southern political dominance in Washington resulted in the annexation of Texas in 1845 (not to mention the Mexican War that inevitably followed it the next year), and in the Kansas-Nebraska Act of 1854. The latter act repealed the Missouri Compromise of 1820 that prohibited the spread of slavery north of latitude thirty-six degrees thirty minutes. Southern dominance in the national politics of the early Republic is reflected as well in the list of its early presidents (including nine of the first twelve through 1853, who presided over 52 of the Republic's first 64 years), House speakers (40½ of the first 64 years), and Supreme Court Chief Justices (51 of the first 64 years to 1853, and on from there, as Chief Justice Roger Taney, a Marylander from a wealthy slaveholding family, died in office in 1864). [134]

The slaveholding interest's highly leveraged national influence began with its Southern local and regional dominance. While less than a third of Southern households held slaves in the 1850s, [135] a significantly greater proportion of Southern political officeholders held slaves. [136] But then as today, many of the true economic elite preferred to wield political power without exposing themselves to the vicissitudes of public office. Southern slaveholders consolidated and maintained their local and regional dominance not just through holding state offices but through more diverse exercise of their

commanding wealth. These combined means gave slaveholders disproportionate control of all local institutions in most areas: municipal governments, courts, police, press, pulpits, banks, businesses, and schools. In some eastern Southern states this influence was still being abetted in the 1850s by undemocratic statutes lingering from earlier times. These measures included disproportionate apportionments of representation in state houses, property requirements for both voting and office holding, and poll taxes, which disenfranchised many poor whites. Public education was generally opposed in the South, [137] because the elite did not need it and they considered that neither blacks nor inferior whites should have it. When required, neither did large slaveholders shrink from naked, violent intimidation to silence dissent. [138] Thus, a regional minority—Southern slaveholders—within a larger national minority—the white population of the South—often came to dictate policy to an increasingly restive and resentful nation.

Meanwhile, in the North the American Industrial Revolution took off during and after the War of 1812. That revolution grew from seeds planted as early as 1793 when the first successful textile mill opened in Pawtucket, RI, capitalizing on a crucial cost advantage derived from both the cheap price of cotton provided by Southern slave labor and an American technological breakthrough achieved in the same year: the cotton gin. Northern shipping and banking industries fattened on slave-grown cotton alongside New England textile manufacturers, and before 1808, from the slave trade itself. By 1860 Northern creditors held approximately $200,000,000 in Southern debt. [139] However, unlike in the South, Northerners reinvested the indirect profits they derived from slave agriculture in a broad spectrum of new industries. This aggressive expansion created an ever-growing appetite for new roads, bridges, canals, and railroad lines, and for public and private schools to turn out the increasing numbers of educated workers needed to run the Northern industrial engine. Thus, by 1860 the North had 1,300,000 industrial workers, whereas the South had only 110,000. [140]

In the South a different dynamic was unfolding. While the South did build a skeletal rail network in the 1850s and had about 110 public lines operating within the eleven future Confederate states, the North had 14,000 more miles of track than the South when the Civil War began. The two greatest sources of wealth in the antebellum South remained slaves and land. The University of Houston Digital History website informs us that the proportion of the total white population owning slaves declined from about a third in 1850 to less than a fourth by 1860, even as the proportion of slaves in the Southern population had increased. Similarly, in 1860, 17% of the farming population in the rich cotton-growing regions of the South held two-thirds of all acres. As soil erosion and exhaustion diminished the availability of older cotton land, scarcity and heavy demand forced the price of fertile land and slaves to rise beyond the reach of most, and in newer cotton-growing regions, yeomen farmers were pushed off the land as large planters expanded their holdings. In Louisiana, for example, nearly half of all rural white families owned no land.

This concentration of wealth into fewer Southern hands was simultaneously a cause and a consequence of the changing nature of Southern Slavery into a more quasi-industrial and impersonal system characterized by increasing subdivision of labor and scientific management practices. Historian Edward Baptist documents how personalized production quotas for individual slaves were introduced on some large plantations in the southwest, which would slowly be increased to ensure for the owner the absolute maximum of health-destroying physical labor output from each component of his "property." [141] Baptist reported quotas being enforced by measured torture regimens in which the number of lashes inflicted each day was based on the size of the shortfall in a slave's daily quota. The changes in the conditions of Southern slave labor in that period reflected concomitant changes in Northern industrial labor conditions, but they did so in a horrifyingly distorted magnifying mirror. At the same time a large forced migration was taking place in the 1850s, filling Southern roads with coffles of slaves *en route* from the depleted soils of the Tidewater to the more profitable slave fields farther south and west. Thus, the slave population was shifting geographically precisely toward the areas where the new harsher, more brutal control practices were spreading, as it was shifting demographically to become more concentrated in fewer, more powerful hands. In the process, enslaved spouses, parents, and children often were cruelly separated, and little slave communities were everywhere torn apart. A small-to-medium-sized slaveholder often knew all of his slaves by name and perhaps something about each one. Large slaveholders, many of whom were absentees who left the management of their estates to overseers, mostly did not.

Thus, while white Americans in both the North and South continued to share in the tainted fruits of slave agriculture, the two regional cultures were moving apart from each other and toward confrontation. Many Northern whites who cared little about the plight of Southern slaves increasingly came to despise the institution of Slavery, both because of its corrosive and coercive effects on white national democratic institutions, and because of its intrinsic devaluation of the dignity of free labor. The latter sentiment was expressed most eloquently in 1847 by Congressional Representative David Wilmot of Pennsylvania, no friend to Southern slaves. Arguing on the floor of the House for his proposal, the "Wilmot Proviso," to ban the expansion of Slavery into the lands that the United States expected to seize from Mexico in the war stemming from the recent annexation of Texas, he said:

> I make no war upon the South nor upon slavery in the South. I have no squeamish sensitiveness upon the subject of slavery, nor morbid sympathy for the slave. I plead the cause of the rights of white freemen. I would preserve for free white labor a fair country, a rich inheritance, where the sons of toil, of my own race and own color, can live without the disgrace which association with negro slavery brings upon free labor. I stand for the inviolability of free territory. It shall remain free, so far as my voice or vote can aid in the preservation of its character. [142]

Repeated secession threats and encroachments on white democratic norms had fanned Northern resentment in the decades leading up to the Civil War. Among these affronts were the Nullification Controversy (1832); the Post Office Censorship Controversy (1835); the Congressional Gag Rule Controversies (1836–44); The

Fugitive Slave Law of 1850; and the aforementioned repeal of the Missouri Compromise of 1820 by the passage of the Kansas-Nebraska Act (1854). Most egregious among these many insults to Northern democratic sensibilities was the especially reprehensible Fugitive Slave Law (FSL). This bill forced Northerners to regard slaves as not merely inferior humans, which most unfortunately did, but as mere inhuman property. The act criminalized even the most minimal humanitarian aid or comfort provided by Northerners to an escaped slave, and it deprived alleged escaped slaves of any vestige of due process of law. Worse in many eyes, it empowered slave catchers effectively to impress Northerners into posses for the purpose of capturing and returning escaped slaves, under threat of punishment with huge fines for noncompliance. (The fines of up to $1,000 allowed by the FSL amounted to over three years' pay for a typical wage-earning tradesman.) Southerners, in their turn, were deeply embittered over the subsequent passage by nine Northern states of "personal liberty laws," which exempted their citizens from the onerous requirements of the FSL.

In the midst of this rising tempo of provocations and irritants, a voice of moral condemnation—that of "radical" abolitionism—began to be heard in the North, first faintly, and then more insistently. [143] Abolitionist activities ranged from sermonizing, pamphleting, publishing, and political agitation to more direct measures associated with occasional dramatic rescues of fugitives, and the Underground Railroad, which provided courageous covert assistance to fleeing slaves. [144] Prominent in abolitionist ranks were several self-emancipated former slaves (**FIGURES 157–159**). Among these were the great orator and writer, Frederick Douglass; the intrepid Harriet Tubman, who personally helped rescue seventy families from Slavery in the course of thirteen missions into the South; and Isabelle Baumfree (Sojourner Truth), a tireless and passionate advocate for abolition. (Douglass and Sojourner Truth also were early advocates for women's rights, seeing the oppression of women and that of people of color as intimately related issues.) Between June 1851 and April 1852, Harriet Beecher Stowe, an activist from a prominent white abolitionist family, published a novel in serial form in *National Era Magazine*. The novel was published in book form in March 1852 under the title, *Uncle Tom's Cabin*. Stowe's searing moral indictment of Slavery sold over a million copies, including over 300,000 the first year, galvanizing abolitionist sentiment in the North and provoking bitter, outraged reactions in the South, where the book was banned. Slaveholders' fears were stoked not only by abolitionist agitation but by slave resistance. The resistance of the oppressed took the form of a slow leak of escaping slaves (mostly from Border and Middle South states), occasional sabotage, and even more occasional, but often exaggerated, accounts of domestic poisonings. In planters' minds the memory of the brief but violent Denmark Vesey and Nat Turner slave revolts of the 1820s and 1830s also lingered.

In this same period the leadership of both regional sections increasingly understood that Slavery needed to expand westward with the growing nation if it was to survive at all. [145] Slaveholders needed the expansion economically because the soil in many of the older slaveholding areas in the East had reached or was approaching exhaustion, [146] and because slave-

157. Frederick Douglass was a tireless abolitionist activist, author, and publisher. Although the White House was built by black slaves and maintained by black servants, Douglass became the first black leader to address a president within its walls. He was the only African American to attend the Seneca Falls Convention, a gathering of women's rights activists in New York, in 1848. In the powerful speech he delivered there he said, "In this denial of the right to participate in government, not merely the degradation of woman and the perpetuation of a great injustice happens, but the maiming and repudiation of one-half of the moral and intellectual power of the government of the world." *Image from the Library of Congress.*

holders understood that their commanding voice in national affairs would be submerged by other burgeoning economic interests unless they could share in the opportunities of the West. By 1860 the size of the white population of the Tidewater (primarily the coastal regions of Virginia, North Carolina, and Maryland)

158. Harriet Tubman was a fearless practical abolitionist. She risked her life to lead hundreds of family members and other slaves from the plantation system to freedom through an elaborate secret network of safe houses. She also aided the Union Army during the war, working as a spy behind Confederate lines. After the Civil War Tubman dedicated her life to helping impoverished former slaves and the elderly. *Image from the Library of Congress.*

159. Born Isabella Baumfree ca. 1797, Sojourner Truth devoted her life to the abolitionist cause and helped to recruit black troops for the Union Army. Her most famous speech, "Ain't I a Woman?" was delivered extemporaneously in 1851 at the Ohio Women's Rights Convention. Over the years her activism expanded to embrace many other causes, including prison reform, women's property rights, and universal suffrage. *Image from the Library of Congress.*

had been stagnant for over a decade, and many eastern slaveholding planters were holding on economically only by "growing" slaves for sale further south and west. [147] A rational fear also was growing that without a western "escape valve," slaveholders could one day find themselves with more slaves' mouths to feed than fertile land for slaves' hands to work, a prospect that threatened both financial ruin and social instability for the white South.

The political need for the planter class to expand its dominion westward was equally as urgent. Because the free states had enjoyed a greater rate of increase in population since the nation's founding (when Virginia had both the greatest slave and free populations among the thirteen original states), the South had seen its

share of representation in the House and the Electoral College diminish. In the 1850s, even a monolithic Southern voting block—on occasions when that could be mustered—required Northern allies in the House and Senate to dictate policy. These allies would be few and far between in the future, because the National Democratic Party, long the guardian of slaveholder interests, had broken apart along regional lines.

Events began sliding toward a crisis in 1850, after the Mexican Cession of 1846–48. In 1850 California was admitted as a free state without a compensating admission of a new slave state. The question of the future of Slavery then acquired incandescent urgency in 1854 with the passage of the Kansas-Nebraska Act, which left it to the settlers of those territories to decide whether their lands would ultimately enter the Union as free states or slave states. Hostile groups of free soil and slaveholding settlers then rushed into Kansas, hoping to bring the territory into the Union as either a free, or a slave state. This abdication of Federal responsibility led to "Bleeding Kansas," a protracted violent confrontation between 1855 and 1861—essentially, a two-sided guerrilla war—in the Kansas Territory. In 1857 any hope that Congress might end or mediate this dispute was snatched away by the Supreme Court. The Taney court passed one of the worst and most fateful decisions in the Supreme Court's checkered history. In the case of *Dred Scott v. Sandford,* the court ruled that: (1) a person born a slave could never, under any circumstances, become a U.S. citizen; and (2) the Federal government had no authority to regulate Slavery in the Federal territories. (Seizing the opportunity created by a case brought by a slave trader against the State of New York, Taney was planning to go much further when the secession crisis intervened. He had already drafted a decision that would have declared all Northern state laws banning slavery unconstitutional!) [148]

In that same year of 1857 a fraudulently elected proslavery convention in Kansas drafted the LeCompton Constitution, aiming to have Kansas enter the Union as a slave state. The repeated failure of President James Buchanan to force its approval through Congress over the objections of the majority of Kansas voters elicited a recurring chorus of Southern condemnations. (The eastern portion of the Kansas Territory ultimately was admitted to the Union as the free state of Kansas on January 29, 1861. But by then six Southern states

had already seceded, and Texas followed two days later.) In October of 1859, while the bloodshed in Kansas was continuing, the abolitionist John Brown's ill-fated raid on the Federal arsenal in Harpers Ferry, VA, intended to incite a slave rebellion, seemed to many Southerners to definitively confirm their worst fears about Northern intentions.

As foretold in 1850 by the late John C. Calhoun, the presidential election of 1860 was the final spark that ignited the conflagration. Leading the only successful third party insurgency in American history, a gangly frontier lawyer and former Congressman armed with a paradoxical mix of homespun philosophy, folksy humor, and keen, closely reasoned arguments captured 39.1% of the popular vote (though he was not even on the ballot in several Southern states) in a four-way race and a victory in the Electoral College, to become the 16th president of the un-United States. While there is ample evidence that Abraham Lincoln despised Slavery his entire life, he could see no authority in the Constitution to abolish it. Thus, for both principled and pragmatic reasons, Lincoln had run on a policy of containing Slavery within its existing borders. Slavery having been abolished in the Northern states, he had every reason to hope that if Slavery's westward expansion could be blocked, then time was on his side, and the "peculiar institution" might die a natural death without need of Federal intervention. As early as 1844, when a candidate for Congress from Illinois, Lincoln wrote to a friend:

> I hold it to be a paramount duty of us in the free states, due to the Union of the states, and perhaps to Liberty itself (paradox though it may seem) to let the slavery of the other states

alone, while on the other hand, I hold it to be equally clear, that we should never knowingly lend ourselves directly or indirectly to prevent that slavery from dying a natural death—to find new places for it to live in, when it can no longer exist in the old. [149]

For their part, secessionist leaders agreed with this same analysis that if Slavery could not expand, it would die. Lincoln's fondest hope was the "Slave Power's" greatest fear. Neither did Southern slaveholders relish existing as a despised and retrograde minority within a national government and polity that they were accustomed to having dominated. So, despite the formidable obstacle erected by the Supreme Court to any practical implementation of Lincoln's containment platform, Southern disunionists rolled the dice and gambled on secession before the odds against them grew worse.

On December 20, 1860, South Carolina, ever the most centrifugal state, and the only state in which the majority of white households owned slaves, became the first state to secede. The other six states of the Lower South, which were those with the largest relative slave populations after South Carolina—Mississippi, Florida, Alabama, Georgia, Louisiana, and Texas—quickly followed suit. The first shot of the Civil War was fired on January 9, 1861, when the ship *Star of the West,* which was attempting to resupply the Federal garrison at Fort Sumter in Charleston Harbor, was forced to withdraw by South Carolina shore batteries. As the inept outgoing president, James Buchanan, fiddled while Rome burned, the Southern states seized sixteen Federal forts, six Federal arsenals, five Federal barracks or camps, two Federal mints, the Pensacola Navy Yard, a lighthouse, ships,

customs houses, post offices, and numerous other articles of Federal property throughout the Lower South. [150] They had also organized numerous new local militias and had approximately 100,000 men under arms. On February 8, 1861, the original seven seceding states formed the Confederate States of America, though its legitimacy was never formally recognized by any other government on earth. Twenty-four days later, Abraham Lincoln was inaugurated on March 4. Then on April 12, Confederate batteries opened fire on Fort Sumter after the Federal garrison commander, Major Robert Anderson, refused to yield the fort. With ammunition running low, his food exhausted, his fortification in ruins, and no hope of reinforcement or even resupply, Anderson lowered his flag and surrendered on April 15, 1861. The Civil War had begun in earnest.

At the start of the war the Federal army had numbered only about 16,000 men; many of whom were posted out west on garrison duty, and about a third of whose officers and some enlisted men resigned and returned to their Southern homes by the eve of war. To meet the emergency, on April 15, 1861, President Lincoln issued a call for 75,000 volunteers to come to the defense of the Union. (Those who answered Lincoln's initial call later came to be known as the "First Defenders.") Middle South leaders by then understood that events had tied the survival of Slavery in their own states inextricably to the survival of the Confederacy. Moreover, they understood that once the Union chose to fight unilateral secession by force of arms, the remaining slave states within the Union could never again use secession threats to protect Slavery in their own states. They understood that once the CSA was defeated, the secession option would be permanently closed to them. Thus, seeing that war was now certain and imminent, the somewhat less enslaved states of the Middle South—Virginia, Arkansas, Tennessee, and North Carolina—cast their lots with their more zealous Lower South neighbors and seceded. The least enslaved Border South states of Maryland, Delaware, Kentucky, and Missouri remained loyal—if only just—even after hostilities began. In the end, every state with a relative slave population of at least 25% seceded, and every state with a relative slave population less than 25% remained loyal. But even in the seceding states, local regions unsuitable for large plantation agriculture, such as the central hills region of Texas, the "Free State of Jones" in Jones County, MS, the "Free State of Winston," in Winston County, AL, Appalachian Tennessee and Georgia, and of course, the western counties of Virginia, were strongholds of Unionist sentiment. Some remained so throughout the conflict. (Unionist sentiment was strong in North Carolina at least initially. In that state's secession referendum of January 29, 1861, before the attack on Fort Sumter, Unionists defeated the measure by about 640 votes out of 94,000 cast.) In all, nearly 116,000 Southern white Unionists from the seceded states fought for the Union in the war that followed, and at least a battalion served in the Union Army from every seceded state except South Carolina. [151] In the loyal Border South states, both sides recruited many men.

Not all soldiers served by choice. While volunteers flocked to the colors on both sides, some on either side had little choice but to serve. Before the end, conscription laws were enacted by both the Confederacy (April 1862)

and the Union (March 1863). In the North, conscription generally kicked in when a municipality failed to fill its assigned recruitment quota. If called upon to serve, an affluent Northern man could usually opt out by paying a fee of $300 (about a year's pay for a typical wage-earning Northern tradesman in 1860) or by paying a substitute to serve in his place. But while some Northern men of means used their wealth to avoid military service, others used their wealth to make themselves officers by raising and equipping their own units. A much greater number of Northern men, who could have avoided serving, simply did their duty and entered the ranks. In the end the vast majority of Union soldiers remained volunteers. In the South, male military service was closer to being universal, with one irksome exception. Some 75% of able-bodied white men in the Confederate states between the ages of eighteen and forty-five wore a uniform at some point during the war. The irksome exception to compulsory service was that many affluent Southern men were excused from service without even needing to pay a fee. Beginning in October of 1863 a wealthy planter could exempt one white man, including himself, from military service for every twenty slaves he owned—a privilege others resentfully termed the *twenty negro law*, or cruder words to the same effect.

Fighting to Defend Slavery— In the Secessionists' Own Words!

To be sure, the South went to war for a combination of inextricably linked economic, political and cultural reasons. But at the base of all these reasons' tangled, intertwined roots nestled John Chapman's serpent: Slavery. First and foremost, secessionist leaders committed their states to war in an effort to preserve the basis of the economic system that provided the region's wealth and its leaders with their positions and status. From the American Revolution to 1861 the prevailing Southern white viewpoint concerning Slavery gradually but relentlessly had transformed from one of an unfortunate legacy and transitory evil to that of an essential, permanent good, and even a divine blessing. The nation's Founders, most of whom, including many slaveholders, considered slavery an embarrassment, carefully avoided use of the words *slave* or *slavery* in the U.S. Constitution, although that document clearly recognized the institution as lawful in three places. However, by 1861 most Southern leaders could not even imagine the South without the institution of Slavery at its core. Thus, on March 21, 1861, newly installed CSA Vice President Alexander Stephens declared, in his "Cornerstone Speech":

> The new [Confederate] Constitution has put at rest forever all the agitating questions relating to our peculiar institutions—African slavery as it exists among us—the proper status of the negro in our form of civilization. This was the immediate cause of the late rupture and present revolution. Jefferson, in his forecast, had anticipated this, as the 'rock upon which the old Union would split.' …
>
> Our new government is founded upon exactly the opposite ideas [than that all men are created equal]; its foundations are laid, its cornerstone rests, upon the great truth that … slavery, subordination to the superior race, is his [the African slave's] natural and normal condition. [152]

Lower on the social ladder, many humble white Southern yeomen, who owned no slaves, lived off or depended in one way or another on the slave economy, likewise identified with it, and aspired to one day own slaves themselves. Slaveless white farmers often rented slaves from their wealthier neighbors seasonally, and most depended on the local infrastructures that were built and maintained by slaves or were supported by the profits from slave labor. While often resenting planter aristocrats for their arrogance and contempt of lesser whites, poor Southern whites nevertheless generally participated in the patrols that captured runaways and returned them to their masters, consoling themselves that at least they were better off than slaves. For as historian Chandra Manning argues persuasively, Southern Slavery was not just an economic interest. Much to the contrary, it pervaded every aspect of Southern culture:

> [Southerners thought] Slavery was worth fighting for because it served many fundamentally important purposes that white men considered vital to themselves and their families, whether or not they owned slaves. Black slavery in the antebellum south buttressed the ideals of white liberty and equality. It stabilized an otherwise precarious social structure. Slavery undergirded white Southerners convictions of their own superior moral orthodoxy. In addition, it anchored the individual identity of white Southern men as men in a firm conception of their rights, duties, and social roles, and it intertwined with the Southern notion of honor. Finally, slavery supplied an unambiguous mechanism of race control in a region where 40 percent of the population was black. Nonslavehold-

160. The quintessential Southern Unionist, Virginia-born Major General George Henry Thomas, the "Rock of Chickamauga." One of the Union's best field commanders, Thomas was underappreciated by his superiors, who sometimes called him "Old Slow Trot." He was disowned by his own Southern slaveholding family, who probably called him "traitor," if they spoke of him at all, but he was beloved of his men, who called him "Old Pap," and he was lionized by the Northern public and pro-war press, who called him first, the "Rock of Chickamauga," and later the "Sledge of Nashville." *Image from the Library of Congress.*

161. General Thomas' statue in Thomas Circle in the U.S. capitol, at the intersection of Massachusetts Avenue NW and Vermont Avenue NW. Long may it stand. *Image licensed under the Creative Commons Attribution-Share Alike 3.0 Unported license. Dowloaded June 10, 2018 and retouched.*

ing Confederate soldiers' willingness to fight for slavery grew from a much deeper source than the calculation of economic interest … It grew from white Southern men's gut-level conviction that survival—of themselves, their families, and the social order—depended on slavery's continued existence. [153]

Thus, in the Southern political discourse and rhetoric of the day, any perceived threat to

Slavery was a threat to Southern independence and white liberty. The white antebellum South was enthralled to Slavery even as much as its slaves were bound to their masters. In their declarations of causes for secession or in other contemporaneous documents, every state that seceded before the beginning of armed hostilities at Fort Sumter and which stated their reasons for secession, identified Slavery or rights pertaining directly to the protection and portability of slave property as either the only cause

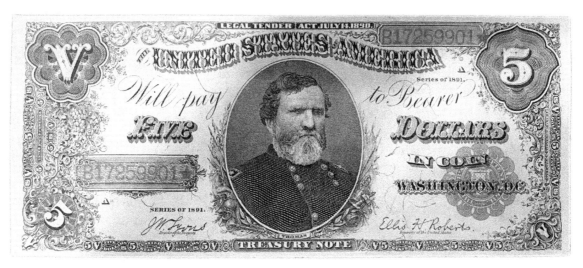

162. An all-too-rare U.S. $5 bill honoring General Thomas, issued ca. 1890. *Image from www.antiquemoney.com/five-dollar-bills-from-the-1890s/ (June 10, 2018)*

or the first cause for their fateful rebellion. The first substantive paragraph in the Declaration of Causes for Secession of Mississippi, Confederate President Jefferson Davis's home state, is wonderfully definitive on the preservation of Slavery as the singular and sufficient motivation behind Mississippi's act of secession:

> Our position is thoroughly identified with the institution of slavery—the greatest material interest of the world. Its labor supplies the product, which constitutes by far the largest and most important portions of commerce of the earth. These products are peculiar to the climate verging on the tropical regions, and by an imperious law of nature, none but the black race can bear exposure to the tropical sun. These products have become necessities of the world, and a blow at slavery is a blow at commerce and civilization. That blow has been long aimed at the institution, and was at the point of reaching its consummation. There was no choice left us but submission to the mandates of abolition, or a dissolution of the Union, whose principles had been subverted to work out our ruin.

The Tragic Choice for Southern Federal Soldiers

Many Southerners who had not favored secession before hostilities began bowed to the inevitable when war came. Professional soldiers like Robert E. Lee, James Longstreet, and numerous other Southern career military officers had sworn oaths to defend the U.S. Constitution. Thus Southern secession confronted them with a tragic choice between loyalty to country and fidelity to their oaths versus loyalty to home state and family. Most, like Lee and Longstreet, chose their home states and families. This much had been foreseen, and counted on, by the "fire-eaters" who had pushed the South over the cliff into war.

But a few outstanding patriotic Southern spirits like Major General George Henry Thomas honored their oaths to country.

During the second bloodiest battle of the war, Chickamauga, things went badly for the Union. The Federal Army of the Cumberland, already in retreat, was threatened with a full-blown disastrous rout. That was when General Thomas (**FIGURES 160–162**), a Virginian from a slaveholding family, tenaciously held his position on a small rise in the path of Confederate General James Longstreet's advancing corps. After a third of the Union army, including its commanding general, had been driven from the field, Thomas took command of the army and stood "like a rock" [154] athwart Longstreet's path atop Horseshoe Ridge that day and earned for himself an admiring sobriquet. Thomas's resolute stand attracted the remnants of other retreating Federal units to his lines, and there he stopped Longstreet's advance. In answer to the South's "Stonewall Jackson," the Union thereaf-ter had its "Rock of Chickamauga." The Union owed its salvation in no small part to this and other Southern-born patriots.

Conclusion

It is fitting to accord the noble statesman, author, abolitionist, suffragist, and champion of all oppressed peoples, Frederick Douglass, the last word in this section. The quote chosen is from an 1877 essay in which he incorporated a well-known passage from Lincoln's second inaugural address:

> There was a right side and a wrong side in the late war, which no sentiment ought to cause us to forget, and while today we should have malice toward none, and charity toward all, it is no part of our duty to confound right with wrong. [155]

NOTES AND REFERENCES

1. Wells, Cheryl A. *Civil War Time: Temporality and Identity in America*. Athens, GA: University of Georgia Press, 2005.

2. Harrold, Michael C. *American Watchmaking: A Technical History 1850–1930*. NAWCC Bulletin Supplement Number 14 (Spring 1984).

3. McIntyre, Thomas P. "Waltham Watch and the Civil War: The impact of the Civil War on the fortunes of the Waltham Watch Company." *mcintyre.com/present/WalthamGoesToWar.pdf*

4. Alexis McCrossen, *Marking Modern Times: A History of Clocks, Watches, and Other Timekeepers in American Life*, University of Chicago Press, 2013. On page 73, McCrossen states that in 1865 alone, the last year of the Civil War, the Swiss exported 226,000 watches to the United States, more than the cumulative output of American watch manufacturers to that date. She states that the British exported about 30,000 watches a year into the United States throughout the war, for a five-year total about equal to the cumulative output of all domestic makers in the same period. McCrossen quotes from the famous speech by Edouard Favre-Perret delivered at the Primary College at La Chaux-de-Fonds, Switzerland, on November 14, 1876, after his return from the Centennial International Exhibition in Philadelphia, and his tour of the Waltham watch factory earlier that year.

5. NPR. *Professor: Civil War Death Toll May Be Really Off*. npr.org/2012/05/29/153937334/professor-civil-war-death-toll-may-be-really-off

6. The "Gettysburg Address," the most famous and arguably important speech in American history, delivered on November 19, 1863, at the newly dedicated Soldier's National Cemetery in Gettysburg, PA, near the site of the Civil War's most famous battle. According to *abrahamlincolnonline.org/lincoln/speeches/gettysburg.htm*, "There are five known copies of the speech in Lincoln's handwriting, each with a slightly different text, and named for the people who first received them: Nicolay, Hay, Everett, Bancroft and Bliss. Two copies apparently were written before delivering the speech, one of which probably was the reading copy. The remaining ones were produced months later for soldier benefit events. Despite widely-circulated stories to the contrary, the president did not dash off a copy aboard a train to Gettysburg. Lincoln carefully prepared his major speeches in advance; his steady, even script in every manuscript is consistent with a firm writing surface, not the notoriously bumpy Civil War-era trains. Additional versions of the speech appeared in newspapers of the era, feeding modern-day confusion about the authoritative text."

7. In late 1860 the inside game still had plenty of life and possibilities left within it for slaveholders to defend their interests. Up until the very moment when slaveholders finally took the plunge over the cliff and drove secession resolutions through the Lower South, all the formidable checks and balances of American Democracy were still at their disposal. The Taney Supreme Court was dominated by Southerners friendly to slaveholding interests; Southern Congressional and Senate delegations were still potent, if no longer dominant; and every Southern senator enjoyed effectively unlimited filibuster powers to block disfavored legislation. (The Senate did not pass its first cloture rule until 1917.) The Dred Scott decision of 1857 would have made it very difficult for Lincoln to have implemented his stated confinement policy for Slavery, even with congressional majorities to command (which he did not have!); the same Taney Court had nixed the North's muscular personal liberty laws in 1859, and even more pro-slavery rulings may well have been coming. Likewise, a president who had just won a four-way election with only just over 39% of the popular vote wielded no overwhelming congressional majorities or popular mandates. Only by vacating their congressional seats and giving the North a compelling reason to end Slavery could secessionists bring about the very calamity they had intended to prevent. That's just what they did.

8. In a five-to-four decision in 1873 the Supreme Court severely undercut the "Equal Protection" clause of the recently enacted Fourteenth Amendment to the U.S. Constitution by ruling that the amendment only protected rights of Federal citizenship and not state citizenship. At the time, Federal citizenship rights were limited to travel between states and use of the nation's navigable waterways. This reactionary, minimalist interpretation of the Fourteenth Amendment negated its protections for citizens against encroachments on civil rights by state governments. Once Reconstruction had ended and white supremacists ruled the South once more, this decision left black communities defenseless against state and local government oppression.

9. Foner, Eric. *America's Unfinished Revolution.* New York, NY: Harper Perennial, 2011.

10. Gallagher, Gary W. *The Union War.* Cambridge, MA: Harvard University Press, 2011.

11. Manning, Chandra. *What This Cruel War Was Over.* New York, NY: Random House Vintage Civil War Library, 2007:39–40.

12. The U.S. Treasury paid for the Louisiana Purchase with $15,000,000 (68,000,000 francs) in Federal funds in 1803. The Federal government effectively purchased Florida from Spain for $5,000,000 in 1819, also with Federal funds, when it paid for the damage done by U.S. citizens there. The Federal army paid in a different currency—blood—when in 1815 the 7th and 44th U.S. Infantry, the 1st U.S. Dragoons, and a contingent of U.S. Marines helped defend New Orleans from British Invaders. In 1835 Congress approved $5,500,000 in Federal funds to effect the removal of Cherokee Indians from their ancestral lands in Georgia. In 1836 the Federal government agreed to pay the Chickasaw $3,000,000 for their lands in Mississippi, Alabama, Kentucky, and Tennessee. The Seminole Wars in Florida (1816 intermittently to 1858) cost the Federal Treasury some $20,000,000, not to mention the Federal army blood that flowed along with that money. All of these expenditures were subsidized by tariffs on imported goods. Perhaps that's why about a third of the South voted in Congress with two-thirds of the North in most of the tariff debates. It is also worth noting that the secession declarations of the five states that issued them altogether mentioned tariffs exactly once. In that one instance the State of Georgia's declaration concluded that the matter of tariffs had been permanently settled for fifteen years by the Act of 1846. Indeed, tariff rates on dutiable items had fallen almost continuously from 1846 to 1861. The Civil War was not about tariffs.

13. While there was no certainty that Southerners in the seceded states would renege on all or part of their massive financial obligations to Northern investors (see REF. 120), many of those same Northern investors would have remembered how they and their predecessors periodically had reneged on or swindled their way out of massive foreign debts themselves. Thus, Northern investors reasonably feared that the opportunity to repudiate their Northern debts with impunity might have been a major unstated motivation for unilateral secession in the first place. Indeed, many Southerners

famously had skipped out on their debts by interposing a national boundary between themselves and their creditors once before. Especially after the financial Panic of 1819, when Texas was part of Mexico, the phrase "Gone to Texas" had become so ubiquitous in the Lower South that it became commonly short-handed as "GTT."

14. Glatthaar, Joseph T. *Soldiering in the Army of Northern Virginia: A Statistical Portrait of the Troops Who Served under Robert E. Lee.* Chapel Hill, NC: University of North Carolina Press, 2011:154.

15. Noe, Kenneth W. *Reluctant Rebels: The Confederates Who Joined the Army after 1861.* New ed. Chapel Hill, NC: University of North Carolina Press, May 14, 2010.

16. McPherson, James M. *For Cause & Comrades: Why Men Fought in the Civil War.* Oxford, UK: Oxford Press, 1997:117.

17. McPherson, James M. *For Cause & Comrades: Why Men Fought in the Civil War.* Oxford, UK: Oxford Press, 1997:118.

18. Manning, Chandra. *What This Cruel War Was Over.* New York, NY: Random House Vintage Civil War Library, 2007:21.

19. A letter written by "Enlisted Soldier, Third Wis.," to the *Wisconsin State Journal*, October 1862, Quiner Papers, Reel I, vol. I, p. 176, citation in Manning, 39. (See reference 11 herein.)

20. Civil War Letters of Major Charles Harvey Brewster, Adjutant, 10th Massachusetts Infantry.

21. Sergeant Cyrus Boyd, 5th Iowa Infantry, February 10, 1863, cited in Manning.

22. After the war, the line in the song, "Battle Hymn of the Republic," was changed in most renditions from "Let us die to make men free" to "Let us live to make men free."

23. McPherson, James M. *For Cause & Comrades: Why Men Fought in the Civil War.* Oxford, UK: Oxford Press, 1997:123.

24. White, Jonathan W. *Emancipation, the Union Army, and the Reelection of Abraham Lincoln.* Baton Rouge, LA: Louisiana State University Press, 2014. Lincoln's more precise portion of the soldier vote was 78%.

25. Slotkin, Richard. *No Quarter: The Battle of the Crater, 1864.* New York, NY: Random House, 2009:11.

26. Based on data from the 1860 U.S. Census, about 53% of the American workforce was engaged in agriculture (40% in the North, and 84% in the South). Because there were about 3,950,000 slaves in the United States in 1860 and most were engaged in agriculture, that means about 44.5% of the *free* labor force was involved in agriculture nationwide. Given initial Union and Confederate free populations of 21,500,000 and 5,500,000, respectively, with approximately 3,500,000 of the nation's 3,950,000 slaves living within the Confederacy, this means about 39% of the North's free labor force and about 66% of the South's free labor force were engaged in agriculture in early 1861. For comparison, the industrial workforces in the North and South were 1,300,000 and 110,000 out of total free populations of 18,500,000 and 5,500,000, respectively. About 26% of the population, which probably included the majority of wage-earning laborers, factory workers, and tradesmen, as well as fee-charg-

ing professionals, lived in cities. Thus, on the eve of war a significant portion of the U.S. population, especially in the South, still operated within a primarily barter economy.

27. Olmsted, Frederick Law. *The Cotton Kingdom: A Traveler's Observations on Cotton and Slavery in the American Slave States.* New York, NY: Mason Brothers, 1861:158.

28. Smith, Mark M. *Mastered by the Clock: Time, Slavery and Freedom in the American South.* Chapel Hill, NC: University of North Carolina Press, 1997:2.

29. George Oscar French Civil War Letters, 1862—MSA 414, in a letter dated August 28, 1862, posted from Camp Bradley, Brattleboro, Vermont, *vermonthistory.org/documents/transcriptions/french/french1862.pdf*, page 5.

30. McCrossen, REF. 4, Chapter 2, page 60.

31. Cater, Douglas John. *As It Was: Reminiscences of a Soldier of the Third Texas Cavalry and the Nineteenth Louisiana Infantry,* State House Press, 2007; quoted in Wells.

32. Wells, Cheryl A. *Civil War Time: Temporality and Identity in America.* Athens, GA: University of Georgia Press, 2005:14.

33. McCrossen, REF. 4, page 68, "If imperfect instruments, timepieces were nevertheless considered vital to the conduct of the war from the draftee and the West Point general alike."

34. Trudeau, Noah A. *Gettysburg: A Testing of Courage.* New York, NY: Harper Collins, 2002:282.

35. Wells, Cheryl A. *Civil War Time: Temporality and Identity in America.* Athens, GA: University of Georgia Press, 2005:57.

36. Union Major General August V. Kautz. *The Company Clerk.* Philadelphia, PA: J. B. Lippincott & Co., circa 1863.

37. Sala, G. A. *My Diary in America in the Midst of War.* London, UK: Tinsley Brothers, 1865.

38. Mellen, Paul. "Major Jonathan Ladd, Paymaster, Story in Time," *NAWCC Bulletin,* Nov/Dec 2013.

39. "I'm All Right Yet," Letters from the Civil War, Sgt. James C. Beitel, 153rd Regiment, Pennsylvania Volunteers, 1862-1863, *htdocs.com/docs/James_Beitel/*

40. McCrossen, REF. 4, page 70.

41. Civil War History: Death of McPherson. *battlefields.org/learn/articles/death-mcpherson*

42. Krick, Robert K. Armistead and Garnett: The Parallel Lives of Two Virginia Soldiers. In: Gary W. Gallagher, ed. *The Third Day at Gettysburg & Beyond.* Chapel Hill, NC: University of North Carolina Press, 1994):122; and Lt. Col. Edmund Rice (19th Massachusetts Infantry). In: *Battles and Leaders of the Civil War,* vol 3, p. 388.

43. Chaffin, Tom. *The H. L. Hunley: The Secret Hope of the Confederacy.* New York, NY: Hill and Wang, 2010.

44. Sears, Stephen W. *Gettysburg.* New York, NY: First Mariner Books, 2004:165 and subsequent pages.

45. September 23, 2018 Jones and Horan Auction, Lot Number 110: *jones-horan.hibid.com/catalog/142459/-live-webcast-horology--jewelry-and-portrait-miniatures-/?cpage=3*

46. Loomes, Brian. *Watchmakers & Clockmakers of the World*. Vol. 2. London, UK: N.A.G. Press, Ltd., 1976 (1978 reprint).

47. *Sons of Union Veterans of the Civil War. suvcw.org/past/edwinruthvenpeckens.htm*

48. Bates, Samuel P. *History of Pennsylvania Volunteers, 1861–5*. Vol. II, Harrisburg, PA: B. Singerly, State Printer, 1869.

49. Luzerne in the Civil War—History of the Fifty-Second Regiment. In: *History of Luzerne, Lackawanna and Wyoming Counties, PA, with Illustrations, and Biographical Sketches of Some of Their Prominent Men and Pioneers*. New York, NY: W. W. Munsell & Co., 1880,

50. Mott, Smith B. ed. *The Campaigns of the Fifty-Second Regiment Pennsylvania Volunteer Infantry First Known as "The Luzerne Regiment" Being the Record of Nearly Four Years' Continuous Service, from October 7, 1861, to July 12, 1865, in the War for the Suppression of the Rebellion*. Philadelphia, J. B. Lippincott Co., 1911.

51. Although it may be surprising to many readers, it was a common practice in American armies before and during the Civil War for enlisted men to elect their own line officers (i.e., Lieutenants and Captains).

52. *www.gentlemansgazette.com/iwc-an-american-swiss-brand/*

53. *forums.watchuseek.com/f11/standard-french-swiss-lepine-key-wound-calibers-19th-century-4274666.html*

54. Treasurer's report for 1863, American Watch Company records.

55. *americanhistory.si.edu/collections/search/object/nmah_1050581* and also in Stephens, Carlene, *On Time: How America has Learned to Live by the Clock*, Bulfinch Press (2002)

56. Price, Ron. *Origins of the Waltham Model 57: Evolution of the First Successful Industrialized Watch*. *NAWCC Bulletin* Special Order Supplement Number 7, 2005.

57. Geller, Clint B. *A Study of E. Howard & Co, Watchmaking Innovations: 1858–1875*. *NAWCC Bulletin* Special Order Supplement Number 6, 2005.

58. Clare, William Keating. Durham, NC: 9th NY State Militia (83rd NY Infantry), Papers, 1863, Special Collections, Duke University Libraries, Letter to William, Gettysburg Battlefield, July 5, 1863.

59. Nevin, John I. Pittsburgh, PA: Papers, Box 1, Folder 4, Library and Archives Division, Historical Society of Western Pennsylvania, diary entry of July 3.

60. Guelzo, Allen C. *Fateful Lightning*. Oxford, UK: Oxford University Press, 2012:275.

61. Gerald, Judge G. B. The Battle of Gettysburg. *Waco Daily Times-Herald*, July 3, 1913. Robert L. Brake Collection, U.S. Army Military History Institute, Carlisle Barracks, PA, Major G. B. Gerald, 18th Mississippi Infantry.

62. Price, Ron. *Origins of the Waltham Model 57: Evolution of the First Successful Industrialized Watch*. *NAWCC Bulletin* Special Order Supplement Number 7, 2005:12–13 and references therein.

63. Ehrhardt, Roy. *Encyclopedia and Price Guide, Volume I: American Pocket Watches*. Heart of America Press, 1982:95.

64. Civil War History: Military Pay. *civilwar.org/learn/articles/military-pay*

65. U.S. National Park Service. *nps.gov/civilwar/facts.htm*

66. The man to whom this famous quote is attributed was Sir David Lionel Goldsmid-Stern-Salomons. Salomons was the preeminent twentieth-century authority on the life and work of Abraham-Louis Breguet (1747–1823) and the foremost collector of Breguet timepieces of all time. A barrister, philanthropist, member of parliament and founder of the English Society of Engineers, Salomons was far from alone in his admiration for Breguet's work. Arthur Wellesley, the 1st Duke of Wellington and the victor at Waterloo, reportedly paid 3,000 guineas for his own Breguet watch, and he "always wore it." In the late eighteenth-century and early nineteenth-century courts of Europe, time was told on a Breguet watch. In a later time Sir Winston Churchill habitually wore a Breguet watch, which he affectionately referred to as his "turnip."

67. Collord, George L. III. American System Standards, Methods, and Automatic Machinery. Part II, Second Essay. In: *Boston: Cradle of Industrial Watchmaking. NAWCC Bulletin* Special Order Supplement Number 5, 2005.

68. As the storm clouds gathered in 1860, future Union General William Tecumseh Sherman, who at the time was Superintendent of the Louisiana State Seminary of Learning & Military Academy in Pineville, LA, sent a letter to Prof. David F. Boyd of that same institution. In it, he wrote, "… [W] here are your men and appliances of war to contend against them [the North]? The North can make a steam engine, locomotive, or railway car; hardly a yard of cloth or pair of shoes can you make. You are rushing into war with one of the most powerful, ingeniously mechanical, and determined people on Earth—right at your doors. You are bound to fail. Only in your spirit and determination are you prepared for war. In all else you are totally unprepared, with a bad cause to start with."

69. Foote, Shelby. *The Civil War, A Narrative. Volume Two: Fredericksburg to Meridian.* New York, NY: Random House, 1963.

70. Whitehorne, Joseph W. A. *Self-Guided Tour: Battle of Cedar Creek.* Washington, DC: Center of Military History, United States Army., 1992:10.

71. Bearss, Edwin C. *The Petersburg Campaign, Volume 1.* El Dorado Hills, CA: Savas Beatie, 2012: p. 110 and also footnote #OR 40, part 2, p. 176.

72. Schofield, U.S. Major Gen. John M. *46 Years in the Army.* Personal memoirs.

73. American Civil War Museum on-line catalog item #0985.03.00140a

74. Coatsworth, Dave. "A History of Railroad Time in the United States." *mb.nawcc.org/attachments/ railroadtime-pdf.463705/* More information about "railroad watches" can be found at the following websites: *ph.nawcc.org/Railroad/Railroad.htm* ; *mb.nawcc.org/wiki/Railroad-Time-Service-Watch-Rules* ; and in REF. 63.

75. McIntyre, Thomas P. "Watches and American railroads, the Early Days: A short history of the watch on American railroads from 1853 to 1883." *mb.nawcc.org/attachments/early-20railroad-20watches2-pdf.482616/*

76. Engle, Stephen D. *Yankee Dutchman: The Life of Franz Sigel.* Fayetteville, AR: University of Arkansas Press, 1993.

77. Foote, Shelby. *The Civil War, A Narrative. Volume One: Fredericksburg to Meridian.* New York, NY: Random House, 1958:290.

78. Geller, Clint B. E. Howard & Company watch dials. *NAWCC Bulletin*, No. 285 (August 1993):387.

79. E. Howard & Company Factory Records website, *sites.google.com/site/ehowardwatch/home/*

80. Geller, Clint B. A guide to cases for E. Howard & Company watches, *NAWCC Bulletin*, No. 295 (April 1995):147.

81. Geller, Clint B. The origin and evolution of the E. Howard & Company divided-plate keywind movement. *NAWCC Bulletin*, No. 324 (February 2000):17.

82. Five hundred, or perhaps 501, movements engraved "Howard & Rice" (H&R) were assembled at the Howard clock factory in Roxbury, primarily from BWCo Model 1857 material but with some Howard modifications, particularly to the escapements. (The BWCo's principal successor firm, AT&Co, designated the watch model they inherited from their bankrupt predecessor in 1857 as the "Model 1857," even though the basic design dates to approximately 1854.) Apart from one known outlier, all known H&R movements have serial numbers between 6,001 and 6,500. Like the earlier BWCo products, nearly all H&R watches have unsigned dials, but a few of the last ones to be finished have dials signed either "Howard & Rice" or "E. Howard & Company."

83. The origins of the E. Howard & Co. movement naming convention, originated by Percy L. Small and later popularized by F. Earl Hackett and Col. George Townsend, are discussed in REF. 57 and REF. 81, and references therein.

84. Kinabrew, J. N. Jr. Watch repairing in New Orleans in the 1860s: The Fournier/Barbier records. *NAWCC Bulletin*, No. 304 (October 1996):625–633.

85. The most comprehensive listing of Swiss watchmakers available is by Kathleen L. Pritchard. *Swiss Timepiece Makers, 1775–1975.* West Kennebunk, ME: Phoenix Publishers, 1997.

86. The putative provenance of Confederate Major General William Mahone's watch traces to the Thorpe Collection of American Military History and was previously published in the *North-South Trader's Civil War—Volume XXIV*, No. 6.

87. Priestley, Philip T. *British Watchcase Gold & Silver Marks 1670 to 1970: A History of Watchcase Makers and Registers of Their Marks from Original Assay Office Records in England, Ireland, and Scotland.* NAWCC (2018).

88. Baillie, G. H. *Watchmakers and Clockmakers of the World.* London: NAG Press, 1966.

89. Geller, Clint B. "A Civil War Watch," *NAWCC Bulletin*, No. 297 (August 1995):512.

90. John P. Reynolds (1840–1919). In: Patrick, J. L., ed. *In Her Hour of Sore Distress and Peril: The Civil War Diaries, Eighth Massachusetts Volunteer Infantry.* Jefferson, NC: McFarland & Co. Publishers, 2013.

91. Letter from Major John Hodges Jr., to his mother, dated "Port Hudson, Louisiana, July 15, 1863," in which he states, "I have been an acting Brigadier general before Port Hudson."

92. Slotkin, Richard. *No Quarter: The Battle of the Crater, 1864.* New York, NY: Random House, 2009:7.

93. Higginson, Thomas, ed. *Harvard Memorial Biographies, Volume II.* Carlisle, MA: Applewood Books. Originally published in 1866, p. 306, in a contribution by Captain Thorndike Deland Hodges, 35th USCT, the late John Hodge's older brother.

94. Slotkin, Richard. *No Quarter: The Battle of the Crater, 1864.* New York, NY: Random House, 2009:56–57, 166, 203, 264, and 330.

95. Charlton County Historical Society. History of St. George. *charltoncountyarchives.org/saintgeorge-histo.html*

96. *civilwar.org/learn/biographies/john-hunt-morgan*

97. Lincoln is popularly alleged to have said, "I hope to have God on my side, but I must have Kentucky," but there is controversy over whether he ever actually put it exactly that way.

98. Brent, Joseph E., A Preservation Plan for the Tebbs Bend Civil War Battlefield *tebbsbend.org/history.html*

99. Kentucky History: The Battles of Cynthiana, *explorekyhistory.ky.gov/items/show/97*

100. Schenck, John S., De La Vergne, Earl W., Ensign, D.W. *History of Ionia and Montcalm Counties, Michigan. quod.lib.umich.edu/m/micounty/bad0939.0001.001?hi=0;rgn=main;view=fulltext;q1=Nantais*

101. Ramage, James A. *Rebel Raider: The Life of General John Hunt Morgan.* Lexington, KY: The University Press of Kentucky, 1986.

102. Michigan Supreme Court Historical Society. *micourthistory.org/justices/joseph-copeland/* (which gives no source for the rumor)

103. Beatie, Russell H. *The Army of the Potomac: Birth of Command, November 1860–September 1861.* Boston, MA: Da Capo Press, 2002.

104. Hatch, Thomas. *Glorious War: The Civil War Adventures of George Armstrong Custer.* New York, NY: St. Martins Press, 2013:146.

105. *civilwarwiki.net/wiki/A_Brief_Overview_of_the_East_Cavalry_Field_Fight_(Gettysburg),_July_3,_1863* and references therein.

106. Robert Underwood Johnson (1853–1937), *Battles and Leaders of the Civil War.* Originally printed by The Century Company, 1884; reprinted by Filiquarian Legacy Publishing, 2012. Johnson was a writer, editor, and important nature preservation advocate, an associate of John Muir.

107. Andrew, Rod Jr. *Wade Hampton: Confederate Warrior to Southern Redeemer.* Chapel Hill, NC: University of North Carolina Press, 2008:11, quotes a British traveler, James Stuart, that Hampton, "not only maltreats his slaves, but stints them in food, overworks them, and keeps them almost naked. I have seen more than one of his overseers whose representations gave a dreadful account of the state of slavery on his plantations, and who left his service because they would no longer assist in the

cruel punishments inflicted … but I do not mention such a fact … merely on such authority. General Hampton's conduct toward his slaves is [a] matter of notoriety."

108. Wittenberg, Eric M. *Protecting the Flank at Gettysburg: The Battles for Brinkerhoff's Ridge and East Cavalry Field, July 2-3, 1863.* El Dorado Hills, CA: Savas Beatie, 2002:109.

109. Eric M. Wittenberg, *At Custer's Side: Civil War Writing on James Harvey Kidd,* The Kent State University Press, 2001:132.

110. Jeb Stuart had a highly accomplished military career, but not beyond legitimate criticism. He deserves a share of the credit for several of Stonewall Jackson's victories, and his command performed superbly in shielding the AoNV from Union cavalry during its retreat after its defeat at the Battle of Gettysburg. But Stuart had a penchant for attention-grabbing stunts of sometimes dubious military value, a trait that was of a piece with his ostentatious appearance. He also had a habit of deflecting blame for his occasional failures and of rejecting valid criticism. His audacious circumnavigations around the rear of the Union army during the Peninsula Campaign (March–July 1862) and the Maryland Campaign (September 1862) made great newspaper copy but were criticized by his military peers. He is generally considered to have used the discretion that Robert E. Lee gave him during the AoNV's advance into Pennsylvania in June 1863, unwisely. That army was famously drawn into battle at Gettysburg, which they entered with inadequate intelligence of Union force dispositions. But Stuart certainly had panache—quite literally. When he was shot off his horse at Yellow Tavern, he likely was wearing his trademark red-lined gray cape and hat cocked to the side with a black ostrich plume. The romantic figure he cut may partly explain the price of $131,450 for which his gold English watch with French-made case sold at Heritage Auction Galleries in December 2006.

111. Geocities.org social media website archives: *oocities.org/rlperry.geo/ColonelGeorgeWGallupPage.html*

112. Letter of Major General George W. Morgan, recounted in Kolakowski, Christopher I.: The Civil War at Perryville: Battling for the Bluegrass. *battleofperryville.com/bl_morgan.html*

113. *nytimes.com/1862/10/11/archives/the-evacuation-of-cumberland-gap-reason-of-the-evacuation-of-the. html*

114. Kolakowski, Christopher I. *The Civil War at Perryville: Battling for the Bluegrass.* Stroud, Gloucestershire, UK: The History Press, 2009.

115. Cozzens, Peter. *The Darkest Days of the War: The Battles of Iuka & Corinth.* Chapel Hill, NC: University of North Carolina Press. 1997:18–19.

116. Smith, Charles H. [Major, US Army Retired, 27th OH Volunteer Infantry, Brigade Historian]. *The History of Fuller's Ohio Brigade, 1861–1865; Its Great March, with Roster, Portraits, Battle Maps and Biographies.* A. J. Watt Press, 1909.

117. McKinstry, James A. With Col Rogers When He Fell. *Confederate Veteran,* 1896.

118. Bryner, Byron Cloyd. *Bugle Echoes: The Story of the Illinois 47th.* Baltimore, MD: Philips Brothers, Printers, 1905.

119. Catton, Bruce, *This Hallowed Ground: A History of the Civil War,* Random House, 1955:177, among many other places.

120. Boyd, James Penny. *The Life of General William T. Sherman.* Publishers Union, 1891:109.

121. Morton, John Watson. *The Artillery of Nathan Bedford Forrest's Cavalry: "The Wizard of the Saddle."* Publishing House of the M. E. Church, 1909:1.

122. civilwar.org/learn/civil-war/battles/parkers-cross-roads

123. Clausewitz, General Carl von. *On War.* 1832, and reprinted many times thereafter.

124. Fuller's Official Report on his command's action at the Battle of Atlanta: "HDQRS. FOURTH DIVISION, SIXTEENTH ARMY CORPS, Near Atlanta, Ga., August 2, 1864." The report is reproduced in its entirety in REF. 106 (Johnson).

125. John C. Calhoun was referred to as "the very apostle of slavery" by Congressman Joshua Reed Giddings of Ohio in a speech before the House of Representatives in January of 1845. Giddings may not have been the first to confer that title upon Calhoun, one that Calhoun probably did not find objectionable, but the appellation was commonplace both during and after his life.

126. Excerpted from a speech written by the dying Senator John C. Calhoun of South Carolina and read on the floor of the U.S. Senate by Senator James M. Mason on March 4, 1850. Calhoun, who had been present for the speech but was too frail to deliver it himself, died 27 days later, on March 31.

127. Chapman, John Jay. *William Lloyd Garrison.* Boston, MA: Atlantic Monthly Press, 1913:chap. 2.

128. The New Jersey Abolition Act of 1804 slowly rid New Jersey of slavery, but it freed few slaves, nor was the act intended to. The law kept slaves born before 1804 in bondage for life and stipulated a long grace period for slaveholders to sell children born of slave mothers after 1804 southward prior to the deadline. A few slaves were still in bondage in New Jersey when the Thirteenth Amendment was ratified on December 6, 1865. New Jersey's Abolition Act was similar in character to those of other Northern states that had acted before her.

129. Varon, Elizabeth R. *Disunion!: The Coming of the American Civil War, 1789–1859.* Littlefield History of the Civil War Era. Chapel Hill, NC: University of North Carolina Press, 2008:23–24, documents that two prominent South Carolina statesmen, John Rutledge and Charles Cotesworth Pinckney, used a secession threat to push the earliest date on which Congress could choose to abolish the international slave trade back from 1800 to 1808.

130. Von Drehle, David. Why the US is Still Fighting the Civil War. *Time Magazine,* April 7, 2011. content.time.com/time/magazine/article/0,9171,2063869,00.html

131. Yafa, Stephen H. *Big Cotton: How A Humble Fiber Created Fortunes, Wrecked Civilizations, and Put America on the Map.* New York, NY: Viking Press, 2004.

132. Article I, Section 2, of the U.S. Constitution of 1787. This is only one of three passages in the Constitution that clearly refer to the institution of slavery without mentioning either the word *Slavery* or the word *slave.* By 1861 Southern leaders had gotten over their embarrassment about the word and the institution.

133. Freehling, William W. *The Road to Disunion, Volume II: Secessionists at Bay.* Oxford, UK: Oxford University Press, 2007:chap. I:15.

134. Some salient facts of the Southern dominance of the antebellum Republic are laid out here: *accessible-archives.com/2016/10/the-political-power-of-slave-owners/* In addition, in 1860 the nine sitting justices of the U.S. Supreme Court, led by Chief Justice Roger Taney, a Southerner, included five Southerners and three Northerners nominated by Southern presidents.

135. *courses.lumenlearning.com/ushistory1os2xmaster/chapter/wealth-and-culture-in-the-south/*

136. As one yardstick of the preponderance of slaveholders among antebellum Southern political officeholders, one may take the composition of the secession conventions of the original seven C.S.A. states of the Lower South. Ralph A. Wooster, in *The Secession Conventions of the South* (Princeton, NJ: Princeton University Press, 1962), found that of the 1,048 delegates to those seven conventions, 179 (17%) owned no slaves, 432 (41%) owned from one to twenty slaves, and 437 (42%) owned twenty-one or more slaves. By comparison with the broader population, fewer than half of households in any of the seven Lower South states, except for South Carolina, held any slaves. A second source, J. Mills Thornton, in *Archipelagoes of My South: Episodes in the Shaping of a Region, 1830–1965* (Tuscaloosa, AL: University of Alabama Press, 2016:chap. 1:6), states that in the "late antebellum period," a quarter of Southern state legislators owned twenty or more slaves, from which we may reasonably extrapolate that considerably more than half owned at least one.

137. Neighbors, Forrest A. *From Oligarchy to Republicanism: The Great Task of Reconstructionism.* Columbia, MO: University of Missouri, 2017:chap. 6. (Despite the reference to Reconstruction in the title, this book has much to say about public education in the *antebellum* South.)

138. Freehling, William W. *The Road to Disunion, Volume I: Secessionists at Bay, 1776–1854.* Oxford, UK: Oxford University Press, 1990:Part II, Section 6: "Democrats as Lynchers."

139. *digitalhistory.uh.edu/disp_textbook.cfm?smtid=2&psid=3558*

140. *Hunts Merchants Magazine* xliv:316. (1861) The Dunn Agency (later to become Dunn and Bradstreet), estimated Southern indebtedness at $300,000,000. The report of the Massachusetts Bank Commissioners, October 1861, estimated losses to Northern creditors resulting from secession and war at $200,000,000.

141. Baptist, Edward E. *The Half Has Never Been Told: Slavery and the Making of American Capitalism.* New York, NY: Basic Books, 2016:111-144.

142. *Congressional Globe*, 29th Congress, second session, 1847, Appendix, p. 317; reprinted in Gienapp, William E., ed. *The Civil War and Reconstruction: A Documentary Collection.* New York, NY: W. W. Norton Publishers, 2001:17–18.

143. According to Yale Professor David W. Blight, about 15% of the Northern population sympathized with "immediatist" demands for abolition in 1860: David W. Blight. The Civil War and Reconstruction (HIST 119). Yale Courses, Number 5.

144. Bordewich, Fergus M. In *The Underground Railroad: Myth & Reality*, 2007. *fergusbordewich.com/blog/?p=13* "Understanding the Underground Railroad has also been hampered by the seeming dearth of meaningful statistics. However, enough local underground groups published figures on the number of fugitives they aided during a given span of time to make it possible to estimate larger patterns for the system as a whole. Over the sixty-odd years of its existence, from its beginnings in Philadelphia in the 1790s to the Civil War, the underground facilitated the escape of probably something in the order of 100,000 fugitive slaves to safe havens in the northern states and Canada. This is an impressive figure in terms of lives saved. But it must be understood in a larger context. There were 4,000,000 slaves in the United States by 1860. Moreover, most slaves who fled were recaptured and returned to slavery. Although those helped to freedom by the Underground Railroad were a small percentage of the total, their impact on the hearts and minds of Americans was enormous. The underground delivered tens of thousands of fugitives into northern communities where for the first time large numbers of whites encountered former slaves, heard their heartrending stories of enslavement, and began to recognize African Americans as people like themselves."

145. S. C. Posey, of Lauderdale County, Alabama, speaking to the Alabama Secession Convention on January 25, 1861, expressed the predominant white Southern view when he said, "Mr. President, the fierce strife we have had with the Northern States, which has led to the disruption of the Government, is a trumpet-tongued answer to this question. They have declared, by the election of Lincoln, 'There shall be no more slave territory—no more slave States.' To this the Cotton States have responded by acts of secession and a Southern Confederacy; which is but a solemn declaration of these States, that they will not submit to the Northern idea of restricting slavery to its present limits, and confining it to the slave States." In his first inaugural address, on March 4, 1861, Abraham Lincoln said, "One section of our country believes slavery is right and ought to be extended, while the other believes it is wrong and ought not to be extended. This is the only substantial dispute."

146. University of South Carolina Press website: *sc.edu/uscpress/books/2006/3681.html*

147. Earle, Carville. *Geographical Inquiry and American Historical Problems.* Stanford, CA: Stanford University Press, 1992:286–287. "By … 1840, the Chesapeake tobacco economy had sunk into an impoverished state. … The region was beyond agricultural or economic salvation. [Local planters] confronted an almost overwhelming set of regional problems—worn-out and worn-down land; a dual economy and threadbare planter elites; and a bewildering mix of plantation slaves, hired slaves, and free negroes created by slave owners trying to cut costs by manumitting or hiring out slaves." When the cotton boom of the 1850s began a decade later, many of these same planters remained afloat by selling their excess slaves southward and westward, enabling a vast forced southward and westward slave migration. See Baptist.

148. Finkelman, Paul. *An Imperfect Union: Slavery, Federalism and Comity.* Chapel Hill, NC: University of North Carolina Press, 1981:338.

149. Letter from Abraham Lincoln, candidate for Congress, to his friend, Williamson Durley, from Springfield, IL, dated October 3, 1845.

150. Abraham Lincoln Presidential Library and Museum website: *illinois.gov/alplm/museum/Education/Documents/2.Confederate%20Confiscations.pdf*

151. Current, Richard Nelson. *Lincoln's Loyalists: Union Soldiers from the Confederacy.* Boston, MA: Northeastern University Press, 1992:5.

152. The "Cornerstone Speech," delivered by the new C.S.A. Vice President Alexander Stephens, in Savannah, GA, on March 21, 1861, laid out for the Southern people the case for Southern secession and the purpose of what was intended to be the new Confederate nation. The "cornerstone" of the new national culture and society, like that of the Southern United States from which it had been formed, was the institution of Slavery. Thirty-one days earlier, on February 18, 1861, in Montgomery, AL, the newly elected C.S.A. President Jefferson Davis had delivered his inaugural address. In that speech, which Davis expected would be parsed closely in Europe, he studiously avoided any mention of slavery. Davis knew that European support for his new country, which had no navy of its own, and which would urgently need trading partners, was likely to be crucial. He also understood that slavery was by 1861 a despised, odious institution throughout Europe. Thus, he sensibly avoided any mention of the term whatsoever, leaving it to his Vice President to address their domestic Southern audience. This was the purpose of Stephens's Cornerstone Speech.

153. Manning, Chandra. *What This Cruel War Was Over*. New York, NY: Random House Vintage Civil War Library, 2007:32.

154. Commanding the Union XIV Corps during the Battle of Chickamauga, Major General George Henry Thomas successfully defended a position against the Confederate assault as the Union line on his right collapsed. In his book, *The Legacy Road* (Lulu.com, 2015), writer Steve Enyeart wrote, "Thomas rallied broken and scattered units together on Horseshoe Ridge to prevent a significant Union defeat from becoming a hopeless rout. Future president James Garfield, a field officer for the Army of the Cumberland, visited Thomas during the battle, carrying orders from [the commanding Union General William] Rosecrans to retreat; when Thomas said he would have to stay behind to ensure the Army's safety, Garfield told Rosecrans that Thomas was 'standing like a rock.'"

155. Frederick Douglass, in "Remembering the Civil War," 1877.

BIBLIOGRAPHY

Andrew, Rod Jr. *Wade Hampton: Confederate Warrior to Southern Redeemer*. Chapel Hill, NC: University of North Carolina Press, 2008.

Baillie, G. H. *Watchmakers and Clockmakers of the World*. London: NAG Press, 1966.

Baptist, Edward E. *The Half Has Never Been Told: Slavery and the Making of American Capitalism*. New York, NY: Basic Books, 2016.

Bearss, Edwin C. *The Petersburg Campaign, Volume 1*. El Dorado Hills, CA: Savas Beatie, Publishers, 2012.

Beatie, Russell H. *The Army of the Potomac: Birth of Command, November 1860–September 1861*. Boston, MA: Da Capo Press, 2002.

Bordewich, Fergus M. *The Underground Railroad: Myth & Reality*, July 22, 2007. *www.fergusbordewich.com/blog/?p=13*

Boyd, James Penny. *The Life of General William T. Sherman*. Publishers Union, 1891.

Bryner, Byron Cloyd. *Bugle Echoes: The Story of Illinois 47ᵗʰ*. Baltimore, MD: Philips Brothers, Printers, 1905.

Cater, Douglas John. *As It Was: Reminiscences of a Soldier of the Third Texas Cavalry and the Nineteenth Louisiana Infantry*. Abilene, TX: State House Press, 2007.

Cozzens, Peter. *The Darkest Days of the War: The Battles of Iuka & Corinth*. Chapel Hill, NC: University of North Carolina Press, 1997.

Catton, Bruce, *This Hallowed Ground: A History of the Civil War*, Random House, 1955.

Crossman, Charles S. *The Complete History of Watch Making in America*. Boston, MA. Adams, Brown & Co., originally printed serially in the *Jeweler's Circular & Horological Review*, 1885–1887.

Dew, Charles B. *Apostles of Disunion: Southern Secession Commissioners and the Causes of the Civil War (A Nation Divided: Studies in the Civil War Era)*. 15ᵗʰ ed. Charlottesville, VA: University of Virginia Press, 2017.

Earle, Carville. *Geographical Inquiry and American Historical Problems*. Stanford, CA: Stanford University Press, 1992.

Ehrhardt, Roy. *Encyclopedia and Price Guide, Volume I: American Pocket Watches*. Heart of America Press, 1982.

Eldridge, Captain D. *The Third New Hampshire and All About it*. Boston, MA: E. B. Stillings & Co., 1893.

Engle, Stephen D. *Yankee Dutchman: The Life of Franz Sigel*. Fayetteville, AR: University of Arkansas Press, 1993.

Enyeart, Steve. *The Legacy Road*, lulu.com (publisher), 2015.

Finkelman, Paul. *An Imperfect Union: Slavery, Federalism and Comity*. Chapel Hill, NC: University of North Carolina Press, 1981.

Foner, Eric. *America's Unfinished Revolution*. New York, NY: Harper Perennial, 2011.

Foote, Shelby. *The Civil War: A Narrative, Volumes I, II, and III*. New York, NY: Random House, 1958-1974.

Freehling, William W. *The Road to Disunion, Volume I: Secessionists at Bay, 1776–1854*. Oxford, UK: Oxford University Press, 1990.

Freehling, William W. *The Road to Disunion, Volume II: Secessionists Triumphant, 1854–1861*. Oxford, UK: Oxford University Press, 2007.

Gallagher, Gary W. *The Union War*. Cambridge, MA: Harvard University Press, 2011.

Gallagher, Gary W., ed. *The Third Day at Gettysburg & Beyond*. Chapel Hill, NC: University of North Carolina Press, 1994.

Geller, Clint B., coordinating contributor. *Boston: Cradle of Industrial Watchmaking*. NAWCC Bulletin Special Order Supplement Number 5, 2005.

Geller, Clint B. *A Study of E. Howard & Co, Watchmaking Innovations: 1858–1875*. NAWCC Bulletin Special Order Supplement Number 6, 2005.

Glatthaar, Joseph T. *Soldiering in the Army of Northern Virginia: A Statistical Portrait of the Troops Who Served Under Robert E. Lee*. Chapel Hill, NC: University of North Carolina Press, 2011:154.

Guelzo, Alan C. *Fateful Lightning*. Oxford, UK: Oxford University Press, 2012.

Guelzo, Allen C. *Gettysburg: The Last Invasion*. New York, NY: Random House, 2013.

Harrold, Michael C. *American Watchmaking: A Technical History 1850–1930*. NAWCC Bulletin Supplement Number 14 (Spring 1984).

Hatch, Thomas. *Glorious War: The Civil War Adventures of George Armstrong Custer*, New York, NY: St. Martins Press, 2013.

Higginson, Thomas, ed. *Harvard Memorial Biographies, Volume II*. Carlisle, MA: Applewood Books, 1866.

Hoke, Donald R. *Ingenious Yankees: The Rise of the American System of Manufactures in the Private Sector*. New York, NY: Columbia University Press, 1990.

Johnson, Robert Underwood (1853–1937). *Battles and Leaders of the Civil War*, originally printed by The Century Company, 1884; reprinted by Filiquarian Legacy Publishing, 2012.

Kautz, Union Major General August V. *The Company Clerk*. Philadelphia, PA: J. B. Lippencott & Co., circa 1863.

Kolakowski, Christopher I. *The Civil War at Perryville: Battling for the Bluegrass*. Stroud, Gloucestershire, UK: The History Press, 2009.

Loomes, Brian. *Watchmakers & Clockmakers of the World, Volume 2*. London: N.A.G. Press, Ltd., 1976:2 (1978 reprint).

Manning, Chandra. *What This Cruel War Was Over*. New York, NY: Random House Vintage Civil War Library, 2007.

McCrossen, Alexis. *Marking Modern Times: A History of Clocks, Watches, and Other Timekeepers in American Life.* University of Chicago Press, 2013.

McPherson, James M. *For Cause & Comrades: Why Men Fought in the Civil War.* Oxford, UK: Oxford University Press, 1997.

Moore, Charles W. *Timing a Century: History of the Waltham Watch Company.* Cambridge, MA: Harvard University Press, reprinted in 2014.

Morton, John Watson. *The Artillery of Nathan Bedford Forrest's Cavalry: "The Wizard of the Saddle."* Publishing House of the M. E. Church, 1909.

Neighbors, Forrest A. *From Oligarchy to Republicanism: The Great Task of Reconstructionism.* Columbia, MO: University of Missouri, 2017.

Noe, Kenneth W. *Reluctant Rebels: The Confederates Who Joined the Army after 1861.* New edition. Chapel Hill, NC: University of North Carolina Press, May 14, 2010.

Olmsted, Frederick Law. *The Cotton Kingdom: A Traveler's Observations on Cotton and Slavery in the American Slave States.* New York, NY: Mason Brothers, 1861.

Johnson, E. Polk. *A History of Kentucky and Kentuckians: The Leaders and Representative Men in Commerce, Industry and Modern Activities.* Lewis Publishing Co., 1912.

Price, Ron. *Origins of the Waltham Model 57: Evolution of the First Successful Industrialized Watch. NAWCC Bulletin* Special Order Supplement Number 7, 2005.

Priestley, Philip T. *British Watchcase Gold & Silver Marks 1670 to 1970: A History of Watchcase Makers and Registers of Their Marks from Original Assay Office Records in England, Ireland, and Scotland.* NAWCC, 2018.

Pritchard, Kathleen L. *Swiss Timepiece Makers, 1775–1975.* West Kennebunk, ME: Phoenix Publishers, 1997.

Ramage, James A. *Rebel Raider: The Life of General John Hunt Morgan.* Lexington, KY: The University Press of Kentucky, 1986.

Reynolds, John P. (1840–1919), Patrick, J. L., ed. *In Her Hour of Sore Distress and Peril: The Civil War Diaries, Eighth Massachusetts Volunteer Infantry.* Jefferson, NC: McFarland & Co. Publishers, 2013.

Sala, G. A. *My Diary in America in the Midst of War.* London, UK: Tinsley Brothers, 1865.

Sears, Stephen W. *Gettysburg.* New York, NY: First Mariner Books, 2004.

Slotkin, Richard. *No Quarter: The Battle of the Crater, 1864.* New York, NY: Random House, 2009:11.

Smith, Charles H. *The History of Fuller's Ohio Brigade, 1861–1865; Its Great March, with Roster, Portraits, Battle Maps and Biographies.* A. J. Watt Press, 1909.

Smith, Mark M. *Mastered by the Clock: Time, Slavery and Freedom in the American South.* Chapel Hill, NC: University of North Carolina Press, 1997.

Thornton, J. Mills. *Archipelagoes of My South: Episodes in the Shaping of a Region, 1830–1965,* Tuscaloosa, AL: University of Alabama Press, 2016.

Trudeau, Noah A. *Bloody Roads South: The Wilderness to Cold Harbor, May–June, 1864.* Bostons, MA: Little, Brown & Co. Publishers, 1989.

Trudeau, Noah A. *Gettysburg: A Testing of Courage.* New York, NY: Harper Collins, 2002.

Varon, Elizabeth R. *Disunion!: The Coming of the American Civil War, 1789–1859.* Chapel Hill, NC: Littlefield History of the Civil War Era, University of North Carolina Press, 2008.

Weaver, Samuel. *Revised Report to the Select Committee to the House of Representatives, Soldiers National Cemetery, Gettysburg, with Accompanying Documents,* March 19, 1864.

Wells, Cheryl A. *Civil War Time: Temporality and Identity in America.* Athens, GA: University of Georgia Press, 2005.

White, Jonathan W. *Emancipation, the Union Army, and the Reelection of Abraham Lincoln.* Baton Rouge, LA: Louisiana State University Press, 2014.

White, Ronald C. Jr. *A. Lincoln: A Biography.* New York, NY: Random House, 2009.

Wittenberg, Eric M. *Protecting the Flank at Gettysburg: The Battles for Brinkerhoff's Ridge and East Cavalry Field, July 2–3, 1863.* El Dorado Hills, CA: Savas Beatie, 2002.

Wooster, Ralph A. *The Secession Conventions of the South.* Princeton, NJ: Princeton University Press, 1962.

AUTHOR AND SUBJECT INDEX

F:~

G:~

T :~

ABOUT THE AUTHOR

Dr. Geller is a research physicist at a United States government laboratory and lives in Pittsburgh, PA with his wife of thirty-two years. He has collected, researched and written about early American pocket watches since the mid-1980s. This publication is his second full-length book in the horological field, and his first book to focus on aspects of horology relating specifically to the American Civil War.

In 2002, Dr. Geller chaired the "Boston: Cradle of Industrial Watchmaking" NAWCC National Seminar in Boxboro, Massachusetts. In 2006, he chaired the "American Watchmaking II" Ward Francillon National NAWCC Seminar in Cleveland, Ohio. Dr. Geller was made an NAWCC Fellow in 2003, and he received the NAWCC's James W. Gibbs Award for literary achievement in horology in 2009.

Dr. Geller has published in numerous physics and engineering journals and he holds two United States patents for technical inventions. He is also a science fiction/fantasy novelist, the author of the *Gennebar Rising* trilogy.

Dr. Geller can be contacted through the NAWCC and through his blog, *ClintGeller.com*.

ABOUT THE COVERS

Front Cover: The *Friend to Friend* Masonic Memorial in the Gettysburg National Cemetery Annex, immortalizing a famous battlefield incident. Sculpted in polychrome bronze by Ron Tunison and dedicated in 1993, the memorial depicts captured, dying Confederate Brigadier General Lewis Addison Armistead during the immediate aftermath of the ill-fated "Pickett's Charge" on July 3, 1863. Armistead is portrayed handing his watch, with masonic square-and-compass fob, to a young Union captain to be given to Armistead's close friend and former comrade in arms, Union Major General Winnfield Scott Hancock. The Union officer shown receiving Armistead's watch, Captain Henry Harrison Bingham, who confirmed the incident, would subsequently win a Medal of Honor at the Battle of the Wilderness in May 1864. Bingham would be breveted to brigadier general after the war, and would serve a long and distinguished civilian career as a Congressional representative. Armistead, Bingham and Hancock were all freemasons. *Photo by Laura Magone & William Fuller.*

Rear Cover: Private Florentine Ariosto Jones of the 13th Massachusetts Infantry. In his enlistment papers, Jones listed his prewar occupation as "watchmaker." After the war, Jones succeeded George P. Reed as factory superintendent at E. Howard & Company, and then moved on to found the International Watch Company of Schaffhausen, Switzerland in 1868. *Photo from Library of Congress Archives, a sixth plate tintype from the Liljenquist family collection.*

CPSIA information can be obtained
at www.ICGtesting.com
Printed in the USA
LVHW101702140220
647003LV00007B/158